Standards-Based Accountability Under No Child Left Behind

Experiences of Teachers and Administrators in Three States

Laura S. Hamilton, Brian M. Stecher, Julie A. Marsh,
Jennifer Sloan McCombs, Abby Robyn, Jennifer Lin Russell,
Scott Naftel, Heather Barney

Sponsored by the National Science Foundation

EDUCATION

The research described in this report was sponsored by the National Science Foundation and was conducted by RAND Education, a unit of the RAND Corporation.

Library of Congress Cataloging-in-Publication Data

Standards-based accountability under no child left behind : experiences of teachers and administrators in three states / Laura S. Hamilton ... [et al.].
    p. cm.
    Includes bibliographical references.
    ISBN 978-0-8330-4149-4 (pbk.)
    1. Educational accountability—California. 2. Educational accountability—Georgia. 3. Educational accountability—Pennsylvania. 4. Education—Standards—California. 5. Education—Standards—Georgia. 6. Education—Standards—Pennsylvania. 7. United States. No Child Left Behind Act of 2001. I. Hamilton, Laura S., 1968– II. Hamilton, Laura S.

LB2806.22.S73 2007
379.1'580973—dc22

                                                                    2007008952

The RAND Corporation is a nonprofit research organization providing objective analysis and effective solutions that address the challenges facing the public and private sectors around the world. RAND's publications do not necessarily reflect the opinions of its research clients and sponsors.

RAND® is a registered trademark.

Published 2007 by the RAND Corporation
1776 Main Street, P.O. Box 2138, Santa Monica, CA 90407-2138
1200 South Hayes Street, Arlington, VA 22202-5050
4570 Fifth Avenue, Suite 600, Pittsburgh, PA 15213-2665
RAND URL: http://www.rand.org/
To order RAND documents or to obtain additional information, contact
Distribution Services: Telephone: (310) 451-7002;
Fax: (310) 451-6915; Email: order@rand.org

Preface

This monograph presents interim findings from the Implementing Standards-Based Accountability (ISBA) project. It provides descriptive information regarding the implementation of the No Child Left Behind Act (NCLB) in three states—California, Georgia, and Pennsylvania—in 2003–2004 and 2004–2005. Subsequent publications will extend these results for an additional year and will include both multivariate and multilevel analyses of policy decisions and actions at the state, district, school, and classroom levels. This monograph should be of interest to anyone concerned about standards-based accountability (SBA) in general and NCLB in particular.

This research was conducted by RAND Education, a unit of the RAND Corporation. It is part of a larger body of RAND Education work addressing assessment and accountability. It was sponsored by the National Science Foundation under grant number REC-0228295. Any opinions, findings, conclusions, or recommendations expressed in this monograph are those of the authors and do not necessarily reflect the views of the National Science Foundation.

Contents

Figures

Tables

Summary

Since 2001–2002, the work of public school teachers and administrators in the United States has been shaped by the standards-based accountability (SBA) provisions of the No Child Left Behind Act of 2001. NCLB requires each state to develop content and achievement standards in several subjects, administer tests to measure students' progress toward these standards, develop targets for performance on these tests, and impose a series of interventions on schools and districts that do not meet the targets. Together, the standards, assessments, and consequences constitute an SBA system. Many states had such systems in place before NCLB took effect, but, since 2001–2002, every state in the United States has had to develop and implement an SBA system that met the requirements of the law, and its provisions have affected every public school and district in the nation.

In 2002, researchers at the RAND Corporation launched ISBA to gather information on how teachers, principals, and district superintendents are responding to the accountability systems that states have adopted in the wake of NCLB. The study was designed to identify factors that enhance the implementation of SBA systems, foster changes in school and classroom practice, and promote improved student achievement. This monograph provides descriptive information from the 2003–2004 and 2004–2005 academic years to shed light on how accountability policies have been translated into attitudes and actions at the district, school, and classroom levels. Future publications will present results of analyses to identify relationships between these responses and student achievement.

Study Methods

The ISBA study is being conducted in three states: California, Georgia, and Pennsylvania. These states were selected to represent a range of approaches to SBA and to provide some geographic and demographic diversity. The study uses a combination of large-scale, quantitative data collection and small-scale case studies to examine NCLB implementation at the state, district, school, and classroom levels. It focuses on elementary and middle school science and mathematics and is longitudinal in nature with three waves of data collection, 2003–2004, 2004–2005, and 2005–2006. Data were collected using a combination of paper-and-pencil surveys, telephone interviews, and in-person visits. This monograph is based on results from descriptive analyses of survey and case study data collected in the spring of the 2004–2005 school year, with some reference to data collected in the previous school year.

At the state level, we conducted in-person interviews with education department staff and other state-level policymakers, and we gathered documents such as state content standards and technical reports on test quality. A representative sample of 27 districts was selected in each state in 2003–2004, and we gathered information from superintendents using both semistructured telephone interviews and surveys. In each state, 125 elementary and middle schools were randomly selected from the participating districts, and the principals as well as all teachers who taught mathematics or science to students in grades three, four, five, seven, or eight received paper-and-pencil surveys in the spring of each study year. In addition, we conducted site visits at 14 schools during the 2003–2004 year and 16 during the 2004–2005 year to gather richer information from teachers, principals, other school staff, and parents. The survey results presented are weighted to be representative of all districts and schools in each state. In this way, the monograph sheds light on the frequency of various responses, many of which have been observed anecdotally but not studied in a systematic way.

Findings

SBA is, of necessity, a top-down reform, and our findings provide information about educators' responses at each level of the system.

State Accountability Systems Enacted in Response to NCLB Differed Across the Three States

All three states had developed and implemented accountability systems to comply with NCLB, but the details of these systems varied. Systems differed with respect to the content of the academic standards, the difficulty level of their performance standards, their choice of additional indicators, their methods for calculating adequate yearly progress (AYP) and their AYP trajectories, and their school and district support and technical assistance mechanisms, just to name a few areas. Many of the differences were related to pre-NCLB contextual factors, including the degree to which the state had already been engaged in SBA efforts prior to NCLB. For example, California, which had a preexisting accountability system that used a school-level measure of growth, chose to incorporate indicators from that system into AYP calculations, unlike the other states. Differences among the states were greater in terms of science standards and assessments than in mathematics.

Districts and Schools Responded to the New State Accountability Systems Actively and in Broadly Similar Ways, Despite State Differences

In all three states, majorities of school and district administrators described similar types of school-improvement activities. Most district superintendents reported aligning curricula with standards, providing technical assistance to help schools improve and offering a variety of professional development (PD) opportunities for principals and teachers. Principals also said that they took steps to ensure that instruction was aligned with state standards and with state assessments, and large numbers reported providing extra learning opportunities for low-performing students. Other common improvement strategies included promoting the use of student test results for instructional planning, implementing test preparation activities, and adopting interim or progress tests to provide more frequent assessment information. A relatively small number of schools increased instructional time on reading and mathematics. Georgia districts and schools were especially active in promoting science instruction and in adopting interim assessment systems compared with districts or schools in California and Pennsylvania. The emphasis on science instruction is consistent with the fact that, of the three states, only Georgia had in place a comprehensive system of science standards and assessments.

Of all the school-improvement activities reported by superintendents, three were described as the most important: aligning curriculum with state standards and assessments, using data for decisionmaking, and providing extra support to low-performing students. All of these responses, but particularly the first two, suggest that district actions are likely to be influenced by the specific content and features of the state standards and assessments.

Reported Changes at the Classroom Level Included Both Desirable and Undesirable Responses

Teachers noted a variety of ways in which NCLB influenced their instruction. Some of the reported changes, such as efforts to align instruction with standards and efforts to improve their own practices, suggest that NCLB has had some beneficial effects. At the same time, teachers described a number of responses that would probably be considered less desirable. For example, the reported changes included a narrowing of curriculum and instruction toward tested topics and even toward certain problem styles or formats. Teachers also reported focusing more on students near the proficient cut score (i.e., "bubble kids") and expressed concerns about negative effects of the accountability requirements on the learning opportunities given to high-achieving students.

Educators Expressed Support for NCLB Goals but Had Concerns About Specific Features and Effects

Most superintendents, principals, and teachers expressed support for the idea of SBA, but, on average, the groups held different opinions about specific features of these systems. For instance, most administrators thought that state test scores accurately reflected student achievement, a sentiment that only a small minority of teachers shared. Similarly, administrators were more likely than teachers to think that accountability pressures led to improvement in curriculum and student learning. Teachers were particularly attuned to lack of consistency between state accountability requirements and local resources and programs. Teachers associated the implementation of SBA with reduced morale and expressed concerns about negative effects on their teaching. Still, teachers' reports suggested that the emphasis on state standards and assessments has led to some beneficial outcomes. Teachers reported an increased focus on student achievement in their schools as a result of NCLB, as well as increased curriculum coordination and increased rigor of the school's curriculum.

Several Perceived Hindrances May Stand in the Way of Effective Implementation of NCLB

Both teachers and administrators identified a variety of factors that they believed adversely affected their efforts to meet NCLB goals. Most administrators thought that inadequate funding was hampering their school-improvement efforts, and many said that they did not have adequate numbers of highly qualified teachers in mathematics or science. Administrators and teachers alike saw insufficient instructional time and insufficient planning time as barriers. In addition, teachers reported that students' lack of basic skills, inadequate support from parents, and student absenteeism and tardiness hampered their efforts. One of the underlying principles of NCLB is that educators are expected to promote high levels of achievement despite these conditions, but our findings suggest that large numbers of educators consider this expectation unrealistic.

Implications

These descriptive results suggest that NCLB is affecting the work of superintendents, principals, and teachers in a variety of ways, both positive and negative. The findings from this study suggest a need for clearer information about alignment, capacity-building efforts to help educators engage more effectively in school improvement, and more valid measures of teacher and school effectiveness.

Alignment Efforts at All Levels Need to Be Improved

The need for alignment among standards, assessments, and curriculum was a recurring theme among participants in this study. Teachers, in particular, expressed concerns that state assessments were not well aligned with state standards and described efforts to ensure that their own instructional efforts aligned with the assessments that the state had produced. Although all states have taken steps to measure alignment between tests and standards, evaluations of these efforts have suggested that most state tests fail to capture all of the content in the standards, so teachers' lack of confidence in the process is not surprising. States need to communicate to educators the ways in which tests do and do not capture what is in the standards and should take steps to promote better alignment. States and districts also need to assist teachers in their efforts to adopt instructional approaches that are well matched to the standards without leading to excessive test preparation. It is worth noting that many of the actions that superintendents, principals, and teachers reported are likely to lead to curriculum and instruction that reflect the particular features and content of the state standards and tests, so it is critical that states ensure that these elements of their accountability systems are of high quality and well suited to the purpose of guiding instructional improvement.

Teacher and Administrator Capacities for Improvement Need to Be Developed

Superintendents, principals, and teachers noted several areas in which they needed additional assistance. In particular, teachers expressed a need for guidance to help them improve their instruction of English language learners (ELLs) and students with special needs. Assistance designed to help teachers and other school and district staff use data for decisionmaking, devise strategies for improving the learning of low-performing students, and identify effective instructional practices would also be beneficial for improving the impact of SBA.

Better Methods for Measuring School and Student Performance Should Be Explored

The responses of teachers and principals in this study echo criticisms of NCLB's method for measuring progress that a number of prominent individuals and groups have lodged. Educators at all levels reported that the 100-percent proficiency target was unrealistic. Many of the teachers whom we interviewed cited as unfair the fact that AYP is defined primarily in terms of status rather than progress over time, reflecting their view that it fails to give credit for all of the learning gains that teachers and other educators might promote. Moreover, the fact that AYP is defined in terms of proficiency creates incentives to change instruction in ways that might not be desirable, such as by focusing on students near the proficient cut score to the detriment of students performing below or above that level. As an alternative, states could be permitted to explore alternatives that rely on measuring growth and that take into account movement at all points along the score scale. Some states are already making progress toward such a change by experimenting with growth-based measures as part of a U.S. Department of Education pilot program, though that program still requires 100-percent proficiency by 2014 and requires status-based measures to continue to be used. States' efforts to adopt growth measures should be supported but should also be carefully examined to ensure the quality of measurement and that the nature of incentives they create are consistent with the goals of improved student learning.

Teachers' Concerns Should Be Examined and Addressed

In general, teachers expressed less support for NCLB than administrators did. Because the effects of NCLB are dependent on what occurs in the classroom, it is critical to ensure that teachers are responding to state accountability requirements in educationally productive ways. Teachers are in a unique position to see the effects of accountability policies on teaching and learning, and it is important to take their concerns seriously when considering revisions to those policies.

Conclusion

This monograph suggests reasons for both optimism and concern: States are nearing full implementation, but state-to-state differences in the specific features of each accountability system are substantial. SBA is leading to an emphasis on student achievement, and many educators laud this focus, but teacher and administrator responses suggest that a single-minded emphasis on student proficiency on tests has some potentially negative consequences such as a narrowing of curriculum and a decline in staff morale. One of the key challenges facing those who are responsible for designing, implementing, or responding to SBA systems is to identify ways to increase the prevalence of desirable responses and minimize the undesirable ones. Future reports from the ISBA project will provide additional information to help policymakers and educators make well-informed decisions about SBA system development and implementation.

Acknowledgments

A large number of people have contributed to the ISBA study. In addition to the named authors, this work benefited from the contributions of RAND research and support staff, consultants from Vanderbilt University, our survey subcontractor Westat, and the project advisory committee. At RAND, credit should be given for the research assistance provide by Abigail Brown, Mark Hanson, Felipe Martinez, Hilary Rhodes, and Alice Wood; the statistical help provided by Bonnie Ghosh Dastidar, Amelia Haviland, David Klein, and J. R. Lockwood; and the administrative assistance offered by Linda Daly and Donna White. At Vanderbilt, we were aided by the advice and assistance of Mark Berends and Albert Boerema. At Westat, Timothy Smith and Debbie Alexander coordinated the work of a dedicated staff whose efforts are reflected in the high survey response rate and the excellent quality of survey responses. The project advisory committee, consisting of Philip Daro, Geno Flores, Adam Gamoran, Margaret Goertz, Clara Keith, Edys Quellmalz, and Carina Wong, asked insightful questions and offered helpful guidance.

In addition, we were graciously received by staff in the California, Georgia, and Pennsylvania departments of education, who participated in interviews, provided access to information, and helped us understand the complex evolution of their SBA policies. If any errors of fact remain, they are due to our own failings, not the unwillingness of state staff to explain and clarify. We also interviewed staff from teacher, administrator, and school board professional organizations and from other state agencies, elected bodies, and educational interest groups, and we wish to thank them for their time and insights. Credit is also is due to the hundreds of superintendents, principals, and teachers who responded to our interviews and surveys each year and to the 18 schools that graciously participated in our site visits.

Finally, we want to thank our reviewers, Margaret Goertz of the University of Pennsylvania and Vi-Nhuan Le, Catherine Augustine, and Susan Bodilly of RAND. Their thoughtful input improved the final manuscript. We are also grateful to Lisa Bernard, who skillfully edited the document, and to Todd Duft, who guided the document through the production process.

Abbreviations

AFT	American Federation of Teachers
AMO	annual measurable objective
API	academic performance index
ASAM	Alternative Schools Accountability Model
AYP	adequate yearly progress
CAC	Comprehensive Assistance Center
CAPA	California Alternative Performance Assessment
CRCT	Criterion-Referenced Competency Test
CST	California Standards Test
DAIT	District Assistance and Intervention Team
ELA	English and language arts
ELL	English language learner
ESEA	Elementary and Secondary Education Act
ESL	English as a second language
GaDOE	Georgia Department of Education
GPS	Georgia Performance Standards
HOUSSE	High Objective Uniform State Standard of Evaluation
IEP	individualized education program
ISBA	Implementing Standards-Based Accountability
IU	intermediate unit

LEA	local education agency
LEP	limited English proficiency
NAEP	National Assessment of Educational Progress
NATI	National Assessment of Title I
NCES	National Center for Education Statistics
NCLB	No Child Left Behind Act
PAFPC	Pennsylvania Association of Federal Program Coordinators
PASA	Pennsylvania Alternative Student Assessment
PD	professional development
PPI	Pennsylvania Performance Index
PSAA	Public School Accountability Act of 1999
PSSA	Pennsylvania System of School Assessment
PVAAS	Pennsylvania Value-Added Assessment Program
QCC	Quality Core Curriculum
RESA	regional educational service agency
RSDSS	Regional System of District and School Support
SAIT	School Assistance and Intervention Team
SBA	standards-based accountability
SSAS	state single accountability system

CHAPTER ONE

Introduction

The No Child Left Behind Act (NCLB) of 2001 (20 U.S.C. § 6311 et seq.) is arguably the primary policy initiative affecting schools and districts in the United States today, and its standards-based accountability (SBA) provisions are perhaps its most potent component. NCLB requires states to adopt content and achievement standards, to measure student progress toward those standards, and to implement a series of interventions and sanctions in schools and districts that fail to meet their targets. Together, these standards, assessments, and consequences constitute an SBA system. Since 2001–2002, each of the states has been developing and implementing such a system that is consistent with NCLB yet unique to the state.[1] Recent research suggests that these systems have already had a large impact on schools and districts (Center on Education Policy, 2004, 2006).

The Implementing Standards-Based Accountability (ISBA) study was designed to identify factors that enhance the implementation of SBA systems, foster changes in school and classroom practice, and promote improved student achievement. Advocates of SBA often claim that these policies will encourage educators to focus their efforts on improving achievement in core subjects and boost student proficiency, whereas detractors worry that attaching higher stakes to test results will lead to adverse consequences, such as narrowing of the curriculum or excessive test preparation resulting in invalid test scores. Whether NCLB's accountability provisions ultimately turn out to be beneficial or detrimental is likely to depend in large part on how states, districts, and schools implement the provisions and respond to the incentives.

The ISBA study is gathering data from selected states, districts, schools, and teachers longitudinally for three years to address four broad questions:

- What strategies are used in implementing SBA at the state, district, and school levels?
- Which state, district, and school implementation strategies are associated with changes in classroom practice?

---

[1] The term *state* is used in this monograph to refer to all the jurisdictions that are responsible for implementing NCLB, which include the 50 states, the District of Columbia, and Puerto Rico.

- Which features of SBA implementation are associated with student attainment of academic standards?
- How valid are the standards-based test scores as indicators of changes in student achievement?

Answers to these questions will help policymakers, educators, and researchers understand the ways in which SBA policies are implemented at all levels of the system; explain relationships among implementation, instructional practices, and student achievement; and identify successful practices that can be promulgated to make SBA function more effectively. This monograph addresses the first research question. It describes the research project and presents descriptive results from the first two years of data collection. Future publications will expand the analyses to include all three years of data and all of the research questions.

Standards-Based Accountability

SBA is the amalgamation of three ideas intended to improve student achievement that have been part of the educational landscape for some time—academic standards, standardized assessments, and accountability for student outcomes. For example, the nation's governors sounded the call for explicit world-class standards to guide educational practice in 1989 in response to the poor performance of U.S. students on international comparative assessments (McKnight, Crosswhite, and Dossey, 1987; Educational Resources Information Center, 1989; Travers and Westbury, 1989). After much study and discussion (National Council on Educational Standards and Testing, 1992), content standards became a formal requirement of the 1994 reauthorization of the Elementary and Secondary Education Act (The Improving America's Schools Act, Public Law 103-382, October 20, 1994). Standardized achievement testing is a far older idea. Standardized tests began to be used in the United States in the middle of the 19th century, and they have been the most common method for monitoring educational performance for decades (Resnick, 1982). Accountability for outcomes in education can be traced back more than a century to early pay-for-performance agreements in England (Kirst, 1990), although such arrangements are not part of most formal educational accountability systems today. Instead, outcomes-based accountability has taken a number of other forms in the United States, including minimum competency testing and high school exit examinations in the 1970s, and, more recently, grade-level promotion tests. Yet, the combination of these three elements into a single integrated system designed to improve school performance through signals and incentives is relatively new. Some have referred to it as "the new accountability" (Fuhrman, 1999), but we prefer the more descriptive term *standards-based accountability*.

SBA operates through a multilevel, multistep feedback mechanism. Content and performance standards that describe "what students should know and should be able to do" establish goals for the education system. Districts and schools are expected to use these goals to guide their choices of curriculum, professional development (PD), and other school activities. Teachers also use the standards as learning goals when they plan instruction. In this way, the coordinated efforts of policymakers, administrators, and teachers promote students' mastery of the desired content and skills. The standards also guide the development of systemwide student assessments. Student test scores on these assessments are used as an indicator of school success, and incentives are attached to school performance. Schools that do well are rewarded to reinforce good practice. Schools that do poorly are offered assistance and, ultimately, sanctioned so they will change practice and improve services to students. This feedback loop is intended to improve educational practices leading to improved student outcomes. These few basic components are at the heart of SBA, although they can be operationalized in different ways by choosing different standards, tests, assistance policies, and reward structures.

Under NCLB, each state establishes its own SBA system that contains the following seven basic components:[2]

- academic content standards in reading, mathematics, and science indicating what students should know and be able to do
- annual assessments aligned with the academic content standards in reading and mathematics in grades three through eight and once in high school and, in science, once in elementary school, once in middle school, and once in high school
- achievement standards for reading, mathematics, and science indicating the level of test performance that corresponds to "proficient" and other levels of performance (sometimes called *performance standards*)
- annual measurable objectives (AMOs) in reading and mathematics, indicating the percentage of students that is expected to be proficient each year until all are proficient in 2014; AMOs are applied to all students (i.e., the school as a whole) and to designated subgroups, including students from major racial and ethnic groups, low-income students, limited English-proficient students, and students with disabilities[3] (if each group is of sufficient size). (Science results must be made public, but annual measurable objectives are not required for science.)
- an additional academic indicator chosen by the state (for high schools, this indicator must be graduation rate, but each state can select its own indicators for other levels)

---

[2] A more detailed description of accountability under NCLB can be found in Stecher, Hamilton, and Gonzalez (2003).

[3] Many students with disabilities who were exempt from state testing in the past must be included in testing under NCLB.

- adequate yearly progress (AYP) calculations for schools and districts, indicating whether all students and all significant subgroups of students have reached annual AMOs in reading and mathematics (a school makes AYP only if it meets all the requirements for all subgroups)
- interventions and sanctions for Title I schools and districts that do not make AYP for two or more years. After two years, the required interventions include formal planning for improvement, PD, and the requirement that schools offer parents the opportunity to transfer their child to a school that is not low performing (with transportation provided). After three consecutive years not making AYP, schools must also offer students supplemental educational services (i.e., tutoring). The interventions escalate in subsequent years to staffing changes and major governance changes, including takeover by the state.

The law also requires all teachers of core academic subjects to be "highly qualified" in the subjects they teach. For new teachers, this requirement entails passing a subject-matter test, having a major in a subject, or obtaining advanced certification. Existing teachers can use these methods or they can demonstrate subject-matter competency through alternative, state-developed evaluation procedures (see Chapter Three for details about the requirement for highly qualified teachers).[4] Districts must spend at least 5 percent of their Title I funds for PD to ensure that teachers are highly qualified, and this requirement increases to 10 percent if schools have been identified for improvement due to low scores for two successive years.

The NCLB framework specifies the goal of ensuring that all students become proficient in reading and mathematics by 2014. Empirical research on SBA suggests that test-based accountability can be a powerful lever for change, but success in achieving the goals of NCLB is not ensured; this study was designed to understand the factors that influence its effectiveness.

Evidence Concerning SBA Effectiveness

For many educators, the utility of SBA was demonstrated in a few pioneering states in the 1990s. Two of the most prominent examples of SBA occurred in Texas and North Carolina, where scores on state accountability tests rose dramatically after the introduction of SBA systems (Grissmer and Flanagan, 1998). However, some researchers have questioned the validity of these gains and therefore the effectiveness of the reforms, because increases in performance on the National Assessment of Educational Progress (NAEP), which is not associated with high stakes, have not been as large as gains on the statewide tests (Fordham Foundation, 2005; Stephen Klein et al., 2000; Koretz

---

[4] The law also requires that all paraprofessionals meet quality standards.

and Barron, 1998; Linn, 2000). On the other hand, some observers have interpreted small improvements in NAEP scores in states that adopted SBA systems as providing confirmatory evidence of the success of SBA policies in these states (Grissmer et al., 2000). Active debate continues about the impact of high-stakes, test-based accountability systems in the states (e.g., Amrein and Berliner, 2002; Carnoy and Loeb, 2002; Koretz and Hamilton, 2006). In addition, international comparisons provide some evidence that students in school systems with high-stakes testing programs outperform students in systems that do not have high-stakes testing programs (Bishop, 1998). NCLB is testimony to the confidence that U.S. policymakers have in the efficacy of SBA, although, for many, its effectiveness remains an open question.

However, the paths through which SBA changes district, school, and classroom practices and how these changes in practice influence student outcomes are largely unexplored. There is strong evidence that SBA leads to changes in teachers' instructional practices (Hamilton, 2004; Stecher, 2002). For example, researchers have found that teachers shift time away from nontested subjects or topics and toward tested subjects or topics (Jones et al., 1999; Koretz, Barron, et al., 1996; Shepard and Dougherty, 1991; Stecher and Barron, 1999). Much less is known about the impact of SBA at the district and school levels and the relationships among actions at the various levels and student outcomes. This study was designed to shed light on this complex set of relationships, with particular attention to classroom practices that directly affect student learning.

How SBA Is Supposed to Work

The study design and data collection procedures were guided by research on the implementation and the scale-up of educational reforms and by the goal of understanding classroom-level responses. Figure 1.1 provides a simple framework for investigating how NCLB policies are translated into classroom practice and student learning outcomes.[5]

Figure 1.1 highlights the importance of responses at all levels of the education system—state, district, school, and classroom. NCLB requires that states adopt accountability policies (e.g., standards, assessments, AYP targets). Districts and schools develop local policies to promote the state standards and support improvement efforts. Ultimately, the accountability system leads to changes in classroom practices, which directly influence student achievement. Yet, none of this occurs in a vacuum. Contextual factors, including local barriers to implementation and the attitudes and opinions of the stakeholders, affect the ways in which the policies are translated into practice and influence student learning. Our study was designed to gather information

---

[5] At this point, we drop the SBA acronym in the text for the most part and use the language of NCLB, since NCLB is the specific instantiation of SBA that we are studying.

Figure 1.1
ISBA Conceptual Framework

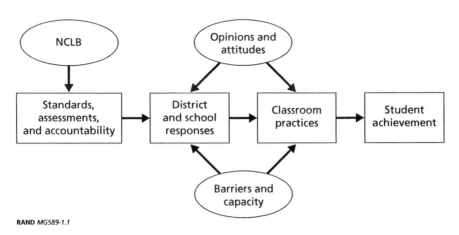

RAND *MG589-1.1*

on implementation at all of these levels, with an emphasis on understanding variations in practice across schools and classrooms. Research points to particular issues that are relevant at each node of the conceptual framework.

District and School Responses to Accountability

District and school leaders must respond to NCLB in informed and constructive ways if the accountability policies are to have positive effects on teachers and students. Research suggests that districts are both implementers of state and federal policy and significant policy generators themselves, i.e., state and federal policies spur additional district-level policymaking (Fuhrman and Elmore, 1990). In the case of new state accountability systems, districts implement the regulations that apply at the district level, and they develop new policies and programs to help students, teachers, and schools meet the demands that the system places on them (Goertz, Massell, and Chun, 1998; Spillane, 1996). The literature highlights specific areas in which districts can have significant influence, and these areas were included in the ISBA research design.

For example, district efforts to provide support, training, and resources can be particularly valuable for helping teachers translate the state policies into classroom practice (Massell, Kirst, and Hoppe, 1997). A large body of research has shown that district and school PD efforts can result in changes in teachers' knowledge and beliefs as well as in their instructional practice (Loucks-Horsley and Matsumoto, 1999). Some researchers have even found direct effects on student achievement for some types of PD (Huffman, Thomas, and Lawrenz, 2003). In contrast, the lack of human capital—including insufficient staffing and limited staff commitment, knowledge, and skills—can hinder efforts to implement wide-scale reform (Burch and Spillane, 2004; Elmore and Burney, 1999; Massell and Goertz, 1999; Firestone, 1989; Spillane and Thompson, 1997). As a result, the study team collected information about policies relating to staffing, staff support, and staff development.

Recent research on the implementation of NCLB found that the most frequent strategy that districts used across the country for schools in need of improvement was increased use of student achievement data to inform decisions (Center on Education Policy, 2005). This enthusiasm for data-driven decisionmaking stems in part from research that suggests that district and school efforts to foster educators' use of data—not only from annual state tests, but from interim progress tests and other classroom-based assessments—is especially prevalent in high-performing schools and districts (Supovitz and Klein, 2003; Symonds, 2003; Casserly, 2002; Edmonds, 1979; EdSource, ongoing; Council of Chief State School Officers and the Charles A. Dana Center, 2002; Snipes, Doolittle, and Herlihy, 2002). Because of the widespread interest in data-driven decisionmaking and the growing body of research examining its use and effectiveness, the examination of educators' use of data is an area of focus for the ISBA study.

A number of other school and district actions have been shown to be important predictors of student achievement in the context of accountability. For example, principals' instructional leadership is related to the likelihood of school change and student learning (Leithwood, 2004; Waters, Marzano, and McNulty, 2003). In addition, the amount of time that districts and schools decide to formally allocate for instruction is associated with student achievement (McKnight, Crosswhite, and Dossey, 1987; Mirel, 1994; Purves and Levine, 1975; Schmidt, 1999; Stevenson and Stigler, 1992). The ISBA study incorporated these and other district- and school-level policies and practices into its data collection efforts.

Classroom Practice

The effects of NCLB on student achievement will occur in large part as a result of the changes that teachers make to their classroom practices. Although teaching styles are fairly resistant to change, research has shown that high-stakes testing can influence both what is taught and how it is taught (Bishop, 1995; Hamilton, 2004). States have used high-stakes tests as "instructional magnets" (Popham, 1987) to persuade teachers to make desired changes in curriculum and instruction. For example, teachers in Vermont reallocated instructional time to include problem-solving and other new elements of the state curriculum or to make their instruction more consistent with the existing state curriculum (Stecher, Barron, et al., 1998; Koretz, Barron, et al., 1996). Similarly, teachers in Kentucky and Washington changed the activities in which students engaged during writing and mathematics instruction to promote the outcomes incorporated into the state assessments (Wolf and McIver, 1999; Borko and Elliott, 1999).

Understanding changes in instructional practice also helps us judge the extent to which NCLB accountability leads to real improvement in student achievement or to inflated test scores (Koretz and Hamilton, 2006). Under certain conditions, accountability systems can produce changes that undermine the validity of test scores, such as a narrowing of curriculum and instruction to focus on tested subjects (Jones et al., 1999) or tested topics within a subject (Shepard and Dougherty, 1991) while ignoring other parts of the standards. High-stakes accountability has also been associated with undesirable instructional behaviors, such as asking students to practice finding mistakes in written work rather than producing writing of their own or having students only solve the type of math story problems found on the test (Shepard and Dougherty, 1991; Smith and Rottenberg, 1991). In some cases, high-stakes testing was found to discourage teachers from using joint or team teaching approaches (Stodolsky, 1988). It can also lead to narrow test-preparation activities (Taylor et al., 2003) or to a focus on students whose performance "counts" the most, such as those on the cusp of meeting the "proficient" standard, at the expense of those well above or well below the standard (Booher-Jennings, 2005). These instructional behaviors may cause test scores to rise without a concomitant increase in student understanding of the standard content.

This monograph explores a variety of changes in classroom practices, including both those considered desirable and those considered undesirable.

Opinions and Attitudes

The study framework illustrated in Figure 1.1 also recognizes that NCLB does not operate in a vacuum, and it is important to look at factors that might mediate the effects of the accountability system. Research suggests that principals' and teachers' beliefs about subject matter, students, and accountability-related reforms are likely to be important predictors of implementation (O'Day, Goertz, and Floden, 1995). For example, self-efficacy (Hoy and Woolfolk, 1993) has been shown to predict teachers' adoption of reform-based practice (Firestone, Monfils, and Camilli, 2001), and it is likely to be an important influence on teachers' responses to SBA. The extent to which teachers believe that they can achieve the specific goals of the reform has been shown to affect their change in behavior (Kelley et al., 2000). The ISBA study gathered information on teachers', principals', and superintendents' opinions and attitudes about NCLB and about various aspects of their districts and schools.

Barriers and Capacity

Research also shows that contextual factors at the school and district levels can act as barriers or supports for implementation of reforms. Local capacity can be built by providing learning opportunities for teachers, including both formal PD and less formal mechanisms, such as teacher learning communities and mentoring programs. For example, Spillane and Zeuli (1999) found that teachers tended not to adopt the kinds of practices that reformers envisioned even when those teachers had been exposed to materials describing these practices; the teachers suggested that more intense learning opportunities were needed. In addition to helping teachers understand the reforms, these learning opportunities can contribute to a shared vision and a sense of community, factors whose absence can hinder improved practice (Cohen, McLaughlin, and Talbert, 1993). Finally, past research also indicates that educators' will and motivation to embrace policy goals and strategies are important facilitators of successful implementation (McLaughlin, 1987; Odden, 1991). The ISBA study gathered information on educators' perceptions of barriers and capacity and examined how these varied by district and school characteristics.

Evidence Concerning No Child Left Behind

Since the ISBA study was initiated, there has been considerable research about the implementation of NCLB. As might be expected with a reform of this scope, much of the initial research was descriptive, documenting the ways in which states implemented the provision of the law and the extent to which they complied with NCLB guidelines and timetables. For the most part, states were meeting the timetables to develop SBA systems, including standards, assessments, AYP targets, and interventions. For example, the National Assessment of Title I (NATI) reported that, as of March 2005, 27 states had completed their first full administration of all required reading assessments, 26 states had done so for all required mathematics assessments, and 22 states had done so for all required science assessments (Stullich, 2006). The rest of the states were pilot testing assessments for implementation by the 2005–2006 deadline. Similarly, all states developed mechanisms to implement the AYP provisions of the law. Thirteen percent of all schools were identified for improvement for 2004–2005; schools in large and urban districts and those with high concentrations of poor, minority, and limited English proficiency (LEP) students were more likely to be identified than other schools (Stullich, 2006). By 2005, all states had developed systems of support for identified schools, and states and districts were implementing the interventions that the law required. In addition, identified schools were undertaking their own improvement efforts, such as increasing the amount of instructional time devoted to reading (Stullich, 2006), and implementing progress tests to provide more immediate assessment data for instructional planning (Olson, 2005).

Yet, the law presented many challenges for states, districts, and schools. Newspaper accounts provided a glimpse of the struggles that were occurring with NCLB accountability across the country. Particularly challenging were the NCLB requirements for parental choice and transfers (Asimov, 2003), supplemental educational services (i.e., tutoring) (Mezzacappa, 2004), and the testing of special education students (Schemo, 2004).

Recently, researchers have started reporting on the effects of the law, both its positive and negative consequences. On the positive side, NCLB was found to have raised learning expectations, focused attention on traditionally low-performing groups, and forced greater alignment between standards and instruction (Center on Education Policy, 2006). The same study also found that schools were making better use of test data and that districts were providing more curriculum guidance and better instructional support for teachers. On the negative side, NCLB has led some schools to reduce or eliminate instruction in nontested subjects, including art, foreign language, and physical education (Dobbs, 2004). Researchers also reported that NCLB increased the demands on districts and schools without providing adequate resources or improving local capacity (Center on Education Policy, 2006).

Finally, researchers have begun to look for local policies and actions that foster school improvement. For example, case studies of restructuring schools in Michigan found that a multiple-strategy approach to improvement was more successful at helping these schools make AYP (Center on Education Policy, 2005). As far as we know, no researchers have yet examined implementation across levels in the manner used in the ISBA study.

How the Monograph Is Organized

This monograph is intended to provide descriptive information from the first two years of the ISBA study. Chapter Two describes the methodological approach, including sampling, data collection, and analysis. In Chapter Three, we present background information on the three states participating in this study as well as study findings related to teacher qualifications. The bulk of the findings are presented in Chapters Four through Seven. In Chapter Four, we present information on educators' impressions of and reactions to their states' NCLB systems. Chapter Five examines school improvement strategies, and Chapter Six focuses on educators' responses to the standards and testing provisions of NCLB. Chapter Seven addresses educators' perceptions about the factors that hinder their efforts to improve schools and raise student achievement as well as parents' perceptions about the effects of NCLB. Chapter Eight summarizes the overarching themes from the study and discusses their implications.

CHAPTER TWO

Study Design and Methods

The ISBA study uses a combination of large-scale, quantitative data collection and small-scale case studies to examine NCLB implementation and outcomes in three states. In each state, we are tracing NCLB implementation at the state, district, school, and classroom levels and gathering information on student achievement so that we can associate implementation factors with student outcomes. We focus on elementary and middle school science and mathematics, though we also collect some information on reading instruction and achievement because reading is a focus of states' accountability systems. The inclusion of both mathematics and science provides an opportunity to contrast a subject that has been a focus of all states' accountability systems with one that has received less emphasis. The study is longitudinal in nature with three waves of data collection: 2003–2004, 2004–2005, and 2005–2006. This monograph is based on results from survey and case study data collected in the spring of the 2004–2005 school year, with some reference to data collected in the previous school year.

Sampling

States

We selected three states—California, Georgia, and Pennsylvania—to represent a range of approaches to implementing NCLB and to provide both geographic and demographic diversity. Table 2.1 summarizes some important demographic features of K–12 public education in California, Georgia, and Pennsylvania measured at the time when data collection began. The states differ in a number of ways that might affect their implementation of NCLB, including the size of their K–12 systems (Table 2.1) and the racial and ethnic characteristics of their students (Table 2.2). California is a large, diverse state that enrolls approximately one out of every eight students in the United States. It has about 1,000 districts that vary greatly in enrollment. More than 100 districts have more than 10,000 students each, but about half of the districts in the state have fewer than 1,000 students. Georgia uses predominantly a county system of school districts with enrollments ranging from 351 to 13,769; most districts enroll between 2,500 and 10,000. Pennsylvania has few large districts—only two have more

Table 2.1
Size of K–12 Public School Systems, 2003–2004

Feature	California	Georgia	Pennsylvania
Districts	1,059	180	500
Schools	9,222	2,040	3,253
Teachers	297,480	96,808	119,888
Students	6,298,413	1,522,611	1,821,146

SOURCES: California data are from Education Data Partnership (2007). Georgia data are from NCES (2004). Pennsylvania data are from Pennsylvania Department of Education (2005b, 2006c).

than 25,000 students—and many that are quite small—128 districts have fewer than 2,000 students.

Pennsylvania is the least diverse of the three states in terms of student race and ethnicity, while California is the most diverse, with two-thirds of all students coming from underrepresented groups (see Table 2.2). Georgia's overall school enrollment in 2003–2004 was 38 percent black, 7 percent Hispanic, and 52 percent white. Pennsylvania had the smallest percentage of students from low-income households (28 percent) compared with California (49 percent) and Georgia (46 percent). All three states had roughly the same proportion of students with disabilities. Neither Georgia nor Pennsylvania had a large number of students who are English language learners (ELLs), in contrast to California, where serving the needs of English learners has been a major educational challenge.

Table 2.2
Student Demographic Characteristics, 2003–2004

Characteristic	California (%)	Georgia (%)	Pennsylvania (%)
White	32	52	76
Hispanic	46	7	6
Black	8	38	16
Asian	8	3	2
Free/reduced-price lunch–eligible	49	46	28[a]
ELLs	25	4	2
Students with disabilities	10	12	14

SOURCES: California data are from Education Data Partnership (2007) and California Department of Education (2006a). Georgia data are from NCES (2004). Pennsylvania data are from Pennsylvania Department of Education (2005b, 2006c).

[a] Pennsylvania percentages for free and reduced-price lunch–eligible students and students with disabilities are from NCES (2004).

Districts

We selected an initial sample of 27 districts per state, stratified by size, to obtain a representative sample that would be adequate for our analyses. Appendix A describes the district and school sampling procedures in greater detail. Unfortunately, we were not able to enroll as many of these districts as we hoped, and we drew a supplemental sample of 23 additional districts to replace those that refused. Eventually, we recruited a total of 68 districts to participate in the 2003–2004 school year, representing an overall cooperation rate of 65 percent. For 2004–2005, we selected a second, supplemental sample of 28 districts to give us more analytic power and to increase the number of districts in which high percentages of schools were not meeting NCLB achievement goals. The total enrollment for 2004–2005 was 89 districts out of a total sample of 132 districts, and the cooperation rate was 67 percent.

Schools

We restricted the school sample to include only "regular" public schools. We excluded charter schools, alternative schools, vocational schools, special education schools, and small schools (as defined by the states for NCLB reporting purposes—those with fewer than 10 students per grade in Georgia and Pennsylvania and those with fewer than 11 students per grade in California). These exclusions reduced the numbers of eligible schools by 4 percent in Georgia and 3 percent in Pennsylvania, and most of the exclusions were charter schools. California had a larger percentage of nonregular schools; the number of eligible schools there was reduced by 22 percent, which included a combination of small, alternative, charter, and special education schools. However, the total count of students in eligible schools in California dropped by only 6 percent.

In 2003–2004, we randomly sampled 297 schools from the cooperating districts, picking between one and five elementary schools and between one and five middle schools per district according to a prearranged plan based on district size. From this sample, 267 schools agreed to participate in the study in 2003–2004, representing a school cooperation rate of 90 percent. In 2004–2005, the same schools were recontacted, and 249 continued to participate. In the supplemental districts, we used the same initial strategy to sample schools as we had the year before; 78 schools were contacted, and 52 agreed to participate. Overall, in 2004–2005, we recruited a total of 301 schools to participate in the study, representing a school cooperation rate of 80 percent.

Teachers

Once schools were recruited, we obtained complete rosters of all teachers in the relevant subjects and grades. From elementary schools, we asked for lists of all teachers who taught mathematics or science to students in grades three, four, or five. We made the same request of middle schools, focusing on grades seven and eight. The study included all teachers in these grades and subjects. The cooperation rate for teachers is the survey response rate of 83 percent in 2004 and 87 percent in 2005 (see below).

Instrumentation

We collected state-level data through semistructured, face-to-face interviews with key personnel in the state department of education, including the state superintendent or designee, the director of assessment, the director of curriculum, and other relevant administrators. We also interviewed other policymakers, including legislators, staff members from the education committees of the legislature, members or staff from the state board of education, and leaders of the teachers' union and the state school boards' association. In addition to conducting the interviews, we collected relevant documents, such as copies of the state content standards and studies that the state conducted to evaluate alignment between standards and tests. We collected state data primarily in fall 2003 but made follow-up contacts thereafter as needed.

At the district level, we gathered information from superintendents using both semistructured telephone interviews and paper-and-pencil surveys. The surveys included questions on district actions related to NCLB, support that districts received from the state, and challenges related to implementing NCLB provisions. The interviews captured more specific information on state-to-district contacts and district-to-school contacts than could be obtained through surveys. We distributed surveys in January and February of 2004 and 2005 and conducted interviews in spring 2004. Appendix C provides a copy of the superintendent survey.

At the school level, we gathered information from principals and teachers using surveys. These surveys addressed local actions related to the components of NCLB (e.g., standards, assessments, supplemental services, student transfers, teacher qualifications) as well as the contextual factors that may have influenced these actions, such as the quality of leadership, the degree of collaboration among teachers, and the extent of PD. We developed a separate teacher survey for each state, which allowed us to use state-specific terminology, though the underlying questions were the same. We administered a common principal survey across the three states. Moreover, the principal and teacher surveys included questions that we administered to both sets of respondents, permitting us to compare principals' responses with those of teachers. Appendix C includes copies of the principal and teacher surveys from one state. We distributed principal and teacher surveys in January and February of 2004 and 2005 and collected responses generally through June of each year.

We pilot tested the draft surveys with relevant groups of respondents (superintendents, principals, teachers). The pilot testing included cognitive interviews, in which similar respondents in the participating states talked through their responses and informed us of any problems they had answering the questions. We made revisions to the surveys as a result of these interviews.

In addition to performing the large-scale data survey collection, we also conducted annual case study visits to elementary and middle schools in two districts in each of the three states. We visited 14 schools (10 elementary, four middle) during the first year and 16 (11 elementary, five middle) during the second year. During these visits, we interviewed principals and teachers, with a total of 89 interviews in the first year and 110 in the second. We asked principals to arrange interviews with teachers in the grades included in our survey sample. We also asked each elementary school principal to include one first-grade teacher, and a few principals set up interviews with kindergarten teachers as well. When possible, we also interviewed school Title I coordinators and other administrative and support staff, for a total of 15 additional interviews in the first year and 23 in the second. In addition, at each school in which principals would allow it, we conducted focus groups with small groups of parents. We conducted focus groups at 10 schools in the first year and 13 in the second. Most of the focus groups included three to six parents, though a few included as many as 10. Because of the self-selected nature of the samples, neither the parent nor the teacher responses should be interpreted as representative of the school as a whole.

The principal and teacher interview protocols we used during these visits focused on NCLB-related changes in the school, the nature and adequacy of technical assistance received, and the use of information from the accountability system. The parent focus group protocol asked parents about their perceptions of the school, their understanding of NCLB, their responses to the choice and supplemental-service provisions, and their use of information from state tests. The case studies were primarily intended to provide richer information than we were able to collect through surveys, and we used the information, in some cases, to revise surveys in subsequent years. In this monograph, we use quotations from the case studies to provide concrete examples of findings from the survey and to illustrate factors that may influence results. Most of the case study information included in this monograph comes from teachers and principals. Since the numbers of parents included in the study were small and we do not have parent survey data to provide representative responses, we have used the parent focus group responses mainly to supplement information that teachers or principals provided.

Data Collection

Data collection occurred in phases, which were generally repeated each year of the study. District recruitment began in July and continued through October. In the second year, we recruited new districts, recontacted continuing districts, and updated records. School recruitment occurred in October through December. We pretested the surveys in November and distributed them in January and February. Survey data collection continued through June; in rare cases, we extended the contact period through the summer if we could maintain contact. School site visits occurred between February and May. In addition, in the first year, we interviewed state policymakers and staff from the state departments of education to build our understanding of the state's implementation of NCLB. We conducted the state interviews in the fall. During the first year, we also interviewed superintendents in all participating districts to supplement the information obtained from the surveys. These open-ended interviews took place in the spring.

Survey Responses

With a few exceptions, survey response rates were quite high. The superintendent response rate for 2003–2004 was 88 percent, and, for 2004–2005, it was 73 percent. (Appendix A provides details about response rates by state.) Principals and teachers responded at even higher rates, 85 and 83 percent, respectively, in 2003–2004 and 86 and 87 percent, respectively, in 2004–2005.

Achievement Data

Each state provides annual school-level student achievement statistics, including mathematics and reading results disaggregated by grade level and NCLB-defined subgroups (in which the number of such students is deemed to be significant). Science scores have only been available in a few grades and only in California and Georgia, since NCLB did not require science testing during the first years of NCLB implementation and states are phasing in these tests incrementally. Subsequent project reporting will analyze associations between changes in student performance as measured by state achievement tests in mathematics and science and specific NCLB policies and school practices as measured by surveys.

Analyses

To analyze survey responses, we generated state-specific sampling and nonresponse weights for each state. Using these weights, we could report estimates of the responses of superintendents, principals, and teachers from regular (or traditional) public schools and districts statewide. Because we excluded some schools that are subject to NCLB requirements but that operate outside a traditional district governance structure, all of the results generalize only to traditional public schools in the respective states. One of the consequences of our sampling strategy in which teachers and principals are nested within schools and schools are nested within districts is that the number of responses grows progressively smaller as we move from teachers to principals to superintendents. As a result, the summary statistics based on teacher responses are more precise than those based on principal responses, which are more precise than those based on superintendent responses. To help the reader interpret the results, we have included estimates in Appendix B of the standard errors associated with the survey responses presented in the body of the monograph.

We analyzed the 43 superintendent interviews using the QSR International® N6® qualitative analysis software package and entered the interview notes into the electronic database. A team of three researchers developed a detailed coding scheme based on the various questions from our interview protocol, the study's overarching conceptual framework, and the major topic areas that emerged from an initial review of the interview notes. We coded the electronic files using this framework and used the software to generate detailed analyses of responses and identify themes within and across states.

We used the case studies primarily to obtain concrete examples to illustrate patterns revealed by the surveys and to afford fresh insight into implementation issues that might be incorporated in future data collection. We recorded each interview on audiotape and transcribed the tapes to provide a searchable archive. In addition, the site visit team of two researchers wrote a summary of each school visit as well as an overall summary of each district visit. Most members of the research team read these summaries as part of the analysis process.

We used state documents and interviews with state policymakers primarily to develop descriptions of state accountability policies, mechanisms for supporting school improvement, and other pressures that influence district and school actions. We wrote up interview notes and assembled them into an archive for analysis. We wrote descriptive summaries for each state and assembled tables to compare specific accountability rules and procedures across states. We clarified disagreements about facts through additional data collection but retained conflicting opinions or points of view.

Technical Notes

To simplify the presentation of results, we use descriptive phrases (e.g., almost all, most) rather than numbers to report the proportion of respondents who gave a particular response. For the sake of clarity, we have adopted the following definitions for these terms. We use *almost all* when 90 percent or more of the respondents answered in a particular way. We use *most* when approximately two-thirds (i.e., 60 to 70 percent) of respondents gave a similar response. *A majority* of respondents means more than 50 percent, and *about half* means between 45 percent and 55 percent. We use *some* when about one-third of respondents (i.e., 30 to 40 percent) gave the same response, and *almost none* or *almost no* denotes fewer than 10 percent of respondents.

Unless otherwise noted, all the results come from the 2004–2005 surveys. We report results from 2003–2004 only if the changes between the years are noteworthy.

All of the figures and tables in the monograph use percentages rounded to whole numbers. When the number of respondents in a particular category is less than 10, we generally report raw values rather than weighted percentage estimates.

To simplify the presentation, we do not report tests of statistical significance in the text. However, as a general rule, we discuss explicitly only statistically significant differences in the text. Readers can use the standard errors in Appendix B to determine whether other differences are statistically significant or whether they might be due to measurement or sampling error. As a very rough guideline, the difference between two percentages is statistically significant (at an alpha level of 0.05) if it is larger than the sum of twice the larger standard error associated with the numbers being compared. In the case of the superintendent survey, in which the number of respondents in each state is small, the standard errors are large, and only very large differences (sometimes 40 percentage points) will be statistically significant.

It is important to note that, because we are carrying out a large number of comparisons, a small percentage of the significant differences will likely be due to chance rather than to actual differences in the responses. Readers should therefore interpret the discussions of significant differences cautiously, especially in cases in which the magnitudes of the differences are small.

CHAPTER THREE

SBA Systems in California, Georgia, and Pennsylvania

Introduction

States have many decisions to make in implementing an SBA system consistent with NCLB (Stecher, Hamilton, and Gonzalez, 2003), and their choices will likely influence what happens in schools and how well students perform. The state implementation decisions include adopting content standards, defining AYP and setting AMOs, selecting assessments in required subjects and grades, identifying schools that make progress toward annual targets based on student achievement and other measures, and taking action to ensure that all teachers are highly qualified to teach the standards in the subjects they teach.

States have considerable flexibility in these choices, and, as a result, states vary extensively in the standards, assessments, and methods for determining whether schools and districts meet their AYP targets. For instance, several national organizations reviewed state standards and found wide variation in rigor and specificity ("Quality Counts at 10," 2006; Finn, Petrilli, and Julian, 2006). The difficulty of state assessments also varies among states—in terms both of their content and of the cut scores that are used to define proficiency (Linn, 2003; Kingsbury et al., 2003; McCombs et al., 2005; Peterson and Hess, 2005). As a result, some states are much further from attaining 100-percent proficiency than others. Similarly, states have adopted different trajectories for their annual proficiency targets for schools. Although all must achieve 100-percent proficiency by 2013–2014, some require greater annual improvement in the early years and others have steeper trajectories toward the end (Porter, Linn, and Trimble, 2005). States have also taken different approaches to meeting the highly qualified teacher requirements of NCLB, particularly for veteran teachers (Walsh and Snyder, 2004; "Quality Counts at 10," 2006). As we noted at the outset, such differences in implementation will likely influence practices at the school level, including instruction, which will, in turn, affect student performance. For example, lack of specificity in state standards may lead teachers to pay greater attention to state tests than to standards (Stecher et al., 2000), leading to potentially inflated test scores.

This study focused on the selected three states to capture some of this variation in implementation. This chapter describes important elements of each state's educational policy context that relate to accountability, including key features of each state's

NCLB accountability system for the 2004–2005 school year. The elements include the accountability systems that were in place prior to NCLB implementation, the testing programs that states have adopted to comply with NCLB, states' methods for defining AYP, the status of their schools with respect to meeting AYP targets, and states' approaches to implementing the highly qualified teacher provisions of NCLB.

Prior Accountability Systems

In all three states, the implementation of SBA was shaped by the existing policy context, including state budget constraints, the structure of educational governance in the state, and the political environment in which the educational reforms were operating. Perhaps the most important factor in determining the direction that each state took with respect to SBA was the state's prior experience with testing and accountability. California already had an elaborate state testing and accountability system. Georgia was just in the process of implementing a state accountability system, and Pennsylvania left accountability primarily in the hands of local school districts. All three states had to adjust their systems to comply with NCLB. This became problematic for California as policymakers attempted to comply with NCLB while maintaining continuity with the earlier approach to evaluating schools. The coexistence of two SBA systems forced educators to deal with sometimes-divergent information that each system provided (Linn, 2005). The next sections describe the existing SBA systems in each participating state and discuss ways in which the states have incorporated features of their existing systems into their new NCLB-compliant accountability systems.

California

California had extensive experience with SBA before NCLB was implemented. The Public School Accountability Act of 1999 (PSAA) created a test-based accountability system that applied to virtually all public schools in the state.[1] This system was intended to provide the public with access to information on school performance and to create incentives for educators to focus on improving student achievement in their schools. The state adopted academic standards and a comprehensive testing program that combined commercially available norm-referenced tests with custom-developed standards-based tests. The emphasis placed on standards-based questions relative to norm-referenced questions gradually increased as the system matured. Under PSAA, the state assigned each school an academic performance index (API) based on student test scores. PSAA required schools to increase their APIs each year by an amount equal to 5 percent of the difference between their prior scores and the state interim target of

---

[1]   Alternative and small schools of fewer than 100 students were eligible for the Alternative Schools Accountability Model (ASAM), in which multiple measures would be used to determine progress. However, with the implementation of NCLB, the state was required to compute a test-based AYP score for all schools.

800 (on a scale with a maximum value of 1,000). Similar targets applied to significant subgroups of students, but, in recognition of the larger measurement error associated with smaller sets of students, PSAA set subgroup targets at 80 percent of the schools' overall targets. The system included rewards and sanctions based on annual gains in a school's API score rather than on attainment of a specific score level. For the first two years, the program gave several types of financial awards, including awards for all schools that met their annual growth targets and for schools that made the greatest gains. After 2000, California's economic outlook worsened considerably, and the program discontinued the reward funding. Schools that did not meet their targets were subject to interventions to improve their performance. The intervention program provided schools with expert help to develop and implement improvement plans. If these plans did not succeed, the state could apply sanctions, including five forms of restructuring: reopening the school as a charter school, reconstituting the school, entering the school into a management contract, taking over the school, or other major restructuring (Ziebarth, 2004).

California's accountability system under NCLB limited federal accountability sanctions to Title I schools, though many of the other features of the prior system were incorporated into the state's system under NCLB. For example, API was used as the additional indicator that NCLB required (in addition to test scores), thus retaining, to some degree, the state's gain-based approach to accountability. However, the overlay of the federal system onto the existing state system created some problems in California. Changes in the way in which accountability was determined and the consequences of these changes frustrated educators. More troubling was the fact that the two systems sometimes led to different conclusions about individual schools' performance. It was common for a school to be told that it had achieved significant growth according to the state system but had not met the AYP benchmark. In fact, in 2004, the state superintendent reported that 317 schools increased 30 points or more on API (a large gain), yet failed to make AYP. In 2005, more than one-third of all schools either met their API targets but did not make AYP (19 percent) or made AYP but did not meet API targets (15 percent) (O'Connell, 2006). Despite this fact, California continued to report both AYP and API results, and many educators continued to believe that the state's system was superior to the federal system.[2]

Georgia

Georgia was implementing test-based accountability for the first time just as NCLB was enacted. In 2000, Georgia's legislature enacted a school accountability system (Georgia's A Plus Education Reform Act, HB1187) modeled on the systems in Texas and North Carolina. Georgia had an extensive state testing program on which to build the accountability system, including tests in reading, mathematics, and science in grades

---

[2] Interviews with state education officials, November 19–20, 2004.

one through eight. The A Plus Education Reform Act was supposed to award a letter grade (A–F) to each school based on both overall student achievement and gains in student achievement; these grades were supposed to be the basis for assigning rewards and interventions. However, the grading system was not fully implemented by the time the state had to respond to NCLB, and the plans were changed to create a system that was in compliance with the federal requirements, although it retained some elements of the A Plus Education Reform Act.

Changes in the accountability system reflected changes that were occurring in Georgia's political leadership. For several years, accountability had been a point of contention between the governor's office and the state department of education. In addition to creating an accountability system, the A Plus Education Reform Act removed the responsibility for accountability from the department of education and placed it in a new Office of Educational Accountability that reported to the governor. In 2003, a new governor was elected from the opposing party. The Office of Educational Accountability was renamed the Governor's Office of Student Achievement. At this time, efforts were begun to reverse the changes in educational governance that had been enacted under the previous governor.

In 2005, Georgia instituted a state single accountability system (SSAS), integrating federal and state accountability provisions. The state's system complies fully with NCLB, with AYP as the primary measure of school performance. Each school receives an annual report that includes a link to the school's AYP report. The annual report also includes a performance index that includes two components for each public school: (1) the percentage of students meeting and exceeding standards and the gain or loss of that percentage from the previous year and (2) performance highlights that list academic measurements for each school that meets or exceeds 80 percent. SSAS expanded to all schools federal sanctions that, at first, applied only to Title I schools. The system includes sanctions for schools that persistently perform poorly. These may include school-level interventions such as appointing instructional coaches, replacing school staff, or making major changes in school governance; or district-level interventions such as the appointment of a local education agency (LEA) support specialist with management authority; and ultimately entering into an improvement contract with the district supervised by the Georgia department of education.

Pennsylvania

Pennsylvania has traditionally been a "local control" state with a limited state testing program. This was starting to change prior to NCLB, when the state enacted empowerment legislation which identified districts as *educational empowerment districts* if more than 50 percent of students in the district scored in the bottom quartile on the Pennsylvania System of School Assessment (PSSA) for two years. (The PSSA was administered only in grades five, eight, and 11.) The state identified 11 districts for improvement under this law in its first year (Pennsylvania Department of Education, 2005b) and gave their local boards wide latitude for improving schools, including reopening them as charter schools, reconstituting them, or entering into management contracts (Ziebarth, 2004).

However, this system was far from compliant with NCLB, and Pennsylvania had to make significant changes to meet the federal guidelines. The changes included revised content standards, additional tests, new performance standard-setting, and a new formula for identifying schools. In the first year, each school's status from the empowerment legislation was transferred into the NCLB system, including the Title I schools. In 2004, the state created the Pennsylvania Performance Index (PPI), a continuous improvement measure that the state could use to recognize significant growth. Pennsylvania allowed schools and districts to appeal AYP status by demonstrating significant growth on the PPI. In 2005, the U.S. Department of Education approved PPI as an alternate AYP measure.

Pennsylvania planned to have its accountability provisions apply equally to all schools and districts rather than just to Title I schools. In particular, state leaders wanted to provide the same technical assistance and sanctions to all schools that failed to make AYP, regardless of Title I status. However, budget constraints made this impossible; benefits as a result of NCLB sanctions such as school choice and supplemental educational services are only being offered to eligible students in Title I schools.

As noted, Pennsylvania has a long history of local control, and the state department of education has traditionally had limited direct involvement in local districts and schools. However, under the new NCLB-mandated accountability system, the department has taken a much more active role in guiding local education policy. These changes led to a debate in the legislature about how much control the department of education should have over districts. The increased role requires more funding, but the legislature has been reluctant to expand the budget of the state department of education.

Pennsylvania has recently implemented a pilot program to provide schools with estimates of student achievement based on value-added models. The state initially implemented this program, the Pennsylvania Value-Added Assessment Program (PVAAS), in phases but has now expanded it to all of the state's districts. Whether it will be incorporated formally into the state's accountability system remains to be seen.

State Academic Content Standards

Academic content standards define the goals for each state's educational system. Schools are expected to use these statements about "what students should know and be able to do" to establish policies regarding curriculum, PD, and other school functions, and teachers are expected to use them to guide instructional planning. Like a majority of states, California, Georgia, and Pennsylvania had already adopted content standards in certain grades and subjects prior to NCLB. The grades and subjects in which content standards were in place in 2003–2004, however, varied across the three states. Table 3.1 indicates the grades in which each state had implemented standards in English language arts, mathematics, and science as of the 2003–2004 school year.

California's content standards outline the skills and knowledge that all students should master at each grade level for all three of these subjects plus others, including history and social science and visual and performing arts. Several organizations have praised them for their clarity and comprehensiveness. In particular, California was one of only three states to receive a grade of A from the Thomas B. Fordham Foundation in its evaluation of state mathematics standards (Finn, Petrilli, and Julian, 2006). Despite contentious debates about the standards when they were adopted, they have now been in place for a number of years, and educators and policymakers are generally satisfied with them.

Georgia's new state content standards, the Georgia Performance Standards (GPS), are being phased in at the time of this writing. The Quality Core Curriculum (QCC), which was in place when NCLB was adopted, described expectations for reading, English language arts, mathematics, science, social studies, foreign languages, fine arts, health, physical education, technology and career education, and agriculture. The QCC contained grade-by-grade standards for grades K–8 and grade cluster standards for 9–12 (i.e., descriptions that apply to a range of grades). However, an external audit conducted by Phi Delta Kappa found that the QCC lacked depth, covered too many topics, and was not aligned with national standards.

In 2002, the Georgia Department of Education (GaDOE) launched a major curriculum revision initiative in mathematics, science, social studies, and English language arts. In 2003, the state board of education adopted the new GPS curriculum, along with a comprehensive plan for training teachers. The new, concept-focused GPS represented a shift away from the previous, fact-based QCC. The revised Georgia curricula have received high marks from the Fordham Foundation, which ranked it fifth in the nation (Finn, Petrilli, and Julian, 2006). The training plan was designed to phase in all subject areas over a five-year period. Content areas were rolled out in two parts: The first year of the training would prepare teachers before they actually started teaching the new content in the second year. Content specialists from GaDOE

Table 3.1
Content Standards in English Language Arts, Mathematics, and Science, by State and Grade Level, 2003–2004

State	English Language Arts	Mathematics	Science
California	Grades K–12	Grades K–12	Grades K–12
Georgia	Grades K–8, high school	Grades K–8, high school	Grades K–8, high school
Pennsylvania	Grades 3, 5, 8, and 11	Grades 3, 5, 8, and 11	Grades 4, 7, 10, and 12

provided each segment of the two-year training program throughout the state to groups of teachers who were expected to return to their districts and redeliver the information to the remaining teachers. Concurrent with this face-to-face training was the development of instructional resources aligned to the GPS. Teams of educators worked with GaDOE staff to create lessons, guidelines, tasks, and instructional resources that would help teachers implement the new GPS.

Plans are under way in Georgia to create performance standards in additional content areas, to develop online resources for all subjects in K–12, and to expand web-based professional learning opportunities for all teachers. English language arts standards in K–8 were completely implemented in 2005–2006. The state will implement new K–8 standards for mathematics and science (the subjects that are the main focus of this study) in 2007–2008. It has scheduled implementation of social studies standards for 2008–2009.

Prior to NCLB, Pennsylvania had reading and mathematics content standards for grades three, five, eight, and 11 (which were the tested grades) and for grades four, seven, 10, and 12 in science. The standards were cumulative. For example, the grade-three standards described what students should know and be able to do by the end of the third grade, so they included material that would have been taught in earlier grades. Moreover, the standards were designed to influence classroom practice but were not intended to indicate what material would be tested at the end of each grade. When NCLB was enacted, the state began to delineate what would be assessed at each grade level. Rather than rewriting the standards, the state produced a supplemental concept in 2004–2005, assessment anchors (now called assessment anchor content standards), for grades three through eight and 11 in mathematics and reading. Pennsylvania's department of education does not intend for the assessment anchors to replace the standards; rather, the anchors are to clarify which standards are going to be assessed at which grade levels on the PSSA.[3]

State Testing Programs

Each state had a testing program prior to NCLB, but the programs varied considerably in the number of grades and subjects tested and, therefore, whether they satisfied NCLB requirements. Georgia's testing system provided all the achievement information required by NCLB. However, as Georgia's content standards were revised, the tests had to be revised to remain aligned with the standards. California tested students in reading and mathematics in most of the required grades prior to NCLB, but it did not test in science. In 2005, California added science testing. California had been

---

[3] See Pennsylvania Department of Education (2004b) for a description of the assessment anchors and a discussion of their role in the state's SBA system.

gradually shifting from norm-referenced tests to standards-based tests in all subjects, and NCLB accelerated this change. Pennsylvania was administering only a common state test in reading and mathematics in "milepost" grades (i.e., one elementary grade, one middle school grade, one high school grade) prior to NCLB. As a result of NCLB, Pennsylvania has had to add state tests in the other grade levels. In addition, Pennsylvania will add science tests in 2007–2008.

All three states also have alternative assessments for students with significant cognitive disabilities (for a maximum 1 percent of each state's student body). Table 3.2 summarizes some of the key features of states' testing programs as of 2004–2005, but, as this summary indicates, many changes are occurring.

Adequate Yearly Progress Definitions

The three study states differed in how they set the AMOs that schools and districts (called *school systems* in Georgia) had to meet each year and in how they computed AYP for schools and districts.[4] All three states used the same method for determining AMO starting points based on schoolwide average proficiency levels from 2001–

Table 3.2
State Testing Requirements, 2004–2005

Testing Requirement	California	Georgia	Pennsylvania
Tested grades and subjects	Mathematics (2–11) English and language arts (2–11) Science (5) (5, 8, and 10 in 2005) Writing (4 and 7) History and social science (8, 10, and 11)	Reading and English and language arts (1–8, 11) Mathematics (1–8, 11) Science (3–8, 11) Social studies and history (3–8, 11)	Reading (3, 5, 8, and 11) (3–8 and 11 in 2006) Mathematics (3, 5, 8, and 11) (3–8 and 11 in 2006) Writing (6, 9, and 11) (5, 8, and 11 in 2006) Science (3–8 in 2007–2008)
Standard assessment	California Standards Test (CST)	Criterion-Referenced Competency Test (CRCT)	PSSA
Alternative assessment	California Alternative Performance Assessment (CAPA)	Georgia Alternative Assessment for students with severe disabilities	Pennsylvania Alternative Student Assessment (PASA)

SOURCES: California Department of Education (2006a), Georgia Department of Education (undated[c]), and Pennsylvania Department of Education (undated).

---

[4] Given our study's focus, we examine basic definitions for the elementary and middle school levels only. Requirements for districts are similar to those of schools: They generally have to meet the same targets, based on all individual student data.

2002.[5] In 2002–2003, this starting point in California meant that 13.6 percent of students in each subgroup had to reach proficiency in ELA and 16 percent in mathematics. Pennsylvania's initial proficiency targets were somewhat higher that year, with 45 percent for reading and 35 percent for math. Georgia's starting points were higher still, with the expectation that 50 percent of students reach proficiency in mathematics and 60 percent in reading and ELA using a score that combined ELA and reading scores into a single score.

The states selected different growth trajectory patterns to achieve the federal goal of 100 percent of students proficient by the year 2014. All three states adopted stair-step trajectories in which the AMO remains the same for a three-year period before increasing (see Porter, Linn, and Trimble, 2005, for a discussion of variability in trajectories across states). After two or three steps, the AMO increases linearly to 100 percent in the final years. However, California's trajectories are much sharper, with just two steps, whereas Georgia's and Pennsylvania's have three steps (see Figures 3.1 and 3.2).

Figure 3.1
Annual Measurable Objectives for Reading and ELA, by State, 2002–2014

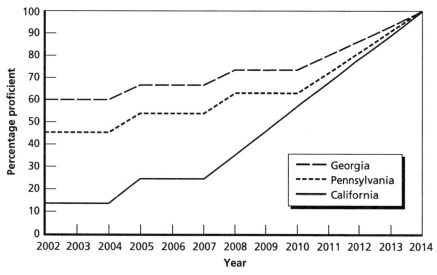

RAND MG589-3.1

---

[5] Each state generally ranked all of its schools from highest to lowest performance based on average student proficiency levels in 2001–2002. It then selected the one school in that list representing the 20th percentile for student enrollment (i.e., this school and all those below it on this ranked list of higher to lower performing schools enrolled 20 percent of all students in the state). The level of proficiency in math and reading and English and language arts (ELA) in that school became the starting point for AMO trajectories.

Figure 3.2
Annual Measurable Objectives for Math, by State, 2002–2014

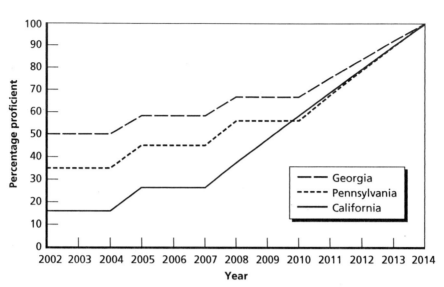

The computation of AYP also differs among the three states. AYP calculations are complicated, involving multiple subgroups, additional indicators, test participation rates, rules governing subgroup size, the use of confidence intervals (in some states), and a number of other features. For the purpose of this discussion, we mention two key ways in which the state AYP calculations differ: subgroup size and additional indicators. All three states report performance for the student subgroups required by law—including African American, American Indian/Alaskan, Hispanic, white, Asian, economically disadvantaged, students with disabilities, and limited English proficient.[6] However, they differ in the minimum number of students needed to qualify as a significant subgroup for reporting purposes. In Georgia and Pennsylvania, 40 students in any one category constituted a subgroup. California set a higher threshold, defining a minimum group size as either 100 students in any school or 50 students if that number constitutes 15 percent of total student enrollment in a school. As demonstrated by Porter, Linn, and Trimble (2005), decisions about subgroup size can have large effects on AYP determinations.

The states also varied in what they chose as their additional measure of academic progress in elementary and middle schools. Georgia and Pennsylvania initially selected attendance as the additional indicator. California selected the state's API as the second indicator, requiring schools to either achieve a schoolwide API of 560 (this target increases over time) or demonstrate improvement by at least one point over the previous

---

[6] California defined three separate Asian subgroups: Asian, Filipino, and Pacific Islander. Georgia and Pennsylvania also included the subgroups of multiracial and multicultural, respectively.

year. However, in 2003–2004, both Pennsylvania and Georgia received permission to change their requirements. Pennsylvania decreased the attendance target from 95 percent to 90 percent and allowed schools to meet the attendance target either by reaching the 90-percent threshold or by showing an increase in attendance from the previous year. Georgia allowed districts to select among several options, including attendance as well as writing test scores; percent of students exceeding standards on reading, ELA, math, science, or social studies tests; and percent proficient on science or social studies tests. Table 3.3 summarizes these features as well as other aspects of state definitions and rules regarding AYP for the 2003–2004 and 2004–2005 school years.

Table 3.3
State Accountability Systems and Key Definitions, 2003–2005

System	California	Georgia	Pennsylvania
AMO: proficiency targets 2003–2004	ELA: 13.6% Math: 16.0%	ELA & reading: 60% Math: 50%	Reading: 45% Math: 35%
AMO: proficiency targets 2004–2005	ELA: 24.4% Math: 26.5%	ELA & reading: 66.7% Math: 58.3%	Reading: 54% Math: 45% Reported by grade span
Multiyear averaging	None for AMOs	3-yr avg for AMOs	2-yr avg allowed
Confidence interval	Only for schools with <100 valid scores	95% z-test can be used as alternate test for all schools & subgroups	95% z-test can be used as alternate test for all schools and subgroups
Safe harbor	10% reduction in percent not proficient and meets 2nd indicator	10% reduction in percent not proficient and meets 2nd indicator	10% reduction in percent not proficient; 75% confidence interval using standard error of difference in proportions
Minimum group size	100 students, or 50 if that makes at least 15% of enrollment	40 students or 10% of students enrolled in AYP grades, whichever is larger (75-student cap) excluding participation rate	40 students
Participation rate	2-yr avg allowed	3-yr avg allowed	2-yr avg allowed; in 2005: reported by grade span; 3-yr avg allowed
Additional indicator	API: 560+ (increases over time) or growth of at least 1 point	Menu of options, e.g., attendance or retention rates, percent of students proficient on other state academic assessments	Attendance: 90% or improvement from previous year

SOURCES: California Department of Education (2003, 2004a, 2004b, 2005a), Georgia Department of Education (2003a, 2003b, 2004, 2005), Pennsylvania Department of Education (2003, 2004b, 2005a, 2005c, 2006a), and Simon (2004a, 2004b, 2004c, 2004d, 2005).

AYP Status of Schools

Based on 2003–2004 testing, more than one-third of the schools in California did not make AYP (see Table 3.4). In Georgia and Pennsylvania, the rates were 18 and 23 percent, respectively. If a school does not make AYP in the same subject for two years in a row, it is identified for improvement and the school district must intervene to help it perform better. Continuing failure to make AYP results in a school being placed into corrective action, and, after five years of identification, into restructuring. These designations entail more intensive interventions and sanctions. Although Georgia had a lower percentage of schools failing to make AYP in 2004–2005 (shown in 2005–2006 columns) than Pennsylvania, it had a higher total percentage across the other NCLB-designated categories. This situation probably reflects the fact that Georgia implemented the Title I accountability system requirements of the 1994 reauthorization of the Elementary and Secondary Education Act (ESEA), also known as the Improving America's Schools Act, earlier than Pennsylvania did, so struggling schools there are further along in the identification and remediation processes. By 2005–2006, of the three states, California had the highest percentage of schools in corrective action and restructuring. Although all three states must address the needs of poorly performing schools, California is facing the greatest current challenges in required district and state intervention.

A greater proportion of elementary schools met AYP targets than did middle schools in all three states, particularly in Georgia. For example, based on 2003–2004 test data, 50 percent of Georgia middle schools met AYP, compared with 95 percent of

Table 3.4
2004–2005 and 2005–2006 NCLB Status
(based on 2003–2004 and 2004–2005 testing, respectively)

School Status	California (%)		Georgia (%)		Pennsylvania (%)	
	2004–2005	2005–2006	2004–2005	2005–2006	2004–2005	2005–2006
Made AYP	65	62	82	79	77	79
Identified for improvement	13	10	12	10	5	5
Corrective action	2	4	1	2	1	3
Restructuring	3	4	4	3[a]	2	3

SOURCE: Data retrieved from state department of education Web sites April 17, 2007.

NOTE: Schools must make AYP for two consecutive years to exit from improvement status, so some schools may be counted in both the Made AYP and Identified for improvement rows. The percentages in the last three rows are mutually exclusive.

[a] Years four through nine of school improvement.

elementary schools. In California and Pennsylvania, roughly twice as many elementary schools made AYP as middle schools (see Table 3.5).

Specific AYP Targets Missed by Schools

As noted earlier, AYP determinations involved a number of factors, including meeting AMOs for all students and for defined subgroups, having a high test-participation rate, and satisfying an additional indicator that varied by state. We examined the AYP status of the schools in our study sample to see which of these factors were related to missing AYP.[7] These results are based on sampled principals' self-reports, so they are not definitive, but they provide suggestive evidence about the most challenging aspects of states' AYP determinations.

Table 3.6 shows the percentage of schools in our study sample that missed specific targets (out of all study schools that did not make AYP). This information is provided for 2003–2004, the first year of our data collection, as well as for the previous year. Across all three states, subgroup AMO requirements appeared to be the most consistent obstacles to making AYP. In California and Pennsylvania, all schools that missed AYP missed it for at least one subgroup target. This finding is consistent with other research on NCLB, which finds that a significant percentage of schools succeed in the aggregate but do not make AYP for one or more specific subgroups (Kim and Sunderman, 2005; Novak and Fuller, 2003; U.S. Government Accountability Office, 2004). Among those schools that miss AYP for only one subgroup, the subgroup that fails to make AYP most often is students with disabilities. School personnel seem acutely aware of this, and, in most of our case study schools, teachers expressed concern and

Table 3.5
Schools and Districts in State Making AYP, 2003–2005

Schools or Districts	California (%)		Georgia (%)		Pennsylvania (%)	
	2003–2004	2004–2005	2003–2004	2004–2005	2003–2004	2004–2005
All schools	65	56	80	82	81	77
Middle schools	44	39	50	57	70	61
Elementary schools	75	60	95	96	86	85
All districts	59	56	34	45	58	62

SOURCES: California Department of Education (2006b, 2005b, 2005c), Georgia Department of Education (undated[a]), Pennsylvania Department of Education (2006a), Commonwealth of Pennsylvania (2005).

[7] Statewide data for these analyses were not readily available in all three states. As a result, we used estimates based on our weighted school data. This school sample included any school in which a principal responded to our survey. In the future, we hope to conduct these analyses using data for all schools in each state.

Table 3.6
Sampled Schools Failing to Meet Specific Targets, as a Percentage of All Sampled Schools Not Meeting AYP in 2002–2003 and 2003–2004

Missing Item	California (%)		Georgia (%)		Pennsylvania (%)	
	2002–2003	2003–2004	2002–2003	2003–2004	2002–2003	2003–2004
Participation rate	15	2	45	6	39	4
Additional indicator	0	0	35	36	46	15
Schoolwide AMO	60	30	11	7	26	55
Subgroup AMO	95	100	77	81	83	100

NOTE: See Table B.1 in Appendix B for standard errors and additional information.

frustration that these students were being "blamed" for the school's failure to meet AYP and that this was negatively impacting those students' self-esteem. As one teacher put it, *"every finger is pointing at special education."*

State Awards

NCLB asks states not only to implement sanctions, but also to establish reward systems. All three of our sample states have instituted programs to recognize schools' academic achievement. California and Georgia reward both growth and absolute levels of achievement, while Pennsylvania focuses on the absolute AYP standard.

California law provides for monetary awards for schools achieving their API goals; the Certificated Staff Incentive Award program targets the highest-growth schools, and another program provides college grants for top-performing high school students. However, the state has not funded the programs since 2001. Currently, exemplary schools can apply for the California School Recognition Program. Application criteria include the learning environment, family and community participation, and academic performance reflected by API and AYP scores. The program selects approximately 5 percent of California's public schools for awards each year, alternating annually between elementary and secondary schools. Those selected for recognition receive a California Distinguished School plaque and flag.

Prior to NCLB, Georgia had begun to implement a pay-for-performance award system based on the grading scheme that was part of the state's accountability system. Schools set goals for themselves in four categories—academic achievement, client involvement, educational programming, and resource development—then had a year to achieve the goals. Schools submitted reports at the end of the school year and program administrators scored them on their accomplishments. In 2003–2004, pay for performance was applied only to high schools. In 2005, as part of the announcement of Georgia's Single Statewide Accountability System, Georgia's Office of Student

Achievement introduced a system of awards recognizing schools for either improving or excelling in student achievement. School awards are administered at four levels: platinum for making AYP for the last three years and showing the greatest gain or highest percentage of students meeting or exceeding standards (98th percentile), gold for the 97th percentile and making AYP for the last two years, silver for the 96th percentile and making AYP for the last two years, and bronze for schools in the 95th percentile and which are not in identified-for-improvement status. The system recognizes schools with banners and certificates. Financial awards are provided if the Georgia state assembly appropriates funds. Georgia also provides monetary rewards to its Title I Distinguished Schools—schools that make AYP for three or more consecutive years.

The Pennsylvania Department of Education, in partnership with the Pennsylvania Association of Federal Program Coordinators (PAFPC), began implementing a reward program in late 2004. A keystone-shaped award is given to schools that have made AYP for two consecutive years. The PAFPC funds the awards.

State Technical Assistance

In addition to the technical assistance that districts provide to schools in the improvement process, NCLB also envisions a role for states as technical assistance providers for both schools and districts that have been identified for improvement.

Of the states in our study, Georgia has been particularly active in developing and implementing a new coordinated system of school support involving regional teams. California has established a new infrastructure, but its implementation is still in progress. Meanwhile, the continued functioning of several previous school support programs creates multiple layers of assistance but a potentially more fragmented system. Pennsylvania has not created new infrastructure but is instead relying heavily on its long-established network of independent regional agencies to take the lead in providing assistance to schools and districts. All three states have developed new resources for school and district improvement that have been made available online, though Georgia offers assistance in more areas than the other two states and has made some components of this online assistance mandatory. The next sections describe in more detail the individual state systems.

California
California established the Statewide System of School Support in 2002, which includes the 11 centers of the Regional System of District and School Support (RSDSS) and two federally funded Comprehensive Assistance Centers (CACs). The RSDSS and CACs work to build districts' capacity to support their low-performing schools, provide school support teams for schools identified for improvement, provide PD services, and broker and coordinate other types of assistance. Low-performing schools may also receive

financial support through the Immediate Intervention/Underperforming Schools Program and the High Priority Schools Grant Program. Schools that fail to show improvement after two years in these programs receive additional support from School Assistance and Intervention Teams (SAITs)—teams of experienced educators from provider organizations that the state approves and trains and that districts contract to support schools by assisting with self-assessments and developing improvement plans. County educational offices also provide support to schools. The state department of education is also establishing District Assistance and Intervention Teams (DAITs) analogous to the SAITs to assist school districts that have reached the corrective stage of program improvement. When schools receiving assistance from SAIT (or districts from DAIT) fail to meet their annual targets and exit the state's monitoring oversight, they are then eligible for one of the aforementioned NCLB-mandated sanctions. Online resources available through the department of education's Web site include California's nine Essential Program Components Supporting Student Achievement and surveys to help schools and districts assess how well they are implementing these components.

Georgia

Georgia's department of education established the Division of School Improvement in July 2003, and the division has worked to develop a coherent statewide system of support for all schools with intensive support for schools identified as needing improvement The state-level infrastructure provides support from the GaDOE Division of School Improvement working collaboratively with multiple partners (such as the 16 regional educational service agencies [RESAs], the Georgia Learning Resources System, and educational technology training centers, among others) as well as school improvement tools and resources. Five regional support teams, responsible to the state department of education, organize and manage individual school improvement teams in conjunction with the Division of School Improvement's collaborative partners. The regional teams consult with individual schools identified for improvement to develop an integrated improvement plan, and they assign an experienced, trained Leadership Facilitator to work with the school on site on a regular basis. Georgia has also required all schools in the state to complete an online needs assessment based on Robert Marzano's *What Works in Schools* research (Marzano, 2003). In addition, the state's school improvement Web site provides numerous resources for school and district improvement, including data analysis tools, planning templates, and links to external resources.

Pennsylvania

Pennsylvania provides extensive technical assistance through its long-established regional educational offices. These 29 intermediate units (IUs) are regional educational consortia that member districts govern that provide a variety of support services, such as PD, curriculum guidance, planning assistance, instructional materials services, management consulting, and student enrichment programs. Pennsylvania adopted an IU capacity-building initiative and is working through the IUs to direct district and school improvement efforts. The state meets with IU staff monthly during the school year and provides extensive summer training as well as funding for improvement efforts. IU staff receive training on all new state initiatives. The state also provides summer PD through the governor's Institute for Professional Development, which is available by application to any interested teacher. Training sessions target different populations and can cover a range of topics such as curriculum or use of data to guide school improvement. In addition, the state department of education also provides tools for improvement through its Web site, including linked strategic planning frameworks—*Getting Results!* for schools and *Leading for Learning!* for districts—and data analysis tools and protocols. Another resource that the state provides is a tutoring program called the Educational Assistance Program.

Implementing NCLB's Highly Qualified Teacher Provisions

The highly qualified teacher provisions of NCLB are intended to ensure that students have access to competent, knowledgeable teachers. NCLB requires that, by 2005–2006, all students be taught by a "highly qualified" teacher, meaning that teachers must hold a college degree, be fully certified or licensed in the state, and demonstrate content knowledge in the subject they are teaching. They may demonstrate content knowledge in the following ways:

- New elementary school teachers must pass a state test of literacy and numeracy.
- New secondary school teachers must pass a test or have a college major in the subject they teach.
- Veteran teachers may pass the state test, have a college major in the subject they teach, or demonstrate content knowledge through a High Objective Uniform State Standard of Evaluation (HOUSSE), a uniformly applied process designed by the state.

However, states have latitude within this framework, and highly qualified teacher status hinges on state licensing and testing requirements that vary in rigor. In the case of veteran teachers, states have adopted different methods of proving subject-matter mastery.

The three states in this study have responded in different ways to the highly qualified teacher provisions. Both California and Georgia give veteran teachers who are not considered "highly qualified" (for example, because they are middle school teachers with a K–8 instead of subject-specific credential) the choice of taking a test to prove subject-matter expertise or complying with the state's HOUSSE evaluation procedures. Teachers may meet HOUSSE evaluation requirements through years of teaching experience in the content area; college coursework; activities related to the content area at the school or district, regional, state, or national level; scholarship in the content area; "and/or teacher effectiveness." Pennsylvania has not adopted a HOUSSE evaluation system. Instead, Pennsylvania requires all teachers to pass subject-matter tests to obtain certification. The highly qualified teacher provisions of NCLB appear to be creating greater challenges in California than in Georgia or Pennsylvania. In 2003, California reported that only 48 percent of teachers were highly qualified according to NCLB, and only 35 percent of teachers in high-poverty schools were highly qualified (Education Trust, 2003). In 2004, the latest year for which data are available, teachers in compliance with NCLB regulations taught 74 percent of California classes (California Department of Education, undated). California has many teachers who have emergency or temporary credentials, in part due to the state's class size reduction initiative in the 1990s. To reduce class size, California districts hired approximately 30,000 new teachers, and many of these teachers did not have full credentials. Like many other states, California's compliance problems are particularly acute in middle, small, rural, and alternative schools, as well as in the area of special education.

In contrast, Pennsylvania trains more teachers than it hires, and, in 2003, 95 percent of teachers in Pennsylvania were highly qualified; 93 percent were highly qualified in high-poverty school districts (Education Trust, 2003). According to Pennsylvania state officials, the primary problem that Pennsylvania has faced is with middle school teachers. Like many states, Pennsylvania allows teachers with elementary certification to teach in the middle grades (seven and eight). As a result of NCLB, these teachers now need to be certified in a subject area, and the situation is similar in Georgia and California. In 2003, 94 percent of teachers in Georgia were highly qualified (Education Trust, 2003). Superintendents in our sample of districts provided some information about the challenges associated with these provisions. About one-third of superintendents in California reported that the new requirements made hiring and retaining teachers more difficult (Table 3.7), though fewer reported this problem in 2005. Superintendents in Pennsylvania reported the least negative impact of the requirements—

Table 3.7
Superintendents Reporting Difficulty Hiring and Retaining Teachers Due to NCLB Requirements

Difficulty Reported	California (%)		Georgia (%)		Pennsylvania (%)	
	2004	2005	2004	2005	2004	2005
Retain existing teachers	34	16	17	18	11	9
Hire new teachers	38	18	26	44	13	19

NOTE: See Table B.2 in Appendix B for standard errors and additional information. Response options included not a hindrance, a minor hindrance, a moderate hindrance, and a major hindrance.

only 11 to 13 percent reported increased difficulty in retaining teachers or hiring new teachers in 2004.

In 2003–2004, we also asked superintendents whether the problems were greater for teachers in specific subjects or grade levels (see Table 3.8). In general, they had greater problems hiring and retaining qualified secondary teachers than elementary teachers and hiring qualified mathematics and science teachers than English language arts teachers. In California and Pennsylvania, finding qualified middle school teachers was a greater problem than finding teachers for elementary school or high schools. This problem may be related to the same issue discussed above, that the qualifications for middle school teachers changed the most with the advent of NCLB. Nationally, middle school teachers in 2004–2005 were more likely to report that they were considered not highly qualified according to NCLB than elementary teachers. Although 2 percent of elementary teachers reported not being highly qualified under NCLB, 8 percent of middle school English and 12 percent of middle school mathematics teachers reported not being highly qualified (Stullich, 2006).

Principals' actions to address the requirements for highly qualified teachers reflected the differences among these states. For example, most elementary school principals in Pennsylvania (63 percent) reported that they did not undertake any additional actions to meet the requirements for highly qualified teachers. By comparison, only 10 percent of elementary principals in California and only 30 percent of elementary teachers in Georgia undertook one or more actions. In contrast, at the middle school level, more than 85 percent of principals in all three states reported taking at least one action to address the highly qualified teacher requirements. Principals who did have to act used a variety of strategies to ensure that all classes were taught by highly qualified teachers (Table 3.9). The most common actions among these principals was to impose stricter hiring rules, to require current teachers to pass subject-matter tests, and to

Table 3.8
Superintendents Reporting Slightly More or Considerably More Difficulty Hiring or Retaining Teachers Due to NCLB Requirements, by Teacher Type, 2004

Teacher Type	California (%)	Georgia (%)	Pennsylvania (%)
Elementary school teachers	15	41	0
Middle school teachers	73	51	52
High school teachers	47	61	15
English language arts teachers	46	39	6
Mathematics teachers	66	66	17
Science teachers	66	68	26

NOTE: See Table B.3 in Appendix B for standard errors and additional information. Response options included easier, no change, slightly more difficulty, and considerably more difficulty.

Table 3.9
Principals Taking Specific Actions to Meet Requirements for Highly Qualified Teachers, Among Principals Who Took Any Action, 2004

Action Taken	California (%)		Georgia (%)		Pennsylvania (%)	
	Elem.	Middle	Elem.	Middle	Elem.	Middle
Change classroom assignments	7	47	38	61	16	25
Increase class size	2	0	13	7	5	8
Impose stricter hiring rules	83	83	62	74	26	78
Increase use of substitute teachers	0	6	5	0	12	10
Require current teachers to obtain certification	80	79	67	81	72	81
Fire or transfer teachers who are not highly qualified	17	15	18	27	5	17
Require current teachers to pass subject matter tests	35	56	53	68	52	60

NOTE: See Table B.4 in Appendix B for standard errors and additional information. Response options included yes and no.

require current teachers to obtain certification. At the middle school level, 47 percent of principals in California and 61 percent of principals in Georgia reported changing classroom assignments. Increasing class size, firing or transferring teachers, and using substitute teachers were less frequently used strategies. Principals reported less use of most strategies in 2005 (e.g., "require current teachers to obtain certification" decreased for California elementary school principals from 80 percent (nine) to 47 percent (11) and for Pennsylvania elementary school principals from 72 percent (12) to 28 percent (six) probably because many of these actions were already in progress.

Most principals did not find the rules regarding highly qualified teachers to be a hindrance in their efforts to improve student performance, although this differed by state. Well over half of elementary school principals (54 percent in California, 69 percent in Georgia, and 84 percent in Pennsylvania) responded that it was not a hindrance, and approximately half of middle school principals in all three states responded that it was not a hindrance.

Summary

The three states participating in this study approached the accountability and teacher quality provisions of NCLB in different ways, and their choices related directly to the policy context that existed in the states prior to NCLB. In particular, the states had different accountability systems in place when NCLB was passed, and this prior experience with SBA colored their implementation decisions. California and Georgia had testing systems that complied with many NCLB requirements, whereas Pennsylvania had very limited state testing and began expanding its assessment system in response to NCLB. However, California had a functioning accountability system based on growth, which had to be modified to comply with NCLB. The states also varied in the nature and breadth of their standards. These differences and others discussed in this chapter illustrate the variation in SBA implementation that would have been found across all states at the time of NCLB. The differences underscore the importance of considering state context when examining the effects of SBA on districts, schools, and students. They are especially relevant to the material presented in the next chapter on educators' reactions to state standards and assessment systems.

CHAPTER FOUR

Educators' Opinions About Standards, Assessments, and Accountability

Gathering information about educators' opinions about their state accountability systems is important for understanding the actions they take in response to the systems. The study probed educators' opinions about key components of NCLB, including academic content standards, annual assessments, and AYP determinations, as well as educators' responses to the pressures associated with accountability. In general, teachers and administrators were familiar with the components of NCLB accountability, had mixed opinions about the accuracy of test scores and AYP status determinations, and reported both positive and negative effects of accountability.

State Content Standards

Standards are at the core of the accountability system, so it is important that educators be knowledgeable about them. Almost all teachers and principals in California, Georgia, and Pennsylvania reported that they were familiar with their state standards in mathematics and science. Familiarity was especially high for mathematics; almost 95 percent of mathematics teachers and principals reported either having a thorough understanding of the mathematics standards or being familiar with the main points.[1] Responses were similar for science in California and Georgia; however, in Pennsylvania, only slightly more than half of the teachers were familiar with the state science standards. This result is likely because Pennsylvania had adopted science standards only in grades four, seven, eight, and 12 and did not administer a science assessment in 2004–2005.

---

[1] At the time of the surveys, the Pennsylvania Academic Standards for Mathematics were being supplemented with the Pennsylvania Assessment Anchors and Eligible Content for Mathematics. The Georgia Quality Core Curriculum (QCC) for Mathematics (and for science) was being supplemented with the Georgia Performance Standards (GPS) for Mathematics (and for science). Three-quarters of the principals and two-thirds of the teachers in Georgia and Pennsylvania reported being familiar with the additional material, as well.

Usefulness of State Content Standards

Most teachers in California and Georgia agreed that the mathematics and science standards were useful for planning their lessons (see Figure 4.1). These responses suggest that the standards documents were not "left on the shelf" but that teachers used them for curriculum and lesson planning. As one elementary school teacher in California commented, "In both subjects [math and science] . . . teaching is based on the standards. So you have some place to start your teaching, and that has helped, rather than just doing random things. So it's helped me stay focused." Teachers in the case study schools generally noted that standards were useful for bringing focus and consistency of instruction within and across schools. For example, they reported that state standards made sure teachers were on the same page and prevented teachers from teaching simply what they knew and liked best.

Pennsylvania teachers were somewhat less likely to agree that the standards were useful for instructional planning in mathematics and were considerably less likely to agree in science. The reports from Pennsylvania science teachers were consistent with the fact that Pennsylvania had science standards only for selected grades and had not yet administered science tests.

Coverage of State Content Standards

Although teachers reported using the state standards to help plan their lessons, they also reported concerns about the breadth of the standards (see Figure 4.2). Most

Figure 4.1
Elementary School Teachers Agreeing That Standards Are Useful for Planning Their Lessons, 2004–2005

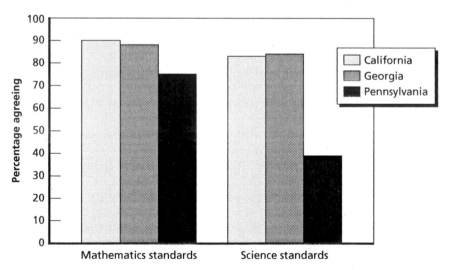

NOTE: See Table B.5 in Appendix B for standard errors and additional information.
RAND MG589-4.1

Figure 4.2
Elementary School Teachers Agreeing with Statements About Content Coverage of State Standards

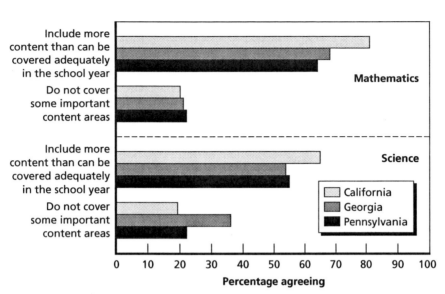

NOTE: See Table B.5 in Appendix B for standard errors and additional information.
RAND MG589-4.2

elementary school teachers in all three states agreed that the mathematics and science standards covered more content than they could address in a year. In such a situation, teachers must decide on their own whether to cover some standards fully and omit others or whether to cover all the standards incompletely. Pennsylvania had created assessment anchors to help teachers understand which aspects of the standards would be included in state assessments, and the responses reported here reflect teachers' opinions about the more focused anchors (not just the standards). Teachers were somewhat more likely to agree that the mathematics standards were too broad than to agree that the science standards were too broad.

In addition, about 20 percent of the elementary school math teachers and 20 to 30 percent of the science teachers in all three states thought the standards omitted important material in math or science (for similar results from middle school teacher, see Table B.5 in Appendix B). These teachers faced the dilemma of teaching the content though it was not included in the standards and would not be on the assessment or omitting the content though they believed it was important. Middle school science teachers, who generally have more training in science than do elementary school science teachers, were more likely to report omissions than elementary school science teachers were.

Taken together, these findings suggest somewhat of a mismatch remaining between the content described in state standards documents (and supplementary materials) and the curriculum that teachers believed that they should cover during a school year. Our surveys do not allow us to estimate the extent of the mismatch nor to say whether it reflects overly ambitious (or incorrectly focused) standards, undemanding (or misdirected) teachers, or underprepared students.

State Assessments

Teachers' and administrators' opinions about the accuracy and appropriateness of state assessments provide one indication of the quality of the assessments. In addition, their attitudes toward the assessments are likely to influence their use of test results as well as the impact that the accountability system has on curriculum and instruction. There were considerable differences of opinion among respondents on these issues.

Administrators' Opinions of Validity of State Tests

About two-thirds of the district superintendents in California and Georgia and about one-half in Pennsylvania agreed that the state tests accurately reflected the achievement of students in their districts (see Figure 4.3). Principals also had mixed responses to similar questions about the validity of the state test scores. Georgia principals were more likely to report that test results provided an accurate indication of student achievement than were principals in California and Pennsylvania. These attitudes are consistent

Figure 4.3
Administrators Agreeing That State Assessment Scores Accurately Reflect Student Achievement

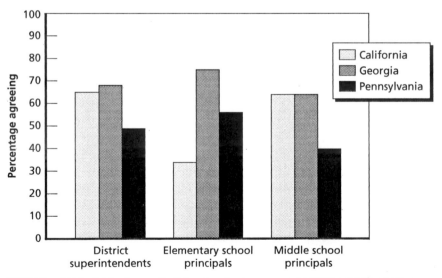

NOTE: See Table B.6 in Appendix B for standard errors and additional information.
RAND MG589-4.3

with administrators' and teachers' reports concerning their use of test results (which will be discussed in Chapter Five).

However, it is important to point out that administrators in districts and schools that made AYP held more positive views about the validity of state tests than administrators in districts and schools that did not make AYP (see Figure 4.4). In all three states, superintendents who reported that their districts met AYP targets were far more likely to agree that test results accurately reflected their students' achievements than were superintendents who reported that their districts did not make AYP. Principals' views on the validity of state tests follow a similar pattern, although the differences in attitudes toward the validity of tests between principals in schools that met AYP and those that did not were not as large as the differences between superintendents.

It is not surprising that administrators in schools and districts that were deemed more successful based on state test results would be more likely to have favorable views of the validity of the test scores than were administrators in schools and districts deemed less successful. However, for SBA to function most effectively, all stakeholders should endorse the measures of progress (the state assessments, in the case of NCLB). If they do not, it may undermine the functioning of the accountability system.

Figure 4.4
Administrators Agreeing That State Assessment Scores Accurately Reflect Student Achievement, by District or School AYP Status

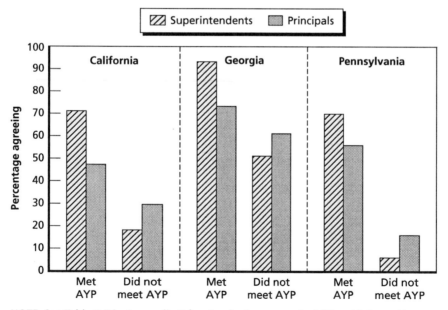

NOTE: See Table B.7 in Appendix B for standard errors and additional information.
RAND MG589-4.4

Teachers' Opinions of Validity of State Tests

Teachers were more critical than superintendents and principals in their views about the state assessments (see Table 4.1). Only about 40 percent of the teachers in California, about 50 percent in Pennsylvania, and about 60 percent in Georgia agreed that the mathematics assessment was a good measure of students' mastery of the content standards. The percentages were even lower for the science assessments (Pennsylvania had not yet administered a science test in 2004–2005). Georgia teachers were more likely to agree that the assessments were good measures than were teachers in the other states, consistent with the opinions of Georgia administrators reported above.

Difficulty and Curriculum Alignment of State Tests

Teachers may have thought that state assessments were not good measures of students' mastery of content standards because they found the state assessments to be too difficult for the majority of their students. In California and Pennsylvania, two-thirds of middle school teachers reported that the tests were too difficult, as did almost half of Georgia middle school teachers. In all three states, middle school teachers were more

Table 4.1
Teachers Agreeing with Statements Regarding State Assessments

Statement	California (%)		Georgia (%)		Pennsylvania (%)	
	Elem.	Middle	Elem.	Middle	Elem.	Middle
The mathematics assessment						
Is a good measure of students' mastery of content standards	42	38	60	57	45	50
Is too difficult for the majority of my students	47	65	31	46	47	64
Includes considerable content that is not in our curriculum	33	32	24	27	25	43
Omits considerable content that is in our curriculum	35	30	26	37	27	49
The science assessment						
Is a good measure of students' mastery of content standards	21	30	46	47	NA	NA
Is too difficult for the majority of my students	64	73	43	45	NA	NA
Includes considerable content that is not in our curriculum	44	54	34	39	NA	NA
Omits considerable content that is in our curriculum	36	28	28	45	NA	NA

NOTE: Reports percentages of teachers in tested grades. Response options included strongly disagree, disagree, agree, strongly agree, and don't know. Table entries are percentages responding agree or strongly agree. See Table B.8 in Appendix B for standard errors and additional information.

likely than elementary school teachers to report that state assessments were too difficult. From the teachers' perspective, the challenges associated with meeting the states'
NCLB targets in mathematics and science appeared to be greater for older students
than for younger ones.

In addition, many teachers believed that the assessments were misaligned with
their curriculum—either by including considerable content that was not in the curriculum or by omitting important content that was in the curriculum. Figure 4.5 shows
the percentage of mathematics teachers who reported that the mathematics assessment
either omitted considerable content that was part of their curricula or included considerable content that was not in their curricula. In mathematics, majorities of middle
school teachers reported considerable misalignment between the assessments and the
curricula, as did a majority of elementary school teachers in California. The percentage of science teachers reporting such misalignment was a bit higher (71 percent of
elementary school science teachers and 74 percent of middle school science teachers in
California; 53 percent of elementary school science teachers and 63 percent of middle
school science teachers in Georgia).

One Georgia eighth-grade mathematics teacher noted some specific problems
with alignment: "With eighth grade, because we're teaching algebra, and the CRCT
does not test algebra, it's testing eighth-grade math, which doesn't exist anymore in
[this district]; then it's difficult because you're not getting tested on what you've been

Figure 4.5
Math Teachers Reporting That State Assessment Omits Considerable
Content in the Local Curriculum or Includes Considerable Content Not in
the Local Curriculum

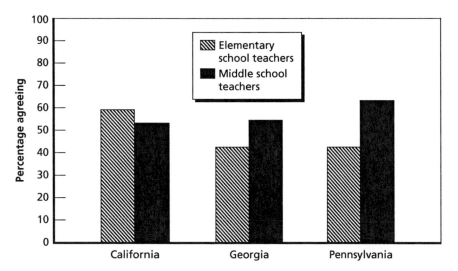

NOTE: See Table B.9 in Appendix B for standard errors and additional information.
RAND MG589-4.5

teaching all year. For all kids, they're tested on the basic skills, things that they should have mastered, but they haven't. And, because we have to follow the pacing chart, because we're doing Springboard, because we're doing this whole curriculum that isn't really aligned with the test, then it puts them at a disadvantage."

For the accountability system to function effectively, the standards should be clear, appropriate, and well understood, the tests should align with the standards, and the curriculum should align with both. These results suggest that alignment among standards, assessments, and curriculum could be improved in all three states and in both subjects.

Adequate Yearly Progress

AYP is the metric that determines whether schools and districts meet their goals for student achievement or are identified for improvement and face interventions and sanctions. For the accountability system to promote improved student performance, teachers and administrations must understand AYP calculation and see a connection between the school's AYP status and their efforts on behalf of students.

Understanding of Accountability System

Despite the complexities of state AYP calculations, three-quarters or more of superintendents and principals in all three states agreed that they had a clear understanding of AYP criteria (see Figure 4.6).[2] In addition, about two-thirds of the principals in all three states reported receiving assistance to understand the state accountability system (see Table B.10 in Appendix B). Interviews with staff in the state departments of education confirmed that all three states had devoted resources to communicating AYP rules and regulations to administrators and teachers (e.g., via memos, email, or Web sites) and that much of each state's technical assistance to schools during the first few years of NCLB focused on clarifying NCLB requirements.

Teachers, who were asked about their understanding of the accountability system in general rather than about AYP specifically, tended to report a lack of understanding of the system (see Table B.10 in Appendix B). Approximately one-half of the elementary and middle school teachers in all three states agreed that the accountability system was so complicated that it was hard for them to understand.[3] Georgia teachers were slightly less likely than California and Pennsylvania teachers to agree that the system was difficult to understand. This result is consistent with previous findings about Georgia educators' reactions to accountability in their state. Responses to these

---

[2]   Superintendent responses to this item come from the first year of data collection (2003–2004) only.

[3]   Part of the difference in responses between teachers and administrators may have occurred because the question was phrased in a negative way for teachers whereas the administrator questions used positive wording.

Figure 4.6
Administrators with Clear Understanding of AYP Criteria

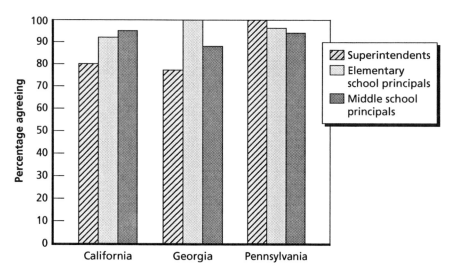

NOTE: See Table B.10 in Appendix B for standard errors and additional information.
RAND MG589-4.6

questions did not change much between 2003–2004 (the first year of the study) and 2004–2005, indicating that, despite an additional year of operating under NCLB, many teachers remained confused by the policy in their states.

In our case study visits, we encountered a number of teachers in schools or districts that had failed to make AYP, usually for the first time, who were misinformed about the reasons that the school or district had failed to make AYP. In these cases, it seemed like the principal or district administration had intentionally downplayed the results, focusing the blame on technicalities that they did not describe clearly to teachers. It appeared that this was the result of an attempt to keep up school morale and help the school community get past the stigma of failing.

Confidence in Ability to Meet AYP Targets

As noted in the introduction to this monograph, research suggests that incentives are most effective when the majority of people believe the goals can be attained with hard work (Kelley et al., 2000). School administrators in California, Georgia, and Pennsylvania were uncertain about meeting future AYP targets for their districts and schools. On the one hand, majorities of superintendents and principals in all three states believed that their schools or districts would meet their AYP targets for the following year (2005–2006) (see Figure 4.7).

On the other hand, only about one-third of superintendents in all three states believed that their districts could attain their AYP targets for the next five years (see Figure 4.8). Similarly, a lower percentage of principals in all three states agreed that

Figure 4.7
Superintendents and Principals Agreeing That Their Districts or Schools Would Meet AYP Targets for the Next School Year

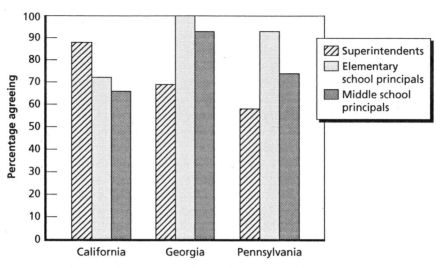

NOTE: See Table B.11 in Appendix B for standard errors and additional information.
RAND *MG589-4.7*

Figure 4.8
Superintendents and Principals Agreeing That Their Districts or Schools Would Meet AYP Targets for the Next Five School Years

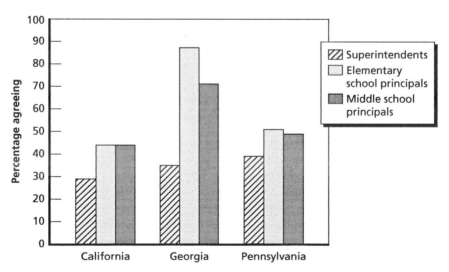

NOTE: See Table B.11 in Appendix B for standard errors and additional information.
RAND *MG589-4.8*

their schools could meet AYP targets for the next five years. The overall pattern of results is not surprising, given that all three states will increase the percentage of students required to be proficient in coming years (see Figures 3.1 and 3.2 in Chapter Three for state trajectories). Georgia principals were far more confident than principals in the other two states; 71 percent of elementary school principals and 87 percent of middle school principals agreed that their schools could meet AYP targets for the next five years. Georgia principals' higher expectations may be due to the facts that they face a more gradual trajectory than California schools and that a greater percentage of students in their state had already reached the proficient level. These attitudes deserve continued monitoring because it may be detrimental to NCLB accountability if future targets are perceived to be unattainable.

Perceived Validity of AYP

About two-thirds of elementary school principals agreed that their school's AYP status accurately reflected the overall performance of their students; however, only half or fewer middle school principals agreed (see Figure 4.9). Superintendents' opinions varied across states, from 30 percent of Pennsylvania superintendents who agreed that their district's AYP status reflected the overall performance of students to 60 percent of California superintendents. As might be expected, since primarily test scores determine AYP status, the wide range of opinions regarding the validity of AYP status mirrors the wide range of opinions regarding the validity of test scores.

Figure 4.9
Superintendents and Principals Agreeing That District or School AYP Status Accurately Reflected Overall Student Performance

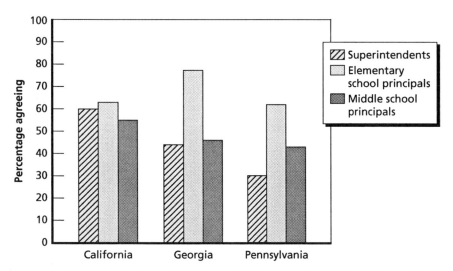

NOTE: See Table B.12 in Appendix B for standard errors and additional information.
RAND *MG589-4.9*

As was the case with test scores, administrators in districts and schools that made AYP held more positive views about the validity of AYP status than did administrators in districts and schools that did not make AYP (see Figure 4.10). The pattern was most dramatic in Georgia, where almost all administrators in districts and schools that made AYP thought the results reflected overall student performance compared with almost none of the administrators in districts that did not make AYP. The overall pattern was similar in California and Pennsylvania, although not as dramatic. In both states, about one-third or more of administrators in successful districts and schools did not agree that AYP status was an accurate reflection of school performance.

California was especially interesting because, as described in Chapter Three, the state assigns its own accountability metric, the API, in addition to AYP. Although more than half of administrators in California viewed AYP as valid, the administrators we interviewed in case studies explained why many preferred the API, which is based on growth over time. As one middle school principal stated,

> The thing with AYP that's so frustrating is that it didn't take into account where you started. Everybody had to hit an arbitrary mark no matter where you started, no matter what you were dealing with. Schools that have high special ed

Figure 4.10
Superintendents and Principals Agreeing That District or School AYP Status Accurately Reflected Overall Student Performance, by AYP Status

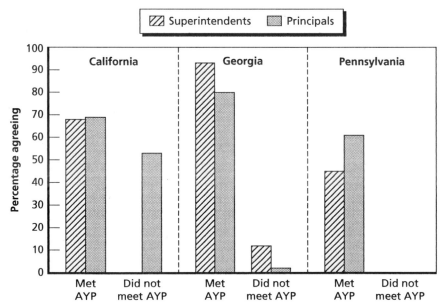

NOTE: See Table B.13 in Appendix B for standard errors and additional information.
RAND MG589-4.10

populations, high ESL [English as a second language] populations, are looked at the same as schools that have one ESL kid and one special ed kid, and that's not right. That's totally ridiculous if you look at it. We're dealing with situations much more difficult.

Further, many teachers in California reported that the differences between AYP and API caused confusion among parents and some staff, particularly when their schools were deemed to be performing well in terms of state API scores but failed to make federal AYP targets. This may explain, in part, why California administrators questioned the validity of AYP. In fact, the California State Superintendent of Public Instruction articulated this point in a public statement: "The fact that 317 of our schools grew 30 points or more [on the API], yet failed to make the federal benchmark, illustrates why I believe a growth model of accountability such as we have here in California more accurately reflects actual student learning" (California Department of Education, 2004c). According to one report, 2,339 schools statewide met API but did not meet AYP in 2003–2004 (Education Trust–West, 2004). These views were reflected at the schools we visited as well. As one California principal put it, "So, being an API-7 school, and not making AYP in this one area, I mean, come on. They've got to look at this bigger picture here."

Teachers' responses suggested other ways in which AYP might not be an effective indicator of school performance (see Table B.40 in Appendix B). For example, approximately half the teachers reported that high-achieving students were not receiving appropriately challenging curriculum and instruction due to the state's accountability system. In addition, the vast majority of teachers in the states believed that the state system left little time to teach content not on state tests. (As we discuss further in Chapter Six, this tendency to focus on tested subjects raised concerns about possible narrowing of curriculum and instruction.)

The Effects of Accountability

Superintendents, principals, and teachers were asked about the pressure they felt as a result of the accountability system and the impact of accountability on the school's instructional program and their own attitudes.

AYP Pressure and Student Achievement Emphasis

Most educators at all levels in Georgia and Pennsylvania and most teachers in California agreed that staff were focusing more on improving student achievement as a result of pressure to make AYP (see Figure 4.11). We asked superintendents about principals' focus on student achievement and principals about teachers' focus, and teachers reported on their individual behaviors. Three-quarters of teachers agreed

Figure 4.11
Educators Agreeing That Staff Were Focusing More on Improving Student Achievement as a Result of Pressure to Make AYP

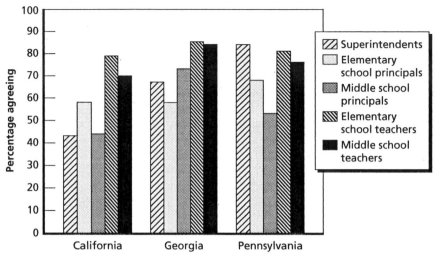

NOTE: See Table B.14 in Appendix B for standard errors and additional information.
RAND *MG589-4.11*

that they focused more on student achievement as a result of pressure to make AYP. Although we do not know exactly what behaviors teachers changed, the fact that a large proportion of teachers was attending more to student achievement is the sort of change that the accountability system was designed to promote. In addition, more than half of the principals in Georgia and Pennsylvania agreed that their staff were focusing more on student achievement, and more than two-thirds of the superintendents in these states agreed that principals were focused more on achievement, which represents a consistent pattern of change due to the accountability system. Less than half of the administrators in California agreed that their subordinates focused more on achievement as a result of AYP, perhaps because California had an accountability system that predated NCLB, which had already shifted staff attention to student performance or perhaps because they thought, as previously noted, that the API metric was more credible.

AYP Pressure and Instrumental Improvement

Responses to other survey items suggested that accountability led to improvements in the academic rigor of the curriculum, staff focus on student learning, students' focus on schoolwork, and, perhaps as a consequence, student learning of important knowledge and skills. Figure 4.12 shows the percentage of superintendents, principals, and teachers reporting that the academic rigor of the curriculum changed for the better or changed for the worse as a result of the state's accountability system (the other results are displayed in Table B.15 in Appendix B). Majorities of superintendents and

Figure 4.12
**Educators Reporting Changes in the Academic Rigor of the Curriculum as a
Result of the State's Accountability System**

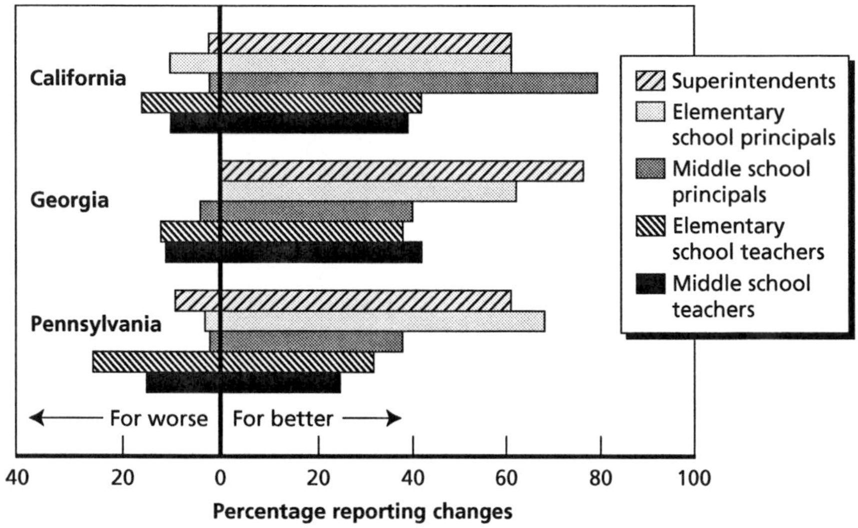

NOTE: See Table B.15 in Appendix B for standard errors and additional information.
RAND MG589-4.12

principals as well as about 40 percent of teachers in all three states reported that the academic rigor of the curriculum had changed for the better in the wake of state accountability. As one California elementary school teacher put it,

> I think standards are great. It keeps us on track as far as—you know something might be a really cute, fun project—but is there academic rigor in it, are they learning from it and how can we make it more rigorous for them so that they are learning?

Parents also seemed to notice the change: One parent in Georgia stated: "I think—as a parent—[NCLB is] extremely beneficial, because I see that the standards are not being lowered. The standards are actually—they're being raised, and children need to rise to that standard."

As a group, Pennsylvania teachers were less likely than others to report that academic rigor had changed for the better and more likely to report that it changed for the worse as a result of accountability. Teachers at one Pennsylvania case study school attributed the negative effect on rigor to the district's pacing guides and interim assessment systems, which they believed led to a lack of mastery of material. On one hand, teachers feel pressure to move on regardless of whether students have mastered content. For example, one teacher commented, "It says on the calendar, 'Today you're going to test cause and effect. Tomorrow, you're going to test double digit addition.' And you test, and you move on. And we do some remediation after we test, based on our test scores, and how our kids did, but I think the frustration is that a lot of us aren't sure that there is a lot of mastery." Several teachers described a phenomenon of coverage without mastery. In addition, some teachers at this school noted that the pace of the calendar was holding higher-level students back.

Two-thirds or more of superintendents and principals and 40 to 60 percent of teachers reported that staff focus on student learning had improved as a result of the accountability system (see Table B.15 in Appendix B). Case studies elaborated on this finding. For example, a middle school principal interviewed in Georgia believed that AYP forced teachers to examine their practices, identify weak areas, and improve their teaching strategies. Similarly, a middle school principal in Pennsylvania said accountability had led them to focus on curriculum and instruction:

> You've got to have a defined curriculum. It's caused us to look at the classroom methods, how you are teaching your classes and the idea of the constant lecture is not a good way to do it. You've got to have a variety of different things. All of that has been good.

Smaller percentages of principals and teachers reported changes for the better in terms of students' attention to their schoolwork; the majority reported no change. NCLB contains no direct incentives for students to change their behavior; they must be motivated to put more emphasis on schoolwork through the efforts of schools and communities. Yet, one-half to two-thirds of principals and about one-third of teachers reported changes for the better in student learning as a result of accountability. Teachers in Georgia were most likely to report a positive change in students' focus on schoolwork, perhaps because Georgia had adopted promotion testing for students (i.e., grades at which students must pass the state test to be promoted) so there were direct incentives for students. Teachers in Georgia case study schools mentioned this additional pressure, noting that it had both positive and negative effects on students.

In general, the perception that academic rigor, teachers' focus on student learning, and actual student learning had changed for the better was more prevalent among superintendents than principals and was more prevalent among principals than it was among teachers (see Table B.15 in Appendix B). Also, in almost every case, 10 percent or fewer of respondents reported that these features had changed for the worse as a result of the state's accountability system.

About half of the teachers reported that their own teaching practices had improved as a result of the state accountability system, while few reported a change for the worse (see Table B.16 in Appendix B). In addition, between 14 and 34 percent of teachers agreed that teachers' relationships with their students had changed for the better, while 5 to 14 percent reported that these relationships had changed for the worse. Georgia teachers were more likely to report changes for the better in both these aspects of teaching than Pennsylvania teachers, with California teachers in between.

Looking more broadly at curriculum, one-half to three-quarters of superintendents and principals reported that the pressure to make AYP had led to better coordination of the mathematics curriculum across grades (see Table B.17 in Appendix B). Similarly, 40 to 50 percent of superintendents and about one-third of principals reported improvements in coordination of the science curriculum across grade levels as a result of NCLB accountability pressures. Between 26 and 64 percent of principals also reported a change for the better in terms of the use of innovative curricular program and instructional approaches.

The vast majority of superintendents in all three states also reported that one impact of NCLB was higher expectations for subgroups of students: 98 percent of district leaders in Pennsylvania, 80 percent in California, and 78 percent in Georgia agreed or strongly agreed that they were increasing academic expectations for special education students or ELLs.[4]

Finally, between one-quarter and one-half of teachers reported that their principal's effectiveness as an instructional leader had improved as a result of accountability, while 19 percent or fewer reported that it had changed for the worse (see Table B.18 in Appendix B). Again, a higher percentage of Georgia teachers than Pennsylvania teachers reported positive changes, with California teacher reports falling in between. Reports from elementary school teachers and middle school teachers were comparable.

AYP Pressure and Morale

Three-quarters of superintendents and one-third or more of principals and teachers in all three states reported that staff morale had changed for the worse due to the state's accountability system (see Figure 4.13). Approximately 10 to 20 percent thought morale had changed for the better. (We asked superintendents about principals' morale and principals and teachers about school staff morale.) The most prevalent negative responses came from superintendents, who suggested that principals may be feeling the accountability pressures more strongly than teachers are. The reports of lower morale were most widespread in Pennsylvania, where majorities of teachers and principals reported that staff morale had changed for the worse and less than 10 percent reported a change for the better. Interestingly, across all three states, teachers in schools that made AYP were just as likely if not more likely as teachers in schools that did not make AYP to report this negative impact on morale.

One partial explanation for the reported decline in morale among teachers may be a disconnect between the approach to teaching being adopted in schools and teachers' own beliefs. Only 30 percent of teachers in Pennsylvania and 29 percent of teachers in California agreed that the state accountability system supported their personal approach to teaching. Slightly more than one-half of the teachers in Georgia (52 percent) reported that the accountability system in that state supported

---

[4] Standard errors for these percentage estimates were 2, 9, and 12, respectively.

Figure 4.13
Educators Reporting Changes in Staff Morale as a Result of the State's Accountability System

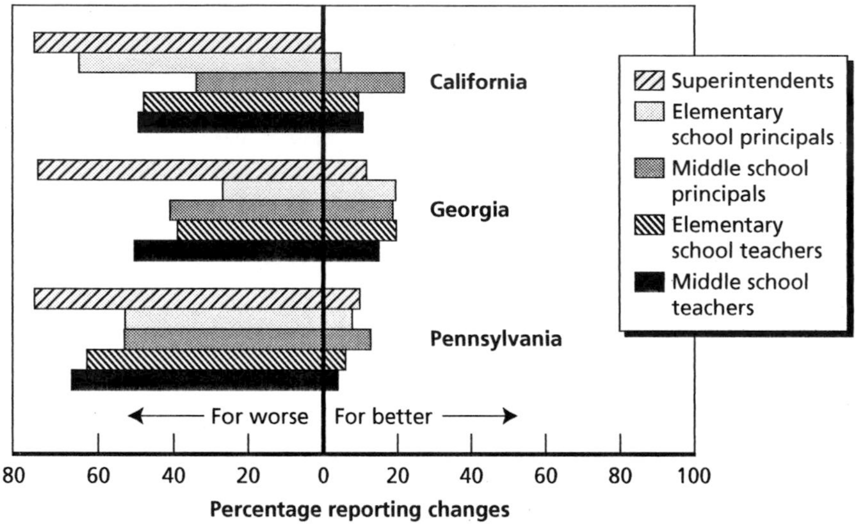

NOTE: See Table B.16 in Appendix B for standard errors and additional information.
RAND *MG589-4.13*

their personal approach to teaching. Thus, many teachers were experiencing some conflict between their own approach and the approach that their state was asking them to adopt as part of the NCLB initiatives. For example, one California teacher told us,

> I know that for teachers, it's this great big machinery that's hanging over your head. You know you've got to do this, you've got to do that, you've got to be this, you've got to be that, to the point where you sort of lose the focus of how about just exploring things for the kids.

Perceived Effects of Accountability System on Students

Despite concerns about morale, most principals and many teachers judged the overall effects of accountability to be positive. Principals were more positive than teachers about the overall impact of the accountability systems, and Georgia educators were more positive than educators in the other two states. More than half of principals in all three states (73 percent in California, 59 percent in Georgia, and 65 percent in Pennsylvania) reported that the state accountability system had been beneficial for students in their school (see Figure 4.14). In comparison, approximately one-third of teachers in California and Pennsylvania and a little over half in Georgia agreed that, overall, the state's accountability system has benefited their students.

Figure 4.14
Teachers and Principals Agreeing That the State's Accountability System Has Benefited Students

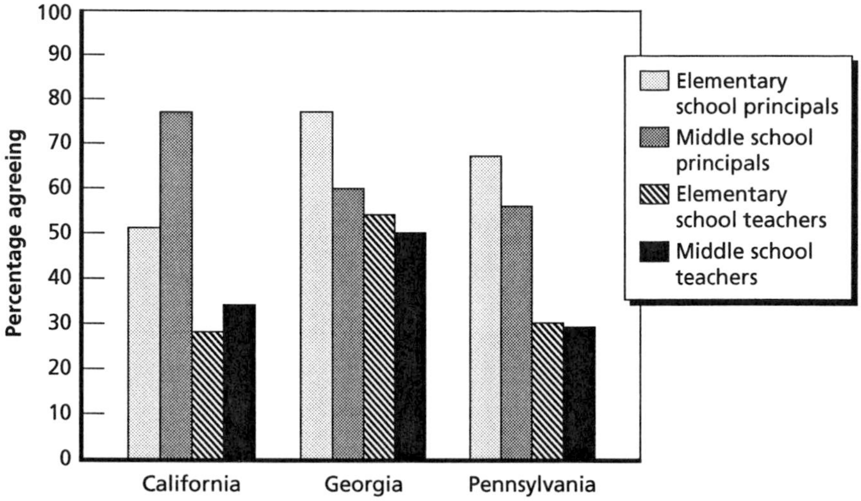

NOTE: See Table B.17 in Appendix B for standard errors and additional information.
RAND MG589-4.14

Summary

Results presented in this chapter suggest that administrators and teachers worked to implement SBA and that state accountability systems had positive effects, though some concerns remain.

- Looking first at broad trends across the three states, most educators were familiar with state content standards in mathematics, although science standards were not yet as well known. Furthermore, teachers found standards helpful for planning lessons, indicating that they were incorporating standards into regular instruction. However, about half of the teachers reported some mismatch between the standards and their curricula: The standards included too much content or omitted some important content or both.

- Teachers also reported a mismatch between state tests and their curricula. Most teachers reported that the state tests were not well aligned with their curriculum and were too difficult for their students. At the same time, most administrators and about half of the teachers thought that the assessments were a good indicator of student performance.

- Assessment results are used to make AYP determinations, and this process can be complicated. Yet, most administrators reported that they understood AYP rules, although about half the teachers found the overall accountability system to be difficult to understand. More importantly (in terms of accountability), the majority of elementary school principals thought that AYP status reflected their students' overall performance. However, the majority of middle school principals and superintendents did not share this opinion. Thus, there appear to be lingering concerns about school designation validity. Although administrators were optimistic that their districts and schools would meet their AYP targets for the following year, most did not believe they would meet AYP in five years, when the requirements would become more stringent. Widespread failure to meet targets coupled with doubts about the meaningfulness of AYP might pose a serious challenge for the accountability systems in the future.

- For the moment, however, the accountability systems appeared to have some positive effects on administrator and teacher behaviors. Reports indicated that schools were focusing more on student achievement, the curriculum was more rigorous, and student learning was improving. In addition, there was greater coordination of the curriculum across grades (potentially helping to address the alignment problems reported above), and teachers reported that principals' leadership had changed for the better. Despite these optimistic findings, some concerns remain. Both administrators and teachers reported declines in morale, and most teachers disagreed with the statement that the accountability system has benefited students (although most principals agreed).

There were few noteworthy differences between responses from elementary and middle schools, but there were some notable differences among the three states. In the area of science, the responses from the states reflected the varying status of science standards and assessments. Responses were more positive in Georgia, which had grade-level standards in place and was already testing science in grades three through eight. Most educators in Georgia were familiar with science standards, and about half thought that the assessments were a good measure of the standards (although about half thought that the tests were too difficult). Responses from teachers in the other states were consistent with the degree to which the state had implemented standards and assessments in science. There were also differences among the states in educators' opinions about accountability and their reports about its impact on curriculum and instruction. In some cases, Georgia educators were more positive than California or Pennsylvania educators. For example, Georgia teachers were more likely to agree that their state's accountability system had benefited students. We can only speculate about the reasons for these differences. Some cross-state differences probably stem from the choices made by states and districts in how to focus school improvement efforts, a topic we address in the next chapter.

CHAPTER FIVE

School and District Improvement Strategies

NCLB's ultimate goal of proficiency for all students in reading and mathematics means that even schools and districts that can currently meet AYP targets will need to improve student performance in future years as those targets increase. In this chapter, we describe the efforts that schools and districts are making to bring about improved student and school performance. The incentive structure that NCLB establishes narrows the focus of improvement to one single, clear goal: increasing students' academic achievement in reading and mathematics.[1] As a result, schools and districts must pay significant attention to student learning and the instruction that produces it if they are to meet NCLB's lofty goal of 100-percent proficiency on state assessments by 2014. In this chapter, we examine the strategies that schools and districts used to improve student performance, the perceived quality and usefulness of these efforts, and the types of assistance that districts and states provided to schools (those that are doing well and those that are not) to help them improve student achievement. In general, educators employed a range of improvement strategies but tended to identify a few as most important—including using data to inform decisions; aligning curriculum, instruction, and assessments; and targeting support for low-performing students.

School Improvement Strategies

Principals' School Improvement Strategies

A majority of principals in all three states reported using a large number of varied strategies to make their schools better in 2004–2005 (see Table 5.1). In many cases, more Georgia principals than California or Pennsylvania principals reported using each of the strategies. Furthermore, more than 90 percent of principals in California, Georgia, and Pennsylvania reported using four common school improvement strategies, including matching curriculum and instruction with standards, using research to guide improvement efforts, providing additional instruction to low-performing students,

---

[1] NCLB now requires science testing in at least three grades (although results do not go into the computation of AYP), but science testing was not required during the years when our data were collected.

and increasing the use of student achievement data to inform instruction. Elementary school principals were more likely than middle school principals to report restructuring the school day to teach content in greater depth. This finding makes sense in light of the greater flexibility afforded by self-contained classrooms and teachers instructing the same group of students all day and the fact that many middle schools may have already employed extended blocks of time for literacy and math prior to NCLB.

Most Important School Improvement Strategies

The three strategies that principals in California, Georgia, and Pennsylvania identified as "most important for making your school better in 2004–2005" were increasing the use of student achievement data to inform instruction, matching curriculum and instruction with standards or assessments, and providing additional instruction to low-achieving students. As shown in Figure 5.1, approximately 40 percent or more of the principals in all three states identified these strategies as one of the three most

Table 5.1
Principals Employing School Improvement Strategies

Strategy	California (%)		Georgia (%)		Pennsylvania (%)	
	Elem.	Middle	Elem.	Middle	Elem.	Middle
Matching curriculum and instruction with standards or assessments	100	100	97	100	100	99
Using existing research to inform decisions about improvement strategies	100	94	100	99	94	94
Providing additional instruction to low-performing students	96	95	98	100	97	98
Increasing the use of student achievement data to inform instruction	93	100	100	94	92	100
Increasing teacher PD	89	90	95	96	64	94
Improving the school planning process	74	85	100	84	81	99
Providing before- or after-school, weekend, or summer programs	84	92	87	86	77	59
Promoting programs to make the school a more attractive choice for parents	60	70	74	62	43	71
Restructuring the day to teach content in greater depth (e.g., a literacy block)	63	36	79	53	61	43
Increasing instructional time (lengthening school day or year or shortening recess)	8	23	58	35	26	20

NOTE: See Table B.20 in Appendix B for standard errors and additional information.

Figure 5.1
Principals Identifying School Improvement Strategies as Most Important

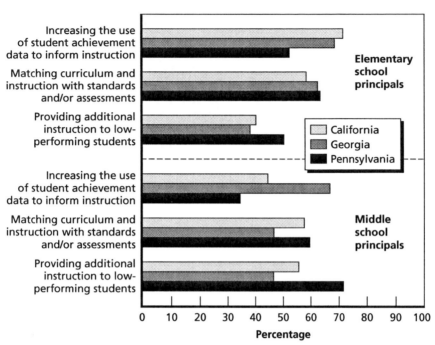

NOTE: See Table B.21 in Appendix B for standard errors and additional information.
RAND MG589-5.1

important they employed in 2004–2005 (none of the other strategies listed in Table 5.1 was selected as often; see the appendixes for the full set of results).

Not surprisingly, principals report using these three strategies: The theory of action underlying NCLB explicitly calls on these elements as important levers of change. Many principals also reported that efforts in these three areas were making a difference. The principal responses are consistent with those from superintendents and teachers, as we will describe further in this chapter. Both surveys and case study visits indicate that teachers, principals, and superintendents emphasized using data; aligning curriculum, instruction, and assessments; and focusing on low-performing students and that these educators and administrators found these strategies helpful for improving teaching and learning. In the following sections, we examine the efforts of individuals at the district, school, and, in some cases, classroom levels within these three domains, exploring the variation both within and across states in the types of activities and reported usefulness of these improvement efforts.

Data-Based Decisionmaking

The theory of action underlying NCLB holds that broader access to assessment results will help administrators and teachers make better decisions. With its focus on regular assessment of student progress toward clear and measurable performance standards and broad public reporting of results from those assessments, NCLB is intended to facilitate increased use of data by providing schools and districts with additional data for analysis, as well as increasing the pressure on them to improve student test scores (Massell, 2001).

Not only did administrators in our sample identify data use as important for their school improvement efforts, but most attributed increased data use to state and federal accountability systems. More than three-quarters of superintendents in our study reported that, because of their state's accountability system, the use of data has changed for the better throughout their districts.

Data-based decisionmaking assumes that, once available, data will be interpreted in ways to inform decisions and potentially improve practice. Thus, we examine the availability of state and local assessment results, the perceived quality and usefulness of these data, and the types of decisions for which schools used them.

Almost all principals in 2004–2005 had access to state test results for both the current and prior years' students, as well as results disaggregated by student subgroups and by subtopics (see Table 5.2 for results from elementary school principals and Table B.23 in Appendix B for results from middle school principals). In general, principals found these results useful for guiding instruction and school improvement.

Table 5.2
Elementary School Principals Reporting That State Test Results Are Available and Moderately or Very Useful (2003–2004 state test results)

Reported Results	California (%)		Georgia (%)		Pennsylvania (%)	
	Available	Useful	Available	Useful	Available	Useful
Reports of last year's test results for the students at your school last year	98	81	98	92	97	84
Reports of last year's test results for the students at your school this year	100	86	98	98	99	93
Test results summarized for each student subgroup	100	72	92	91	100	59
Test results summarized by subtopic or skill	89	71	96	94	100	85

NOTE: Response options included not available, not useful, minimally useful, moderately useful, and very useful. Moderately or very useful is as a percentage of principals who had results available. See Tables B.22 and B.23 in Appendix B for standard errors and additional information.

In addition, in all three states, most elementary school teachers had access to test results disaggregated by subgroup and subtopic (Table 5.3). Teachers were much more likely to find results disaggregated by subtopic or skill useful than results broken down by student subgroup, which differed somewhat from the reports of principals. Unlike the majority of elementary school principals in all three states, less than 40 percent of the elementary school teachers in California and Pennsylvania and about half in Georgia found results broken down by student subgroup to be useful. This difference is consistent with differences in responsibility: Principals overseeing school improvement are understandably interested in information about subgroups (on which the calculation of AYP depends in large part), while teachers may be more interested in information that assists with identifying curricular topics that the class overall may not have understood and required attention.

The fact that only Georgia tested students in grades three through eight in science at the time of our survey limits the availability and use of science test results (California tested science in grade five, and Pennsylvania will not begin testing science until 2008). Only about a quarter of California elementary school teachers reported that state science test results disaggregated by subgroup or subtopic were available, and, of those, approximately one-quarter believed that they were moderately or very useful for guiding instruction. In contrast, these disaggregated results were available to three-quarters

Table 5.3
Elementary School Teachers Reporting Availability and Usefulness of Math and Science State Test Results

Results	California (%)		Georgia (%)		Pennsylvania (%)	
	Available	Useful	Available	Useful	Available	Useful
Math teachers						
Math test results summarized by student subgroup	86	36	88	51	81	27
Math test results disaggregated by subtopic and skill	88	68	94	80	82	66
Science teachers						
Science test results summarized by student subgroup	26	18	74	39	NA	NA
Science test results disaggregated by subtopic and skill	25	27	79	58	NA	NA

NOTE: Response options included not available, available and not useful, available and minimally useful, available and moderately useful, and available and very useful. Percentages in useful columns are percentages of those reporting that the resource was available, which includes teachers in tested and nontested grades in California and Pennsylvania, and that it was moderately or very useful. See Tables B.22 and B.23 in Appendix B for standard errors and additional information.

of Georgia teachers, and, of those, more than half reported that they were moderately or very useful when disaggregated by subtopic or skill.

In general, middle school teachers' patterns of response with regard to math and science test results were similar to those of elementary school teachers (see Table B.25 in Appendix B). Interestingly, in cases in which the state test is not yet administered to students in all grades—science in California and mathematics in Pennsylvania—there were no significant differences in the perceived usefulness of test results between teachers in the tested grades (who received test results for the students in their grade level) and teachers in nontested grades (who received test results for students in other grade levels) at both the elementary and middle school levels. There were, however, a few differences in the reported availability of test results (e.g., more than 40 percent of California teachers in the tested fifth grade reported the availability of science test results broken down by subgroup and by topic compared to approximately 20 to 25 percent of teachers in the nontested third and fourth grades), which is to be expected.

Timeliness of State Test Results

Test results are more useful to educators if they are made available quickly. Surprisingly, principals were much less sanguine than teachers were about the timeliness of state test results. Approximately half or fewer of principals at both levels in all three states characterized the performance information they receive as "timely" (Figure 5.2). In contrast, more than half of teachers at both levels in all states, with the exception of Pennsylvania elementary school teachers, reported receiving state test results in a timely manner.

Perhaps the difference in responses between teachers and principals relates to the different uses they made of the data. One hypothesis is that principals use the data for decisions generally made during the summer before classes start (e.g., year-long planning, notifying parents about public school choice and supplemental service options) and thus need results sooner than teachers. Teachers typically wait until the start of school to consult test results to identify areas in which they need to strengthen their own content knowledge or adjust curriculum during the year and thus have less of a need for results during the summer. Pennsylvania educators at all levels were less likely than their counterparts in the other two states to find state test results timely.

Administrators' Use of State Test Results

Principals and superintendents in all three states reported using state test results for many purposes. Superintendents' priorities for state test data use focused on developing a district improvement plan, focusing principal and teacher PD, making changes to district curriculum and instruction materials, and helping individual schools to develop school improvement plans (Figure 5.3). They were least likely to report using state test data for decisions about allocating resources.

Figure 5.2
**Principals and Teachers Agreeing or Strongly Agreeing That They Receive
State Test Results and Performance Information in a Timely Manner**

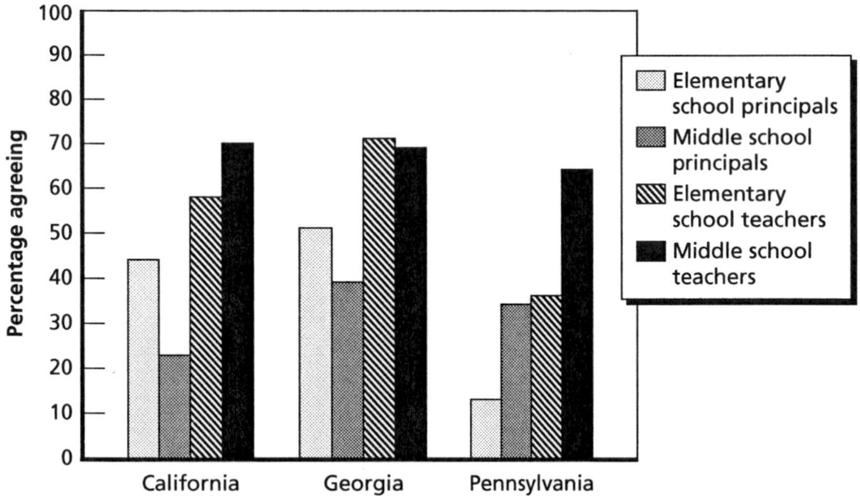

NOTE: Response options included strongly disagree, disagree, agree, and strongly
agree. We asked principals about the receipt of information about their school's
performance and asked teachers about state test results. See Table B.26 in
Appendix B for standard errors and additional information.
RAND *MG589-5.2*

Similar to superintendents, principals reported using data primarily for developing a school improvement plan, focusing PD, making curriculum and instruction changes, and identifying students who needed additional instructional support, as shown in Table 5.4.

In nearly every decision category, more Georgia principals than either California or Pennsylvania principals found the data useful. The differences are most striking in regard to high-stakes decisions. More than three-quarters of Georgia principals at both levels reported that state test results were moderately or very useful for making decisions regarding student promotion or retention, compared with about one-half of California principals and about one-fourth to one-third of Pennsylvania principals. This difference is not surprising, given that Georgia, unlike the other two states, has promotion gateways; that is, to be promoted to the next grade, students must meet grade-level standards on state tests in the third grade in reading (as of 2003–2004), the fifth grade in reading and math (as of 2004–2005), and the eighth grade in reading and math (as of 2005–2006). Georgia principals also were generally more likely to find test results useful for identifying teacher strengths and weaknesses, particularly at the elementary school level where two-thirds of principals found results useful, compared to less than half in California and Pennsylvania. One possible explanation for the pronounced difference in Pennsylvania is that, at the time of the survey, state testing did not yet occur

Figure 5.3
Superintendents Reporting That State Assessment Data Are Moderately or Very Useful for Making Certain Decisions

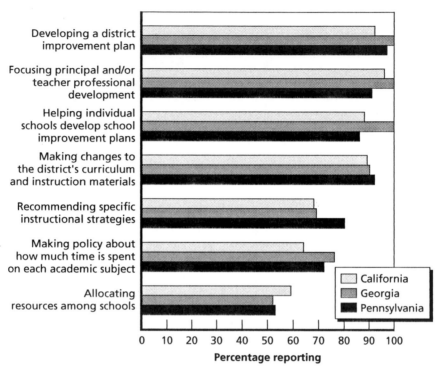

NOTE: See Table B.27 in Appendix B for standard errors and additional information.
RAND *MG589-5.3*

in all grades, so principals did not have relevant data for all teachers' students. And in California, they did not administer science tests in all grades.

Teachers' Use of State Test Results

Both principals and teachers reported widespread use of test results by teachers. More than 80 percent of principals agreed or strongly agreed that teachers in their school review state test results and use them to tailor instruction. Teachers distinguished among a variety of purposes for which they found these data useful. Most mathematics teachers (although less so in Georgia) generally found state test results useful for identifying their own PD needs rather than for identifying students' instructional needs (as shown in Table 5.5). Mathematics teachers at both levels in Georgia were much more likely than their California and Pennsylvania counterparts to find test results useful for tailoring instruction to individual student needs. This finding is consistent with other findings showing more positive attitudes toward and greater use of data in Georgia, though we cannot identify for certain what explains this pattern. The majority of mathematics teachers in all three states, especially in Georgia, also agreed or strongly

Table 5.4
Principals Reporting That State Assessment Data Are Moderately or Very Useful for Making Certain Decisions

Decision	California (%)		Georgia (%)		Pennsylvania (%)	
	Elem.	Middle	Elem.	Middle	Elem.	Middle
Developing a school improvement plan	79	77	100	94	70	88
Focusing teacher PD	73	72	86	83	78	71
Making change to curriculum and instructional materials	69	90	78	83	82	89
Identifying students who need additional instructional support	73	85	96	94	63	65
Making decisions on how much time is spent on each subject	53	70	71	66	47	49
Identifying teacher strengths and weaknesses	47	63	78	60	39	36
Making decisions regarding student promotion or retention	45	57	79	77	22	36
Assigning students to teachers	7	47	57	62	10	26

NOTE: Responses options included not useful, minimally useful, moderately useful, and very useful. See Table B.28 in Appendix B for standard errors and additional information.

agreed that state test results were useful for adjusting curriculum and instruction. Science teachers, particularly in California, were less likely than mathematics teachers to find state test results helpful for all three decision domains. Yet, like their mathematics counterparts, science teachers were more likely to find the results useful for identifying their own PD needs and identifying gaps in curriculum and instruction than for individualizing instruction. In addition, science teachers in Georgia were much more likely than their California counterparts to find state test results useful for all three purposes.

Parents in case study schools also expressed mixed opinions about the use and usefulness of state test results. Some parents appreciated the identification and targeting of student needs through the use of these data. For example, one Georgia parent commented,

> Originally . . . I was not very sure as to where [my child] was really weak . . . and now I know the areas. So immediately when he started back to school . . . he changes classes like constantly because those are the areas that we're targeting, where he had problems. . . . Where he's good in, say, English but he's a little slow in Math. . . . [T]he problem solving . . . he cannot seem to get that. Now he changes class and goes to a special class just for that.

Table 5.5
Math and Science Teachers Agreeing or Strongly Agreeing with Statements About State Tests

Statement	Respondent	California (%)		Georgia (%)		Pennsylvania (%)	
		Elem.	Middle	Elem.	Middle	Elem.	Middle
State test results allowed me to identify areas where I need to strengthen my content knowledge or teaching skills	Math teachers	70	55	89	79	69	60
	Science teachers	46	48	83	80	NA	NA
State test results helped me identify and correct gaps in curriculum and instruction	Math teachers	63	53	86	84	63	58
	Science teachers	38	54	79	74	NA	NA
State test results helped me tailor instruction to individual student needs	Math teachers	54	35	84	78	40	50
	Science teachers	30	41	72	58	NA	NA

NOTE: Excludes teachers who said that they did not receive test results. In math in Pennsylvania, includes only teachers in grades in which state tests were administered in 2004–2005: grades three, five, and eight. In science in Pennsylvania, no state science tests were administered in 2004–2005, and, in California, tests were administered only in grade five and in high school. Response options included strongly disagree, disagree, agree, and strongly agree. See Table B.29 in Appendix B for standard errors and additional information.

Other parents, however, questioned the value of using state test data for targeting student needs for students who perform at proficient or above. A Georgia parent from another school stated,

> [W]hen I think about the CRCT, it seems to me the children that obviously benefit the most from it are the ones that are deficient in whatever area, because then they're identified on that test, and then they can receive whatever extra remedial help they need by taking the classes during the summer and the opportunity to take it over again, or whatever. But, the children that just pass it or exceed expectation, whatever it is, what does it do? I mean it's just another test.

Local Progress Tests

In addition to the annual state tests, many districts or schools administered local tests, and administrators and teachers also used these results. In all three states, many administrators and teachers reported using other student assessment data to guide improvements in teaching and learning. In fact, the vast majority of superintendents agreed or strongly agreed that information from local assessments they administer regularly during the year was more useful than state test results (all of the superintendents in

Pennsylvania, 84 percent in Georgia, and 81 percent in California) (see Table B.44 in Appendix B).

Increasingly, districts and schools are administering progress tests, defined as required tests that are administered periodically (e.g., every six weeks) to monitor students' progress at meeting state standards (also called interim, benchmark, or diagnostic tests). Progress tests were required in one-third or more of districts in all three states, but they were far more popular in Georgia than in the other two states. Eighty-nine percent of Georgia superintendents said that their districts required some or all of elementary and middle schools in their districts to administer progress tests in math and that approximately half required some or all of elementary and middle schools to administer the tests in science (Table 5.6). Although approximately half of the superintendents in California and a third in Pennsylvania required math progress tests in some or all schools, they were much less likely to report this requirement in science. Again, Georgia's history of state science testing in grades three through eight helps to explain this difference.

Consistent with superintendent reports, teachers were more likely to report administering progress tests in math than in science, as shown in Figure 5.4. In addition, teachers in Georgia were more likely than their counterparts in the other two states to report that their districts or schools required them to administer progress tests in 2004–2005 in math or science. Once again, the differences were particularly striking with regard to science progress tests. For example, 30 percent of Georgia elementary school teachers reported administering progress tests, compared with 9 percent in California and 3 percent in Pennsylvania. Interestingly, teacher reports of progress testing were similar or just slightly higher this year compared with last year, with one exception.

Similar to what we found in 2003–2004, teachers using progress tests generally viewed the results as valuable for instruction and, in some cases, more useful than state test results. Because only small numbers of teachers reported administering progress tests in science, we focus here on the results for mathematics. As Figure 5.5 illustrates,

Table 5.6
Districts Requiring Some or All Elementary and Middle Schools to Administer Progress Tests in Math and Science, 2004–2005

Progress Test Required	California (%)	Georgia (%)	Pennsylvania (%)
Elementary schools: math	44	89	38
Middle schools: math	56	89	32
Elementary schools: science	9	55	NA
Middle schools: science	17	43	NA

NOTE: See Table B.30 in Appendix B for standard errors and additional information.

Figure 5.4
Teachers Required to Administer Math and Science Progress Tests

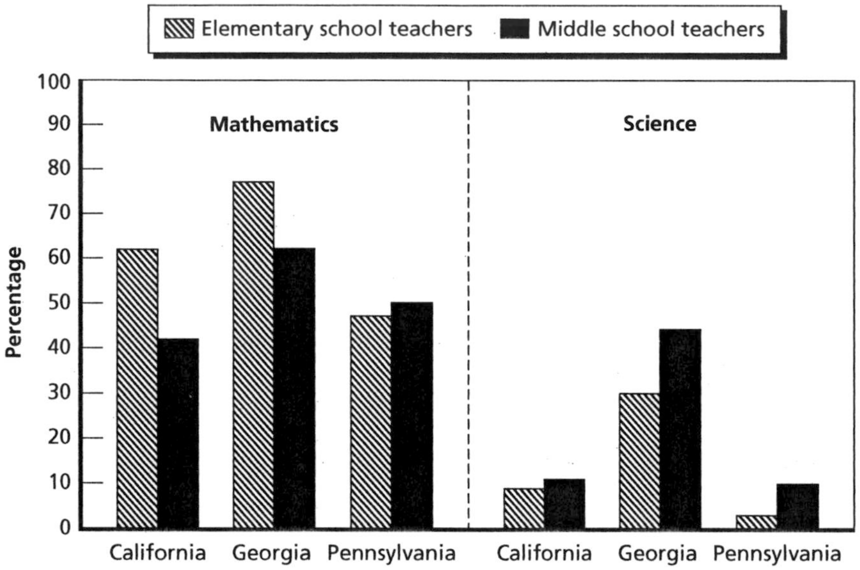

NOTE: See Table B.31 in Appendix B for standard errors and additional information.
RAND *MG589-5.4*

in California and Pennsylvania, elementary school teachers who administered progress tests were more likely to report that these tests, compared with state tests, were a good measure of student mastery of state content standards and that results helped them identify and correct gaps in their teaching. The overall differences were much less pronounced in Georgia, where teachers were almost equally likely to find state and progress tests valid measures and helpful for identifying curriculum and instruction gaps. Similar patterns emerged at the middle school level (see Table B.32 in Appendix B).

There are several potential explanations for the greater likelihood of some teachers finding progress test results useful compared with state test results. As discussed in Chapter Four, many teachers in California and Pennsylvania questioned the validity of state test results. Many noted that state tests were too difficult for the majority of their students or were not well aligned with the curriculum. Specific features of progress tests also may contribute to teachers' opinions. In general, progress tests provided teachers with results more frequently and more quickly throughout the year than state tests. Further, because progress tests are administered during the school year and have quick turnaround, they provide information on students that the teachers are currently teaching, which is not the case for state assessment data. In Georgia, more than half of the teachers reported administering math progress tests every six to eight weeks, as shown in Table 5.7. Teachers in California and Pennsylvania were more likely to report administering them two to three times a year. More importantly, the majority of teachers in all three states reported receiving the results either the same or next day

Figure 5.5
Elementary School Teachers Agreeing or Strongly Agreeing with Statements
About Math State Tests and Progress Tests

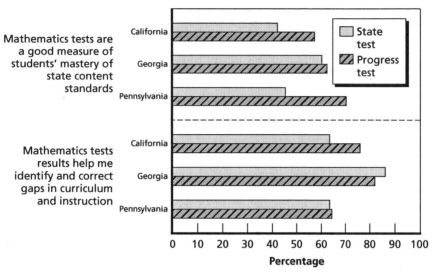

NOTE: State test results include responses from teachers in grades in which state tests were administered in 2004–2005 and who reported having access to these results. For Pennsylvania, this included only teachers in grades three and five. Progress test results include only teachers who reported being required to administer these progress tests. See Table B.32 in Appendix B for standard errors and additional information.
RAND *MG589-5.5*

or within a week. In case study interviews, teachers often noted that this quick turn-around assisted them in applying the data to their instruction and that this timeliness generally did not characterize the speed with which they received state test results. One fourth-grade teacher in Pennsylvania told us, "[The progress test] is quicker, a faster turnaround. I teach it, I test it and I can see who gets it, who doesn't get it and I can go back in and work with that student immediately. It's just more direct."

Finally, most teachers reported that there were no incentives and no consequences for teachers associated with results from progress tests. This lack of consequences may have lessened the pressure on teachers to have their students perform well on progress tests. In contrast, as we reported in Chapter Four, teachers often feel tremendous pressure to prepare students for state tests that contribute to AYP. The further understanding of progress tests as diagnostic, instructional tools intended for an internal audience may also contribute to the large base of support for these results among teachers, who tend to view state tests as accountability tools intended more for an external audience. For example, an eighth-grade science teacher in California explained how he and his colleagues collectively use the district's science progress test results. Implicit in his comments is an appreciation for the diagnostic nature of these tests:

The district is very careful not to bruise any egos with this. But I personally look at it, and we are setting aside two days of professional development for the end of next month [to look at the results]. . . . We're able to diagnose our own approach to the standard, to see which standards seem to be coming across well [and] which standards the students are not understanding. And we can therefore modify our lesson plans to help achieve those needs . . . so that next year . . . we might be more successful in the areas that the students aren't as successful in. . . . [T]he district test is very good because it breaks down each question as to what standard it addresses. So we can get a printout and see . . . specific standards, all the way down to the number and the letter. And what percentage of students were proficient there. If we have more than 50 percent proficiency, that's considered to be good. If there's only 20-percent proficiency, then we need to address that standard, and how that standard is being taught in the classrooms.

Table 5.7
Math Teachers Reporting Progress Tests with Various Features

Feature	California (%)		Georgia (%)		Pennsylvania (%)	
	Elem. (n = 450)	Middle (n = 113)	Elem. (n = 626)	Middle (n = 277)	Elem. (n = 569)	Middle (n = 152)
District or school requires you to administer a progress test	62	42	77	62	47	50
Progress tests administered two to three times per year	57	60	36	28	51	36
Progress tests administered approximately every six to eight weeks	30	21	54	65	32	38
Progress tests administered approximately every two to four weeks	13	20	10	7	17	28
Results are available the same or next day	36	53	57	56	56	50
Results are available within one week	30	24	25	24	25	28
There are consequences for teachers associated with performance on the tests	3	6	9	8	4	7

NOTE: See Table B.33 in Appendix B for standard errors and additional information.

Curriculum and Instructional Alignment

Another popular improvement strategy in all three states was supporting the use of curriculum and instruction aligned with state standards and assessments. Rather than adopting a new curricular or instructional program, respondents were much more likely to report supporting existing curriculum and teachers' implementation of it. In fact, only a small percentage of superintendents and principals reported adopting new math or science curricula in the past two years. (See Table B.34 in Appendix B for results.)

District Curriculum Alignment Efforts

As noted in Table 5.1, virtually all principals reported matching curriculum and instruction with standards or assessments, and more than half in all three states identified this as one of their most important improvement strategies. Yet much of the activity to align curriculum and instruction took place at the district level. In all three states, approximately half or more of superintendents reported undertaking multiple actions to assist schools in aligning curriculum and instruction with state or district content standards in math, as shown in Table 5.8. These actions included the development of pacing plans, instructional calendars, and sample lessons linked to state standards and mapping alignment of required textbooks and instructional programs to state standards and assessments. The most prevalent strategy in math was monitoring and providing feedback on the implementation of state content standards in classrooms (e.g., by reviewing lesson plans or students' work or by conducting walk-throughs).

As might be expected given their current assessment status in science, there was much greater variation across the states in the area of science. Georgia superintendents were much more likely to report undertaking alignment activities with science curriculum and instruction than California or Pennsylvania superintendents (Table 5.9). Because Georgia tested science in grades three through eight at the time of the survey, districts had greater incentives to pay attention to science instruction and its alignment with state tests and standards.

In many of our case study districts, administrators had developed pacing charts, standards calendars, and guides to align curriculum to state standards. Administrators often described their efforts as intended to help teachers know how to cover all of the standards over the course of the year and to ensure that everyone was on the same page. One of the case study districts had identified "highly assessed standards" to help teachers focus on the key standards most likely to be covered on state tests. Teachers and administrators in another case study school, which operated on a year-round calendar, realized that some key topics on the math assessment were not being taught until after the test because the curriculum had been designed with a traditional academic calendar in mind. Staff reported that the school could realize significant test score gains just by rearranging the curriculum slightly to ensure that the concepts were taught before the test.

Table 5.8
Districts Taking Certain Steps to Assist Schools with Aligning Math Curriculum and Instruction with Standards in the Past Three Years

Action Taken	Calif. (%)	Ga. (%)	Pa. (%)
Monitored or provided feedback on the implementation of state standards in classrooms	98	93	82
Mapped out the alignment of required textbooks and instructional programs to state standards	82	86	54
Mapped out the alignment of required textbooks and instructional programs to state assessments	68	88	49
Developed pacing plan or instructional calendar aligned with state standards	60	83	64
Established detailed curriculum guidelines aligned with state content standards	48	75	66
Provided sample lessons linked to state standards	65	70	76
Developed local content standards that augment state content standards	62	51	72

NOTE: See Table B.35 in Appendix B for standard errors and additional information.

Helpfulness of District Alignment Supports

In all three states, more than half of teachers whose districts or states had undertaken curricular alignment efforts in the area of math found them moderately or very useful (Figure 5.6). Interestingly, the action that superintendents cited most frequently—monitoring and providing feedback—was the action that teachers identified least frequently as useful relative to the other four options provided on the surveys.[2]

In case study districts, many teachers and principals viewed district curricular alignment efforts as increasing the centralization and standardization of instruction across classrooms and schools. One California elementary school teacher explained,

> There's more emphasis on teaching to the standards. There's a lot more standardization of what we have to teach and how we have to teach it. I don't know that it's all due to the No Child Left Behind Act, because some of the same things have been coming from different directions at us, but certainly it's much more standardized. There's less flexibility for the teacher or for the individual student.

Many case study teachers and principals—particularly in areas with reported high student mobility—viewed this centralized curricular guidance favorably: mainly for ensuring all students equal access to the same rigorous content. In a few cases, educators also appreciated that these efforts brought greater consistency of instruction and

---

[2]   A similar pattern emerged in response to the same set of questions about efforts to align curriculum and instruction in science. In all three states, teachers were least likely to rate monitoring and feedback as useful.

Table 5.9
Districts Taking Certain Steps to Assist Schools with Aligning Science Curriculum and Instruction with Standards in the Past Three Years

Action Taken	Calif. (%)	Ga. (%)	Pa. (%)
Monitored or provided feedback on the implementation of state standards in classrooms	43	92	40
Mapped out the alignment of required textbooks and instructional programs to state standards	54	76	34
Mapped out the alignment of required textbooks and instructional programs to state assessments	48	72	30
Developed pacing plan or instructional calendar aligned with state standards	24	72	32
Established detailed curriculum guidelines aligned with state content standards	27	70	48
Provided sample lessons linked to state standards	38	67	32
Developed local content standards that augment state content standards	35	47	49

NOTE: See Table B.36 in Appendix B for standard errors and additional information.

Figure 5.6
Elementary School Teachers Reporting That District or State Actions to Align Math Curriculum and Instruction with Standards Were Useful

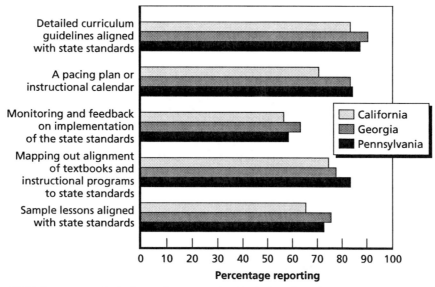

NOTE: Percentages include teachers reporting both that their district or state took these actions *and* that these actions were either moderately useful or very useful. See Table B.37 in Appendix B for standard errors and additional information.
RAND *MG589-5.6*

held teachers accountable. As one California middle school teacher noted, "I do see a change because now we're all on the same page, . . . they try to keep us pacing the same now, we have the same materials—before we didn't have that."

Some parents interviewed in our case study schools also recognized the benefits of curriculum alignment. As one Pennsylvania parent noted, "When you go from one school to the next, they're on the same track that you are. Like say you're doing addition here [at this school], if you move to another school in the district, you're going right into the same program. So you're not completely lost in that way."

Yet for many teachers in our case study schools, this curricular guidance created problems regarding pacing and resulted in a lack of time to teach for understanding and mastery. These concerns about time were voiced in all three states and both levels of schooling. For example, an elementary school teacher in Pennsylvania commented,

> In some ways it's [district standards' calendar] good, but it can also be hurtful when you have a child that doesn't get a concept, and you know, 'Well next week, we did money and now, we're going to do time,' and you know some children just didn't quite get money and you'd like to spend more time, but it kind of pushes us a little bit more.

Similarly, a California elementary school teacher expressed concerns about her district's curriculum guides: "Sometimes you'll find a grade level that has 40 skills to teach in 20 days. There's no depth. It's a mile-wide, inch-deep kind of coverage of skills." Several case study school teachers also complained about not receiving needed guidance on how to modify the curriculum and curriculum guide or pacing plans for special education students.

Several parents interviewed in the case study schools also expressed concerns about the amount of content taught in a school year. For example, one parent from Pennsylvania questioned whether students were mastering curriculum: "They're learning at such a fast speed. I mean they come home. And they're learning all these things: shapes, pre-algebra. And they're in second and third grade, and they're learning stuff. But they're not learning it." Another Pennsylvania parent expressed similar concerns, saying, "I think it's too intense at times. It's too intense. There's no time to sit back and just go, 'OK, let's just take a breather, we did this, let's just relax.' There's no time, it's just a constant go, 'OK we did this, now we need to do this; we just did something, now we need to do this.' So are they really absorbing it? I don't know."

Activities Targeting Low-Performing Students

Targeting of Low-Performing Students

As noted earlier, virtually all principals across the three states provided additional instruction to low-achieving students (Table 5.1). In addition, districts in all three states undertook numerous efforts to further target and support this student subgroup. For example, half or more of the districts in all three states required some or all elementary and middle schools to provide *remedial assistance* to students outside of the school day (Figure 5.7). This was particularly prevalent in Georgia and Pennsylvania, where more than 80 percent of superintendents reported that their districts required this.

More than half of the superintendents in all three states required some or all middle schools to create *separate mathematics classes* for low-achieving students, and more than half of the superintendents in Georgia and Pennsylvania reported this requirement at the elementary school level (Table 5.10). In addition, Georgia superintendents were more likely than their counterparts to require an *increase in the amount of time* spent on mathematics instruction for low-performing students at some or all elementary (94 percent) and middle schools (92 percent). In contrast, less than half of the California superintendents reported this requirement at either the elementary or middle school level.

California districts were more likely to take a different approach to supporting low achievers in math: *eliminating some remedial courses or instruction* and requiring all students to take more challenging math courses or instruction. More than half of the California districts required some or all elementary schools to eliminate some remedial instruction and more than three-quarters required the elimination of remedial courses at the middle school level. Interestingly, many California districts—including about

Figure 5.7
Districts Requiring Some or All Elementary and Middle Schools to Offer Remedial Assistance to Students Outside the School Day

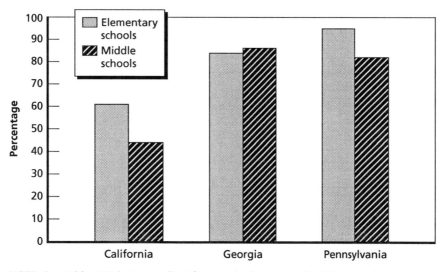

NOTE: See Table B.38 in Appendix B for standard errors and additional information.
RAND *MG589-5.7*

Table 5.10
Districts Requiring Some or All Elementary and Middle Schools to Make Changes Targeting Low-Achieving Students, 2004–2005

Change Required	Calif. (%)	Ga. (%)	Pa. (%)
Creating separate mathematics classes for low-achieving students required at some or all middle schools	56	56	51
Creating separate mathematics classes for low-achieving students required at some or all elementary schools	39	57	54
Increasing the amount of time spent on math instruction specifically for low-achieving students required at some or all middle schools	35	92	49
Increasing the amount of time spent on math instruction specifically for low-achieving students required at some or all elementary schools	44	94	63
Eliminating some remedial math courses or instruction and requiring all students to take more challenging math courses or instruction required at some or all middle schools	76	22	32
Eliminating some remedial math courses or instruction and requiring all students to take more challenging math courses or instruction required at some or all elementary schools	53	19	11
Increasing the amount of time spent on science instruction specifically for low-achieving students required at some or all middle schools	12	33	0
Increasing the amount of time spent on science instruction specifically for low-achieving students required at some or all elementary schools	6	30	0
Requiring all students to take more challenging science courses or instruction required at some or all middle schools	9	43	28
Requiring all students to take more challenging science courses or instruction required at some or all elementary schools	6	33	17
Creating separate science classes for low-achieving students required at some or all middle schools	4	16	8
Creating separate science classes for low-achieving students required at some or all elementary schools	2	3	8

NOTE: See Table B.39 in Appendix B for standard errors and additional information.

half of the same districts eliminating remedial courses—reported creating separate mathematics classes for low achievers. Conversations with district leaders suggested that some districts had eliminated courses with remedial content and replaced them with courses that offered grade-level content to low-achieving students.

In all three states, districts were far less likely to undertake these targeted support strategies in the area of science than in math. However, consistent with more extensive science testing in their state, Georgia superintendents were more likely to report activity in the area of science than their counterparts in the other states. For example, approximately one-third required some or all elementary and middle schools to increase time on science instruction for low-achieving students—compared with no superintendents in Pennsylvania and less than 15 percent in California.

All of the case study schools implemented some form of assistance to low-performing students (or those on the cusp of proficiency, as described in the next chapter). These activities ranged from intervention plans to after- and before-school tutoring to remedial programs during the school day. Several schools offered extra periods of instruction in the tested subjects for low-performing students, which often displaced student participation in nontested subjects such as physical education and music. Although most case study schools provided some type of tutoring or after-school program, teachers and principals in several case study schools reported struggling to get the students in greatest need of assistance to attend. One Pennsylvania principal explained that parents' schedules often contributed to low participation: "Because so many parents pick up their children, and they might have three other kids that they need to pick up at 2:40, they don't want to have to come back for the other kids. I don't have the participation because it's very difficult to enforce if you don't have parental support." In other schools, teachers reported concerns about the quality of tutors and the degree of coordination between tutoring and the regular curriculum.

Concerns About High-Achieving Students

Given this focus on low-performing students, some teachers expressed concerns about the subsequent lack of attention paid to high-achieving students. Some teachers also identified this as a possible unintended consequence of new state and federal accountability. Almost half or more of elementary and middle school teachers responding to surveys in all three states (except Pennsylvania elementary school teachers) agreed or strongly agreed that, "as a result of the state's accountability system, high-achieving students are not receiving appropriately challenging curriculum and instruction," as shown in Figure 5.8.

One parent in Pennsylvania expressed a similar viewpoint:

> I think when you get to the higher levels, my experience has been the kids aren't being challenged. And I blame it on No Child Left Behind. I think those kids are seen as they'll coast along and they'll get high enough scores. But they're not being challenged to really dig deep. . . . And I really do believe that if you want the country to succeed educationally, you ought to do the best with your best and brightest.

Nevertheless, some case study schools were undertaking efforts targeting high-achieving students, such as adding more advanced courses or the international baccalaureate program in the middle schools. Administrators hoped these efforts would attract high achievers back to the school if they had left or retain those who may have

Figure 5.8
Teachers Agreeing or Strongly Agreeing That, as a Result of the State
Accountability System, High-Achieving Students Are Not Receiving
Appropriately Challenging Curriculum or Instruction

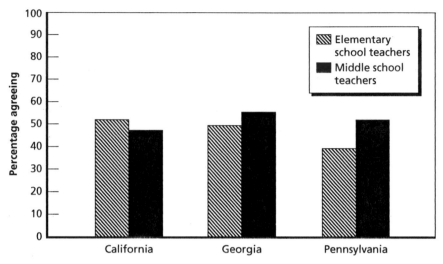

NOTE: See Table B.40 in Appendix B for standard errors and additional information.
RAND MG589-5.8

been considering other school options. Many viewed this population as critical to raising overall school test scores.

Other School Improvement Strategies

District and school administrators implemented a range of other strategies to improve instruction and student performance, including PD, test preparation, and increasing instructional time.

Professional Development Focus

Ultimately, the success or failure of school improvement hinges on what occurs in the classroom. As noted in Table 5.1 at the start of this chapter, most principals reported increasing teacher PD in 2004–2005. Teachers in all three states reported that PD efforts emphasized alignment of curriculum and instruction with state standards and tests, mathematics content and teaching, and instructional strategies for low-achieving students (Table 5.11). In all three states, teachers were less likely to report a PD focus on instructional strategies for special education students and science and science teaching. The former finding—that fewer than one-third of teachers reported that PD emphasized instructional strategies for special education students—is particularly interesting, given that many teachers reported concerns about this subgroup of students

Table 5.11
Teachers Reporting a Moderate or Major Emphasis in PD Activities, 2004–2005

PD Content	California (%)		Georgia (%)		Pennsylvania (%)	
	Elem.	Middle	Elem.	Middle	Elem.	Middle
Aligning curriculum and instruction with state or district content standards	68	52	79	68	70	65
Instructional strategies for low-achieving students	57	45	68	57	47	39
Preparing students to take the state assessments	47	28	74	56	67	58
Instructional strategies for ELLs	57	40	27	17	14	10
Mathematics and mathematics teaching	53	42	57	52	64	44
Interpreting and using reports of student test results	44	24	65	45	36	33
Instructional strategies for special education students	25	25	39	42	33	33
Science and science teaching	28	26	20	32	23	30

NOTE: Response options included no emphasis, minor emphasis, moderate emphasis, and major emphasis. See Table B.41 in Appendix B for standard errors and additional information.

(discussed further in Chapter Seven). There were, however, some differences in what was emphasized across states. Not surprisingly, teachers in California were much more likely than teachers in the other two states to report a PD focus on instructional strategies for ELLs. In contrast, California teachers were less likely to report an emphasis on preparing students for state tests. Less than half the elementary school teachers and approximately one-quarter of middle school teachers reported this focus, compared to more than half at both levels in Georgia and Pennsylvania. This difference is likely due to state policy in California that explicitly discourages narrow test preparation activities. Finally, consistent with other reported activity in the area of data use (see earlier discussion), Pennsylvania teachers were least likely to report a focus on interpreting and using reports of student test results.

Professional Development Support Provided by Districts

Districts also engaged in other avenues of PD to support teacher and principal learning and improvement—such as assigning coaches to teachers and principals—with considerable variation across the states. As Figure 5.9 shows, Georgia districts were much more likely than districts in the other states to assign full-time school-level staff to support teacher development in some or all schools. And of the Georgia districts assigning staff developers in 2004–2005, 85 percent reported using this strategy with all schools. Finally, some districts, particularly in Georgia, reported providing a coach or mentor

Figure 5.9
Districts Providing Technical Assistance to Principals or Teachers in Some or All Elementary and Middle Schools

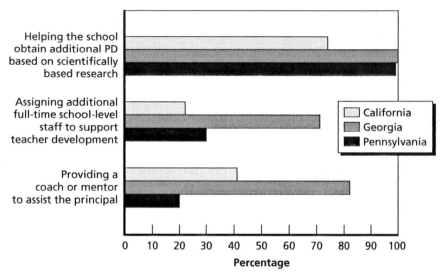

NOTE: Response options included no schools, low-performing schools, high-performing schools, and all schools. See Table B.42 in Appendix B for standard errors and additional information.
RAND *MG589-5.9*

to assist school principals. Interestingly, approximately half of the superintendents in all three states who assigned principal coaches did so only in their low-performing schools (i.e., 82 percent of Georgia superintendents assigned coaches, with 41 percent assigning them to the low-performing schools and the other 41 percent assigning them to all schools).

Test Preparation

The large prevalence of test preparation activities is not surprising, given NCLB's emphasis on school improvement as measured by student performance on state assessments. The majority of principals in all three states reported employing various activities to help teachers prepare students for state tests (as shown in Table 5.12). The most common activities were helping teachers identify content covered on the state test and discussing at staff meetings how to prepare students for the test. Also, roughly half the principals in all three states encouraged or required teachers to spend more time on tested subjects and less time on other subjects. This was consistent with many district efforts, such as requirements that schools increase instructional time in the areas of math and English language arts.

Table 5.12
Principals Reporting Test Preparation Activities

Test Preparation Activity	California (%)		Georgia (%)		Pennsylvania (%)	
	Elem.	Middle	Elem.	Middle	Elem.	Middle
Helped teachers identify content that is likely to appear on the state test so they can cover it adequately in their instruction	94	99	100	100	100	99
Discussed methods for preparing students for the state test at staff meetings	94	95	100	100	99	100
Distributed released copies of the state test or test items	61	61	88	98	96	96
Encouraged teachers to focus their efforts on students close to meeting the standards	85	94	90	93	77	57
Distributed commercial test preparation materials (e.g., practice tests)	59	61	90	88	93	88
Encouraged or required teachers to spend more time on tested subjects and less on other subjects	53	63	47	66	61	45
Discussed assessment anchors with teachers (Pa. only)					100	100

NOTE: See Table B.43 in Appendix B for standard errors and additional information.

There was, however, variation across the states in certain activities. For example, Georgia and Pennsylvania principals were more likely than California principals to distribute released copies of the state tests. Several factors might help to explain the difference across states in the prevalence of test preparation activities. In particular, California has had a statewide test and an accountability system in place since 1999. Administrators, teachers, and students in that state may be more familiar with the content and format of the state assessment than in Georgia or Pennsylvania, which have newer or more recently revised tests or have recently expanded testing into new grade levels. Furthermore, at least some principals interpreted California's discouragement of test preparation activities to mean that they are not allowed to use any material that resembled the state test. One principal told us, "We hear horror stories of 'you'd better not use that practice test because this is too identical to the CST and we'll get dinged' and that kind of thing."

By contrast, our case study visits and superintendent interviews revealed that educators in Pennsylvania felt a particular need to familiarize students and staff with specific question formats since the Pennsylvania System of School Assessment includes open-ended tasks and requires students to write short essays and explain their work on math problems. Superintendents and principals in Pennsylvania also frequently expressed concerns about the alignment between the state standards and the state assessment, which may explain the prevalence of test preparation activities if educators felt that the state assessment was only weakly linked to their normal curriculum and instruction.

Parents from several case study schools in Pennsylvania reported concerns that instructional time was lost to test-preparation activities. An elementary school parent argued, "The teachers have to take so much time to prepare for these tests, to try to motivate the children, to try to teach the children just to get them to pass these tests. The real teaching that should be done is not getting done." Similarly, a parent of a middle school student stated, "It's become teaching towards tests. I don't see a lot of creative teaching." And another middle school parent noted, "I wonder how much instructional time we take away because we're doing all these preparation tests? The whole school is going through them this week."

Efforts by the state departments of education also probably influenced school and district test-preparation activities. Both the Georgia and Pennsylvania departments of education produced and distributed materials to help prepare teachers and students for the state assessments. For example, both maintained online repositories of released test items that were freely accessible to students and teachers. Educators in case study schools and superintendents whom we interviewed from these states frequently noted that they had received test preparation materials directly from the state. By contrast, according to state officials we interviewed in California, the state did not make test-preparation materials available in the same way that Pennsylvania and Georgia did, and principals were told that narrow test preparation was discouraged.

Changes in Instructional Time

Districts and schools also attempted to improve teaching and learning by altering the instructional opportunities that students had to interact with teachers and the curriculum. Superintendents—particularly in Georgia—reported several examples of adjusting time as an improvement strategy. In Georgia, 71 percent of superintendents required some or all elementary schools in their districts to increase *instructional time for all students* by lengthening the school day or year or by shortening recess, compared with only seven percent in California and 15 percent in Pennsylvania (for a table of all results presented in this section, see Table B.44 in Appendix B). Similar patterns emerged at the middle school level. Georgia superintendents also were much more likely than their counterparts to require their schools to increase the amount of *time spent on mathematics instruction for all students*. For example, 73 percent of Georgia district leaders required some or all elementary schools in their district to increase math instruction compared with 10 percent in California and 42 percent in Pennsylvania. Finally, more than half of the superintendents in Pennsylvania and Georgia required some or all elementary schools to institute *full-day kindergarten* in 2004–2005, compared with less than a third in California.

As noted earlier, there also appears to be some efforts in all three states to shift time away from nontested subjects to tested subjects. Roughly half the principals in all three states reported that their schools or districts encouraged or required teachers to spend more time on tested subjects and less time on other subjects (see Table 5.12). In addition, approximately 40 percent of superintendents across the states reported eliminating programs (e.g., art, music) to provide more instruction in core subjects (Table B.44 in Appendix B). (For a more detailed discussion of teachers' allocations of instructional time, see Chapter Six.)

District and State Technical Assistance

Districts and states also play a role in technical assistance. Under NCLB, they must provide assistance to schools that are identified as needing improvement based on annual AYP determinations. Most districts and states also offer other types of support for struggling schools. This section describes how these efforts were being implemented in three states as of the 2004–2005 school year.

Technical Assistance for School Improvement

The provisions of NCLB require districts to ensure that schools receive technical assistance based on scientifically based research; specific areas for assistance include data analysis, identifying and implementing improvement strategies, and budget analysis. The majority of superintendents—especially in Georgia and Pennsylvania—reported that, as a result of NCLB, in the 2004–2005 school year, they were providing "more technical assistance to schools to implement the curriculum, hiring, testing, and reporting requirements of NCLB" (82 percent in Georgia, 80 percent in Pennsylvania, and 61 percent in California agreed or strongly agreed with that statement).

As shown in Table 5.13, superintendents in all three states reported that their districts provided a great deal of technical assistance to schools. The majority of superintendents reported assisting all schools in their districts with data analysis, implementing effective instructional strategies, obtaining research-based PD, teaching standards to special student populations, school improvement planning, complying with NCLB reporting requirements and budgeting.

Some types of technical assistance were far more common in some states than in others. For example, although 81 percent of superintendents in Georgia reported helping all schools obtain more experienced teachers, only 35 percent in California and 23 percent in Pennsylvania reported providing this type of assistance to all schools. Similarly, Georgia superintendents were more likely than their counterparts in the other states to report offering all schools assistance with providing extended learning programs, providing additional instructional materials, and implementing parental involvement strategies. This difference also holds true for types of assistance that involve the assignment of staff to work with schools. As noted, Georgia superintendents

Table 5.13
Districts Providing Technical Assistance to Some or All Schools

Assistance Provided	California (%)		Georgia (%)		Pennsylvania (%)	
	All Schools	Low-Performing Only	All Schools	Low-Performing Only	All Schools	Low-Performing Only
Assisting the school in analyzing assessment data to identify and address problems in instruction	89	3	100	0	97	3
Assisting the school in implementing instructional strategies that have been proven effective	89	11	98	0	93	0
Assisting the school in analyzing and revising its budget to use resources more effectively	65	16	74	4	54	0
Helping the school with school improvement planning	87	2	95	5	64	19
Helping schools prepare complete and accurate data to comply with NCLB reporting requirements	74	3	100	0	71	15
Helping the school obtain additional PD based on scientifically based research	72	2	98	2	98	1
Providing guidance for teaching grade-level standards to ELLs or special education students	79	8	90	8	78	0
Providing before- or after-school, weekend, or summer programs	57	18	86	2	39	24
Providing additional instructional materials and books	57	17	80	18	61	7
Assisting the school in implementing parental involvement strategies	57	10	94	4	41	33
Helping the school obtain more experienced teachers	35	3	81	0	23	1
Assigning additional full-time school-level staff to support teacher development	12	11	55	15	27	3
Providing a coach or mentor to assist the principal	19	22	41	41	11	9

NOTE: Response options included no schools, low-performing schools, high-performing schools, and all schools. See Table B.45 in Appendix B for standard errors and additional information.

were more likely than their counterparts to assign coaches or mentors to principals and full-time staff to support teacher PD.

Although most superintendents reported providing this assistance to all schools, in some cases, they limited this support to their low-performing schools. For example, Georgia superintendents were evenly divided between those who provided a coach or mentor to assist principals in all schools (41 percent) and those who did so only in their low-performing schools (41 percent). Similarly, 33 percent of Pennsylvania superintendents reported assisting only their low-performing schools with implementing parent involvement strategies, while another 41 percent offered this support to all schools.

Though not shown in the table, most superintendents of districts with schools identified for improvement reported providing all three types of technical assistance required by NCLB—data analysis, implementing proven strategies, and budget analysis.

Principals' Perceptions of District Support

The majority of principals agreed that their districts were providing support to schools, as shown in Table 5.14. In all three states, more than two-thirds of principals agreed or strongly agreed that their district provided needed assistance to help schools that were having difficulty improving. For the most part, they were also very positive about district instructional support to school-level staff. The one exception was California elementary school principals: Fewer than half agreed that district staff provided

Table 5.14
Principals Agreeing or Strongly Agreeing with Statements About District Support

Support Provided	California (%)		Georgia (%)		Pennsylvania (%)	
	Elem.	Middle	Elem.	Middle	Elem.	Middle
When schools are having difficulty, the district provides assistance needed to help them improve	66	91	83	82	86	69
District staff provide appropriate support to enable principals to act as instructional leaders	61	82	80	77	66	58
District staff provide appropriate instructional support for teachers	68	74	84	75	74	90
District staff provide support for teaching grade-level standards to special education students (i.e., students with individualized education programs [IEPs])	45	64	77	77	80	80
District staff provide support for teaching grade-level standards to ELLs (i.e., limited English proficient students)	62	74	74	76	84	91

NOTE: Response options included strongly disagree, disagree, agree, and strongly agree. See Table B.46 in Appendix B for standard errors and additional information.

support for teaching grade-level standards to special education students (a sharp contrast to what superintendents reported in Table 5.14).

In schools failing to meet AYP for two consecutive years (i.e., identified as needing improvement), principals reported receiving a variety of supports from districts and states. Because the number of schools identified as needing improvement was very small in some states, we cannot report reliable estimates for the whole state (Table B.47 in Appendix B). We present herein our findings for illustrative purposes only and because they raise important questions. Among the subsample of schools in need of improvement, principals were most likely to receive additional PD and special grants to support school improvement. Some principals also reported receiving a mentor or coach and school support teams. An even smaller number of principals reported receiving additional full-time staff and distinguished teachers.

In the subsample of schools failing to meet AYP for three or more consecutive years (i.e., in corrective action or restructuring)—nine in California and four in Georgia but none in Pennsylvania—principals generally did not report a common set of interventions (Table B.48 in Appendix B). The most common intervention that principals in both states reported was extending the school day or year. Otherwise, one or two principals in either state reported the appointment of an outside expert to advise the school, the reassignment or demotion of the principal, decreased management authority, or the replacement of staff relevant to the school's failure to make AYP. Many principals, particularly in California, did not report any interventions at all. Further, none of the principals—even those in schools that have failed to make AYP for five or more consecutive years (i.e., those in restructuring)—reported major reconstitution of staff, the reopening of the school as a charter school, or contracting with a private management firm to operate the school. This finding is consistent with a recent national study that found that most schools in restructuring are engaging in the least disruptive kinds of actions, such as more intensive efforts to improve curriculum and leadership, instead of more radical actions such as converting to a charter school or being taken over by the state (Center on Education Policy, 2006).

State and Regional Support for Districts

States and regional education offices in our study also provided support to districts. The focus and availability of this support, however, varied among the states. In general, superintendents indicated several similar areas of need for state assistance, as illustrated in Table 5.15. Most superintendents in all three states reported needing support with identifying effective instructional strategies based on scientific research and providing effective PD. More than half in all three states also reported needs for clarifying accountability system rules and requirements. In Georgia and Pennsylvania, most superintendents also reported needs for support in the areas of using data more effectively. Most Pennsylvania superintendents also indicated needs for support with developing standards-based curriculum guides and promoting parental involvement.

Table 5.15
Superintendents Reporting Need for and Receipt of Technical Assistance If Needed

Type of Assistance	California (%)		Georgia (%)		Pennsylvania (%)	
	Needed	Received If Needed	Needed	Received If Needed	Needed	Received If Needed
Identifying effective methods and instructional strategies in scientifically based research	79	53	70	74	88	38
Providing effective PD	74	69	72	92	77	58
Using data more effectively	48	57	74	90	87	55
Clarifying accountability system rules and requirements	84	96	55	86	57	100
Developing and implementing a district improvement plan	43	93	45	6 of 8	50	7 of 8
Developing curriculum guides or model lessons based on state content standards	34	31	50	90	86	62
Promoting parent involvement	37	42	52	60	70	18
Helping the district work with schools in need of improvement	37	78	62	100	39	3 of 7

NOTE: In cases in which the number of principals reporting to have needed or received certain types of assistance was less than 10, we report raw numbers for the state sample rather than estimates for the whole state. See Table B.49 in Appendix B for standard errors and additional information.

Not all superintendents, however, received state or regional support in the areas of stated need. This was particularly true for superintendents in Pennsylvania. Approximately half or fewer of Pennsylvania superintendents who reported a need for support with identifying effective instructional practices, using data, promoting parent involvement, or working with schools in need of improvement received assistance in these areas. For example, 70 percent needed assistance with promoting parent involvement, yet, of these superintendents, only 18 percent received this assistance. In contrast, the most noteworthy area of unmet need in California pertained to research-based instructional support. More than three-quarters of California superintendents reported needing assistance with identifying effective instructional practices, yet, of these superintendents, approximately half received support in this area. Unlike California and Pennsylvania, in nearly every category, a large majority of Georgia superintendents reporting a technical assistance need received that assistance from their state or regional offices, with one slight exception in the area of promoting parent involvement.

In addition to the technical assistance that districts provide to all schools, NCLB also envisions a role for states as technical assistance providers for both schools and districts that have been identified as needing improvement. NCLB requires that states establish systems of support that can include school support teams, distinguished teachers and principals, and provision of assistance from outside entities such as institutions of higher education, educational service agencies, or private providers of scientifically based technical assistance.

Twenty-nine superintendents among the 67 who completed surveys—seven in California, 17 in Georgia, and five in Pennsylvania—reported having schools identified as needing improvement that were eligible for technical assistance from the state. Because the number of superintendents with schools in need of improvement was very small in some states, we provide only a few illustrative examples of the types of assistance superintendents reported that state education agencies provided to these schools (Table B.50 in Appendix B). Superintendents most frequently reported receiving state assistance in the form of special funding to support school improvement, followed by the assignment of school improvement teams and third-party assistance. In Georgia, some schools also received support from a distinguished principal or teacher. Interestingly, in the first year of the study, none of the districts in any of the states reported receiving state support in the form of distinguished principals or teachers and fewer numbers reported working with state-approved school improvement teams or with other third-party support providers.

In districts identified as needing improvement, superintendents also reported a range of NCLB-defined state interventions (Table B.51 in Appendix B). Once again, because the number of superintendents in districts identified for improvement was very small in some states, we do not report estimates for the whole state. The most common intervention from states was help notifying parents of their districts' status. In a few districts in Georgia and Pennsylvania, the state authorized students to transfer to higher-performing districts, and Georgia required several districts to implement new standards-based curricula and deferred or reduced funding. None of the states intervened with structural or staffing changes, such as replacing personnel or restructuring the district.

Summary

In sum, we found evidence that districts and schools were engaged in many improvement strategies in all three of our states. Three of the most important strategies that principals and, to some extent, superintendents identified for helping improve student and school performance were increasing the use of student achievement data to inform instruction, matching curriculum and instruction with standards or assessments, and providing additional instruction to low-performing students. In particular,

- districts and schools made use of a variety of student assessment data including state and local test results. Superintendents and principals found state data especially useful for making decisions regarding improvement plans, focusing PD, and making curriculum and instruction changes. In addition, districts frequently required progress tests in mathematics, especially in Georgia, where nearly all of our surveyed districts required them. In California and Pennsylvania, teachers were more likely to report that progress test results compared to state test results were helpful in measuring student mastery of state content standards and allowing teachers to identify and correct gaps in curriculum and instruction.
- almost all principals reported aligning curriculum and instruction with state standards or assessments and districts actively supported these efforts by providing pacing schedules, calendars, sample lessons, and classroom feedback on the implementation of state standards, as well as mapping the alignment of textbooks and materials to state standards and assessments. Majorities of teachers in all three states viewed these district alignment activities as helpful.
- across the states, schools and districts took some similar approaches to assisting low-performing students. In all three states, approximately half or more of districts required some or all schools to provide remedial assistance to students outside of the school day. In Georgia and, to a lesser extent, Pennsylvania, many districts required schools to increase the amount of time spent on mathematics for low-achieving students. Other popular strategies included the creation of separate classes for low performers (popular at middle schools) and the elimination of some remedial mathematics classes and the subsequent requirement that all students receive more challenging instruction (most frequently reported in California). Simultaneous with this common focus on instruction for low-achieving students was a concern among about half of all teachers in all three states that, as a result of NCLB, high-achieving students were not receiving sufficiently challenging instruction.
- district and school administrators commonly implemented other improvement strategies—including PD, test preparation, and altering instructional time.
- states and districts provided technical assistance in a range of areas to districts and schools, particularly those identified as in need of improvement. Principals in all three states were generally satisfied with the level of support from their districts, while some superintendents—particularly in Pennsylvania—reported areas in which they needed more or better support from their state departments of education.

Several state-specific findings also emerged from this analysis. First, Georgia schools and districts appear to be much more active in promoting science instruction than California and Pennsylvania schools or districts. Given Georgia's history of science standards and testing, it is not surprising that we found more local strategies targeting this discipline in Georgia than we did in the other two states, which have just recently developed science standards and tests in certain grades. Second, Georgia also distinguished itself from the other two states in the area of data-driven decisionmaking: Educators in this state were more likely to report the use of progress tests and more likely to express positive views about the usefulness of state and local test data than their counterparts in the other two states. These differences may be due to a related trend observed in our data: Georgia appears to be providing more overall support to schools and districts. Georgia administrators at the district and school levels were more likely than their counterparts in the other states to report providing and receiving needed assistance in a wide range of areas, including data use, school improvement, PD, and curricular alignment. Third, Pennsylvania districts and schools appear to be at an earlier stage of development in the use of data to drive instructional decisions—likely due, at least in part, to the newness of the state test and the fact that state testing did not yet occur in all grades. As we discuss in the next chapter, many educators in Pennsylvania reported a lack of capacity and need for support in this area. Fourth, California districts appear to be taking a slightly different approach to assisting low-performing students, focusing less on increasing instructional time and providing remedial assistance outside of the school day and more on requiring all students to take more challenging courses and instruction.

CHAPTER SIX

Instructional Practices Related to Standards and Assessments

The school improvement strategies discussed in the previous chapter will exert their effects in large part through the activities in which teachers and students engage in the classroom. In this chapter, we describe how teachers responded to the standards and assessments that their states adopted. We examine the extent to which teachers changed the amount of time they spent on different subject areas, the alignment of instructional activities with state standards and assessments, the perceived effects of the state assessments on teachers' instructional practices, and the instructional strategies that teachers used in their mathematics and science classrooms. Teachers' responses suggest that state testing requirements are influencing their practices. Some of these effects likely benefit student learning, while others raise concerns about excessive narrowing of curriculum and instruction.[1]

Changes in Time Spent on Tested and Nontested Subjects

Although other research has shown that teachers tend to increase time on tested subjects and decrease time spent on nontested subjects, teachers reported relatively few such changes in either year of our survey administration. The time frame of our study may have failed to capture changes that had taken place in prior years. Despite the overall trend, a significant minority of teachers did report changes, particularly in mathematics and ELA. In all three states, teachers were more likely to report increasing than decreasing the time devoted to instruction in mathematics and ELA (Tables 6.1 and 6.2). For example, 22 percent of Georgia elementary school teachers reported an increase in time spent on mathematics, as did 28 percent of California elementary school teachers and 38 percent of Pennsylvania elementary school teachers. These results are consistent with the superintendent and principal responses described in the previous chapter.

---

[1] Although the time frame of our survey focused on the past year, during which NCLB was in place, it is important to keep in mind that many of these teachers had been working in the context of SBA systems that were adopted before NCLB, and some of their responses might reflect the effects of those earlier systems.

Some teachers also reported changes in time spent on science instruction, but the extent of change varied across states and it corresponded to state science testing requirements (see Chapter Three for a discussion of state requirements). In Georgia, where science testing was widespread and had been in place for a few years, middle school science teachers were more likely to report increasing than decreasing the time devoted to science instruction. However, there was no evidence for widespread increases or decreases in time devoted to science instruction in California, and Pennsylvania elementary school teachers were more likely to report a decrease than an increase in science instructional time.

At the elementary school level, teachers were generally more likely to report a decrease than an increase in time spent on nontested subjects (Table 6.1). In a few cases, social studies was the subject for which teachers were most likely to report a decrease in instructional time, especially in California and Pennsylvania, where approximately a quarter of teachers reported a decrease. About a quarter of California teachers also reported decreases in arts and music and in physical education. Middle school teachers reported these changes less commonly, perhaps, in part, because of scheduling constraints in most middle schools, though, interestingly, 20 percent of Georgia teachers reported an increase in time spent on social studies (Table 6.2). The Georgia social studies findings might reflect the fact that Georgia administers tests in social studies to elementary and middle school students. The increases in mathematics and ELA instructional time in California, Georgia, and Pennsylvania in 2004–2005 build on similar increases reported between 2002–2003 and 2003–2004. These findings are consistent with nationwide trends in the wake of NCLB reported by the Center on Education Policy (2006).

Table 6.1
Elementary School Teachers Reporting Changes in Instruction Time from 2003–2004 to 2004–2005

Teaching Subject	California (%)			Georgia (%)			Pennsylvania (%)		
	–	=	+	–	=	+	–	=	+
Mathematics	5	62	28	6	60	22	3	55	38
Science	19	54	21	10	63	11	22	62	8
Reading, language arts, or English	3	59	32	4	62	21	7	63	24
Social studies	28	55	10	11	65	9	25	60	6
Arts or music	23	60	9	9	69	4	2	88	3
Physical education	23	58	11	5	74	5	3	88	3

NOTE: – indicates a decrease in instructional time. = indicates no change in instructional time. + indicates an increase in instructional time. Omitted category is don't know. See Table B.52 in Appendix B for standard errors and additional information.

In case study schools—regardless of whether the school met AYP or was identified as needing improvement—teachers and principals described a wide range of efforts to capture more time for reading and mathematics instruction, including eliminating an instrumental music program, decreasing the number of physical education classes offered each week from five to two, eliminating chorus and assemblies, and refocusing summer school from enrichment opportunities to academic instruction in tested subjects. In some schools, these changes were instituted for all students, whereas in others, the extra mathematics and reading instruction were provided only to low-performing students. Several case study teachers described a dilemma resulting from the pressure to focus on math and reading: Activities that teachers believed kept students in school and engaged in learning were exactly those activities that schools cut due to time constraints from increased pressure to focus on subjects included in AYP.

Parents, too, voiced concerns about shifts in activities. Parents were particularly concerned about the loss of activities that made schools fun and engaging, such as field trips, parties, and arts instruction. One Pennsylvania elementary school parent, for example, described her concerns about the ramifications of these decisions:

> Because of No Child Left Behind, there are kindergarten teachers who they are not allowing them to have fun anymore because it has to be a lot more academic. . . . And teachers really are having a hard time getting that into the curriculum because they have to get so much curriculum into the curriculum. So a lot of what was in school that was fun is no longer. . . . I'm afraid it's No Child Left Behind. I'm afraid what's going to happen is we're going to put so much pressure on these kids that by the time they're in grade school—well, you see it

Table 6.2
Middle School Teachers Reporting Changes in Instruction Time from 2003–2004 to 2004–2005

Teaching Subject	California (%)			Georgia (%)			Pennsylvania (%)		
	–	=	+	–	=	+	–	=	+
Mathematics	1	67	20	5	53	29	2	78	14
Science	9	63	10	5	52	23	7	77	6
Reading, language arts, or English	3	60	14	8	48	23	3	74	9
Social studies	13	59	5	5	51	20	9	75	3
Arts or music	14	48	8	9	52	5	5	74	6
Physical education	5	68	3	8	55	5	3	75	5

NOTE: – indicates a decrease in instructional time. = indicates no change in instructional time. + indicates an increase in instructional time. Omitted category is don't know. See Table B.53 in Appendix B for standard errors and additional information.

now. They hate it. They hate. They hate it. They don't want to go on. . . . They're pushed, they're pushed. They're starting in kindergarten.

The principal in that school said she had heard concerns from parents and tried to reassure them:

> I tell parents it's a very hard balance in these high-stakes times to not overdo with the instruction and with the heavy-duty emphasis on our PSSA. And I know I have to. And then the other half of the equation is to keep an elementary school a place that's fun and active and busy and has all kinds of other things to offer. I think we do a pretty good balance. But I'm not ready yet to give up that balance and to say it's all testing.

Other parents seemed resigned to the fact that these curriculum shifts were necessary. A California elementary school parent shared the following comments:

> I can tell you right now that last year, in second grade, my daughter—zero P.E. And . . . because there was no time because they had to focus on core curriculum. And you know what? I didn't battle that because I really could see that my daughter's teacher was killing herself to make sure that these kids got what they needed, so that they could be ready for that test.

As this quote illustrates, in some schools, the changes affected the primary grades, kindergarten through second, as well as the tested grades. For example, in one school, the principal told us that kindergartners' nap time was eliminated, reportedly to provide more time for academic instruction, although some teachers noted that some kindergarteners could not stay awake to benefit from that instruction. Upper-grade teachers in several other schools described efforts aimed at providing extra mathematics or reading instruction to students in kindergarten through second grade to prepare them for the state tests that they would take in later grades, and the few kindergarten through second-grade teachers we interviewed confirmed these reports.

Another approach to increasing time spent on mathematics and ELL was described by teachers in one Pennsylvania middle school, where staff had been asked to try to integrate mathematics and reading concepts into other subjects. This type of integration was intended to bolster the amount of time during which students received math and reading instruction without formally changing the schedule. A number of the teachers said that this strategy generally did not work well, in large part because they had not received sufficient training on how to implement this type of integration.

The case studies also provided interesting examples to explain survey responses concerning science. In interviews, teachers reported that science generally did not receive as much attention as they thought it should, given that all states' accountability systems would include science testing by 2007–2008. In some schools, teachers reported alternating instruction in science and social studies—sometimes every other week, sometimes every other month. Other teachers reported even less time: One Pennsylvania elementary school teacher estimated that students received "not even one hour of science or social studies a week." Similarly, in one California elementary school, a second-grade teacher reported that science had taken "a big dive and kids are losing out." Her colleague in third grade concurred that "it's basically reading and math all day." At one California elementary school, the amount of time devoted to formal science instruction had been reduced, but teachers were instructed to integrate science into the reading curriculum. Teachers commented on the difficulty of doing this, particularly given the scripted nature of the reading program being used in that school.

At the same time, recall that, in most schools in which we administered surveys, teachers did not report changes in instructional time, and, in a few cases, increased time was spent on nontested subjects. The case studies provide a few examples of such changes. One elementary case study school had purchased a 10-week art program and a drama program to motivate students to attend school. At another school, educators reported that they believed that there was a need to broaden the curriculum to attract back students who had left the public school system because of dissatisfaction over test-related curriculum narrowing.

Alignment of Instruction with State Standards and Assessments

Almost all teachers in the three states reported aligning their instruction in mathematics with state content standards, but the story was somewhat different in science. As shown in Figure 6.1, in California and Georgia, 90 percent or more of elementary and middle school teachers agreed or strongly agreed that they had aligned their instruction with their state's content standards in mathematics. In Pennsylvania, the percentage was slightly lower but still quite high. More than 80 percent of California and Georgia science teachers also agreed that they had aligned their instruction with state content standards in science, but only about one-half of Pennsylvania science teachers agreed with this statement about alignment. The fact that Pennsylvania was not yet administering a science test might be partly responsible for the fact that fewer teachers were attuned to the state standards. Overall high levels of teacher-reported alignment are consistent with the emphasis on alignment as a school-improvement strategy, as described in Chapter Five. At the same time, the fact that teachers report aligning instruction with standards should not be interpreted as evidence that their instruction covers all of the material in the standards, especially given the frequency with which teachers described the standards as too numerous to cover (see Chapter Four).

Figure 6.1
Teachers Reporting Aligning Instruction with State Content Standards

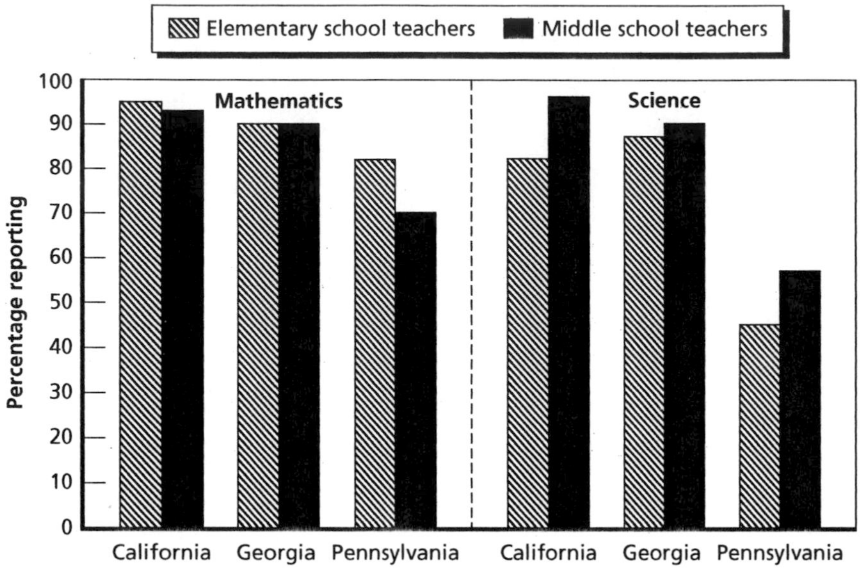

NOTE: See Table B.54 in Appendix B for standard errors and additional information.
RAND *MG589-6.1*

California teachers in grades in which state accountability tests were given were more likely to report aligning their instruction with the standards than with the assessments (Figures 6.2 and 6.3).[2] The difference was especially pronounced for mathematics teachers, with more than 90 percent reporting aligning with standards, compared with approximately 50 percent for assessments. Differences between alignment to assessments and alignment to standards were smaller in the other two states. One reason for this difference could be the lack of access to test-preparation materials such as released items in California as compared with the other states, as discussed in Chapter Four. In Pennsylvania, middle school mathematics teachers exhibited a response pattern opposite that of their counterparts in the other states: These teachers were more likely to report aligning their instruction with assessments than with standards (86 percent versus 71 percent).

---

[2]   For this comparison, we included only teachers who taught in grade levels that the state's testing program included in 2004–2005. For mathematics, this included all teachers in California and Georgia but only teachers in grades three, five, and eight in Pennsylvania. For science, it included all teachers in Georgia and fifth-grade teachers in California. We excluded Pennsylvania science teachers from this comparison due to lack of a statewide science test in 2004–2005.

Figure 6.2
Math Teachers in Tested Grades Reporting Aligning Instruction with State Assessments and State Content Standards

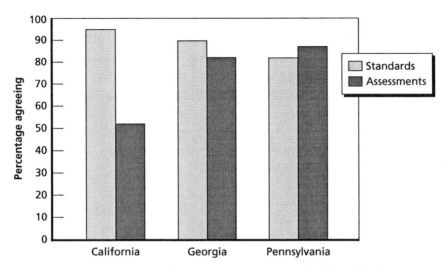

NOTE: See Table B.55 in Appendix B for standard errors and additional information.
RAND *MG589-6.2*

Figure 6.3
Science Teachers in Tested Grades Reporting Aligning Instruction with State Assessments and State Content Standards

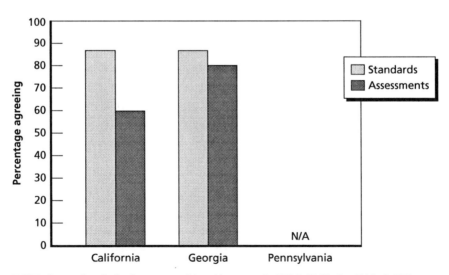

NOTE: Pennsylvania had no statewide science test in 2004–2005. See Table B.55 in Appendix B for standard errors and additional information.
RAND *MG589-6.3*

Effects of State Tests on Practices

Most teachers reported a variety of ways in which the state testing system influenced their instruction, some of which would generally be considered appropriate efforts to improve student mastery of standards and some of which might, in some cases, reduce the validity of test scores.[3] Among the responses listed in Tables 6.3 (elementary school teachers) and 6.4 (middle school teachers), the first four represent efforts to provide more or better instruction in, or exposure to, the subject of interest. The remaining responses address the reallocation of time or resources across topics, activities, or, in one case, students, within the subject. These responses are not necessarily problematic, but they have the potential to result in a reallocation of effort or resources from certain topics, activities, or students to others and therefore could lead to an excessive narrowing of instruction and to inflated test scores. Both of these broad categories of responses were reported frequently, but there were differences in the specific responses within these categories.[4]

Within the category of providing more or better instruction, the most frequently reported response was a search for more effective teaching methods; more than 60 percent of elementary school teachers in each state (with the exception of California science teachers) said their instruction differed in this way by a moderate amount or a great deal because of the state test (Table 6.3). And more than half of elementary school mathematics teachers in each state reported spending more time teaching content. These responses would generally be considered desirable effects of SBA systems because they represent efforts to improve the overall quantity and quality of instruction.

---

[3]   The set of survey questions used in this section differed from most of the others, in that it did not ask directly about frequency or change. We asked a set of questions similar to the one that Koretz and Hamilton (2003) developed to understand teachers' responses to high-stakes testing in Massachusetts. Although we were interested primarily in the kinds of changes that teachers made in response to tests, we decided not to ask directly about change, because this type of question would be appropriate only for teachers who had been teaching prior to the implementation of the state testing program. Instead, we developed a question focused on attribution of practices to the testing program, which allowed us to include all teachers. We asked teachers to describe the degree to which their teaching *differed* because of the state test. Specifically, we asked teachers to "think about ways in which your teaching is *different* because of the [state test] than it would be without the [state test]. How much do the following statements describe differences in your teaching *due to the [state test]*? Teachers could select "no difference," "differs by a small amount," "differs by a moderate amount," or "differs by a great deal." The categories of instructional practice that these questions addressed were designed to capture a range of responses, from the kinds of general improvement in the quality of teaching that many accountability advocates envision to narrowly focused test preparation activities that might detract from the validity of scores (see Koretz and Hamilton, 2006, for a discussion of various instructional responses to test preparation and their implications for the validity of high-stakes test scores).

[4]   Although some of these responses might generally be considered more desirable than others, none of them is definitively negative; even coaching on specific item formats might be considered beneficial in certain circumstances. See Koretz and Hamilton (2006) and Hamilton (2004) for additional discussion of test-preparation activities.

Table 6.3
Elementary School Teachers Reporting That Their Instruction Differs as a Result of Math and Science Assessments

Change in Instruction	Calif. (%)		Ga. (%)		Pa. (%)
	Math	Science	Math	Science	Math
Assign more homework	43	8	29	21	30
Spend more time teaching content	52	29	58	43	53
Offer more assistance outside of school for students who are not proficient	29	8	34	16	21
Search for more effective teaching methods	67	33	74	64	62
Focus more on standards	73	45	77	68	76
Focus more on topics emphasized in assessment	63	35	72	57	73
Emphasize assessment styles and formats of problems	55	20	78	60	74
Spend more time teaching test-taking strategies	53	25	56	42	51
Focus more on students who are close to proficient	37	9	36	23	29
Rely more heavily on multiple-choice tests	24	19	37	42	18
Rely more heavily on open-ended tests	21	18	23	28	50

NOTE: Response options included not at all, a small amount, a moderate amount, and a great deal. Shown are percentages reporting that they engage in each practice a moderate amount or a great deal as a result of the state tests. We did not present these questions to Pennsylvania science teachers because Pennsylvania did not have a statewide science test. See Table B.56 in Appendix B for standard errors and additional information.

Many of the other responses, which might be considered either positive or negative depending on the context, involved reallocation within subjects. Roughly three-quarters of elementary school mathematics teachers said they focused more on state standards than they would in the absence of the state test, and nearly as many said they focused more on tested topics. Percentages of science teachers reporting these reallocation practices were smaller but still substantial. The case studies provided examples of reallocation, including a reduction in time spent on extended investigations and other activities that did not mirror the test formats. One eighth-grade teacher in California told us,

> I can see that there are interesting things I'd like to teach that I can't. I have a project I do every year in math estimating animal population, but it takes a couple of weeks. I'm just not doing it this year. I'm not doing it because I've got to get them ready for these tests. And it's a shame because they get a lot out of it.

Majorities of mathematics teachers also reported engaging in narrower forms of test preparation, such as emphasizing problem styles or formats and teaching test-taking strategies. A seventh-grade mathematics teacher in California explained,

> Because of the pressures of hitting the AYP and APIs, my teaching is geared more toward multiple choice, more toward test-taking skills, test-taking strategies. . . . [T]he month leading up to the test is basically just all review. It's how to take the test, how to be successful on it because of the accountability as a school. . . . Even during my warm-ups I'll give two or three multiple-choice questions now rather than open-ended questions, just to have them practice, get them comfortable. I know [for] a lot of students it's overwhelming, the CSTs, [and] they just get nervous. So my main job is to build their confidence that they can be successful with the test. And by starting at the beginning of the year, I can just slowly get them to build that confidence level up. And then during the course of the period, . . . if they're doing a multiple-choice problem, I'll remind the students . . . "Is there a little trap you could fall into if you choose this?" Or "The test wants you to pick the wrong answer. They don't necessarily want you to. . . ." You've got to keep reminding them of all the different strategies that they can use to look for it to be successful.

In almost all cases, the effects of testing on these practices were greater in mathematics than in science. And among science teachers, Georgia teachers were more likely to report these practices than were California teachers.

A comparison of results for spring 2004 and spring 2005 indicates that the influences of state assessments on instructional practices remained relatively constant, though there were slight decreases in reports of searching for more effective teaching methods and focusing on standards and slight increases in teachers' reported focus on tested topics, assessment styles and formats, and students performing close to proficient, which we discuss below.[5] These changes may suggest that elementary school teachers are increasingly attuned to specific features of their state testing and reporting systems or are more focused on AYP pressures.

Teachers have also changed their classroom assessment approaches in response to the state tests. The highest percentage of teachers reporting such changes was in Pennsylvania, where half the elementary school math teachers said they relied more heavily on open-ended assessments. This is probably because the state math test includes open-ended items; our case study visits suggested that many teachers increased their use of open-ended classroom assessments in part to prepare students for the open-ended section of the state test.

Turning to middle school teachers, the most frequently reported responses to assessments included a focus on standards and on tested content, though narrower

---

[5] Note that the samples of teachers responding to surveys in 2004 and 2005 do not necessarily include all of the same teachers.

forms of test preparation were also common (Table 6.4). In contrast to the results for elementary schools, middle school science teachers in Georgia were more likely than their math counterparts to report a few practices. In particular, they were more likely to report an effect of assessment on their focus on standards and on their use of multiple-choice tests. In general, middle school teachers' patterns of responses were similar to those of elementary school teachers, but many of the responses were less frequently reported among this group than among elementary school teachers.

Middle school teachers were less likely to report an impact of assessments on some practices in 2005 than in the previous year. California and Georgia teachers were less likely to say they relied more on open-ended assessments than they had in the past, whereas Pennsylvania teachers were less likely to report relying on multiple-choice tests. Georgia math teachers and California teachers in both subjects were less likely to report a greater focus on standards than they did in 2004. These results provide no information on actual change in practices; they address only changes that teachers attribute to the state test. The change in California and Georgia teachers' reported focus on standards might indicate an actual reduction in attention to standards, or

Table 6.4
Middle School Math and Science Teachers Reporting That Their Instruction Differs as a Result of Math and Science Assessments

Change in Instruction	Calif. (%)		Ga. (%)		Pa. (%)
	Math	Science	Math	Science	Math
Assign more homework	29	8	29	26	13
Search for more effective teaching methods	58	35	69	67	59
Focus more on standards	66	47	72	77	69
Focus more on topics emphasized in assessment	57	27	73	64	71
Emphasize assessment styles and formats of problems	49	23	71	65	62
Spend more time teaching test-taking strategies	45	26	44	48	39
Spend more time teaching content	45	24	53	59	46
Focus more on students who are close to proficient	19	8	38	30	22
Offer more assistance outside of school for students who are not proficient	26	9	41	33	19
Rely more heavily on multiple-choice tests	23	20	38	54	9
Rely more heavily on open-ended tests	13	11	23	26	33

NOTE: Response options included not at all, a small amount, a moderate amount, and a great deal. Shown are percentages reporting that they engage in each practice a moderate amount or a great deal as a result of the state tests. See Table B.57 in Appendix B for standard errors and additional information.

it could be a result of a growing acceptance of standards as the primary source of information about instructional objectives. In other words, teachers who no longer said they focused on standards more than they would in the absence of the state test may have decided that the standards were worth teaching to, regardless of whether a test was associated with them. More detailed information from interviews or observations would be needed to understand how the responses reported in Tables 6.3 and 6.4 relate to actual changes in practice.

Some teachers reported that they focused their attention on students who were close to proficient, a group that our case study participants and others have called *bubble kids*. In California and Georgia, more than a third of elementary school math teachers said they focused more on students who were close to proficient than they would have in the absence of the state testing program (Table 6.3). The percent of elementary school teachers reporting a greater focus on students near proficient was smaller for Pennsylvania math teachers and for science teachers but was still substantial in most cases. Focus on students close to proficient was reported by some middle school teachers across states and subjects but was slightly less common than among elementary school teachers (Table 6.4). The tendency for some teachers to focus on bubble kids is not surprising in light of the fact that large majorities of principals reported that their schools or districts encouraged this practice, as discussed in Chapter Five. Although we do not know whether the increased focus on students near proficient is resulting in decreased attention to other students, there is some evidence that teachers recognized the risk that this trade-off might be necessary; e.g., roughly half of the teachers across states and levels agreed that, "as a result of the state's accountability system, high-achieving students are not receiving appropriately challenging curriculum or instruction" (see Chapter Four).

Teachers in our case study schools described several examples of bubble-kid strategies. According to one elementary school teacher,

> [T]he high-basic child that's almost proficient . . . that's what we call our target group. . . . Every teacher got a printout of their target group. Every teacher has about four to five kids in their class. We went over strategies on how to make sure you involve them and you get them involved. We talked about seating. These children should be closer up to you. Whenever another child answers a question, refer back to that student and make sure, "Can you tell me what the answer was?" or, "What did Johnny say?" and always keep those four to five kids questioning and making sure they're their target. They're the kids that we need to push up to proficient. So, that's our AYP strategy.

Another teacher described a strategy that reflected a clear understanding of how to maximize AYP gain:

That's something that I learned being a resource teacher, that if you want to make some gains, you look for the students that have the best chance of making a gain in the least amount of time as far as AYP is concerned. So, if a student is, say ten points away, that's not that many questions, so that student has a very high likelihood of making AYP if remediated. . . . I would get them into my morning tutorial. I would target them for my informational classes. I would try to get them into the after school tutorial programs. I would specifically work on their weak domains, not necessarily their weakest domain levels, but the domain where they could make some progress and get to that passing level.

Other teachers, as well as a few parents, expressed concerns about both high- and low-performing students being left behind in the effort to maximize movement from below proficient to above proficient. As one middle school teacher noted,

They don't go to the classroom and say, okay, who are the ones with the really, really bad grades here? Who are the ones who need help? No, they want to get the ones who are in the middle so they can push them to the top. . . . I want to push everyone in my class, everyone in the school, to be better students, to be able to get into the labor force with the most knowledge that they can have. . . . So that's really hard for me.

A Pennsylvania parent expressed a similar concern about some students' needs being neglected and, while acknowledging her lack of knowledge of the reasons, suggesting it might be a result of NCLB:

I hear 'I'm bored' more than anything from my kids. . . . there's so many children in the classroom, and the teachers are spending so much time with children who didn't quite get it. My children are not advanced. But they are above average, they get it. . . . So what's the teacher spending her time on? Based on—I'm guessing—part of the No Child Left Behind, part of getting everyone to the middle.

Instructional Activities in Mathematics and Science

In both mathematics and science, elementary and middle school teachers reported using a variety of instructional activities, but some strategies were especially widespread. For example, 95 percent or more of all teachers reported practices that have been common in classrooms for decades, such as introducing content through formal presentations or direct instruction. Assigning homework was a common strategy, too, especially as reported by mathematics teachers. (Tables 6.5 and 6.6 provide results for elementary and middle school mathematics teachers; responses for science teachers are presented in Tables B.60 and B.61 in Appendix B. The first seven rows in each table focus on general instructional practices, whereas the last five rows address practices related to use of achievement data.)

Table 6.5
Elementary School Math Teachers Reporting Their Instructional Techniques and How They Have Changed in the Past Year

Technique	California (%)			Georgia (%)			Pennsylvania (%)		
	Used	Used less	Used more	Used	Used less	Used more	Used	Used less	Used more
Assign math homework	97	1	19	96	3	16	98	1	11
Have students work on extended math investigations or projects	45	8	13	46	9	16	43	5	12
Introduce content through formal presentations or direct instruction	98	2	13	98	3	14	98	1	8
Provide help to individual students outside of class time	68	5	19	70	5	25	72	5	17
Confer with another teacher about alternative ways to present specific topics or lessons	81	4	20	90	2	23	89	2	19
Have students help other students learn math content	91	2	18	93	2	27	92	2	23
Refer students for extra help outside the classroom	57	4	14	65	3	21	54	2	16
Plan different assignments or lessons based on performance	82	4	27	90	4	29	81	5	18
Reteach topics because performance on assignments or assessments did not meet expectations	93	3	24	96	2	29	89	7	18
Review assessment results to identify individual students who need supplemental instruction	91	2	21	95	1	27	89	2	21
Review assessment results to identify topics requiring more or less emphasis in instruction	90	1	20	94	0	26	87	2	20
Conduct a preassessment to find out what students know about a topic	65	3	13	67	4	17	60	9	11

NOTE: Response options for the frequency questions included never, rarely (a few times a year), sometimes (once or twice a month), and often (once a week or more). Response options for the questions about change from previous year included less than 2003–2004, about the same as 2003–2004, and more than 2003–2004. Used technique columns show percentages reporting that they engage in each practice sometimes or often. See Table B.58 in Appendix B for standard errors and additional information.

Table 6.6
Middle School Math Teachers Reporting Their Instructional Techniques and How They Have Changed in the Past Year

Technique	California (%)			Georgia (%)			Pennsylvania (%)		
	Used	Used less	Used more	Used	Used less	Used more	Used	Used less	Used more
Assign math homework	94	2	12	92	4	19	95	1	13
Have students work on extended math investigations or projects	28	9	7	39	12	13	26	11	10
Introduce content through formal presentations or direct instruction	95	4	10	97	1	14	99	2	5
Provide help to individual students outside of class time	85	2	20	85	4	32	80	3	24
Confer with another teacher about alternative ways to present specific topics or lessons	81	7	20	84	4	33	72	1	17
Have students help other students learn math content	86	3	17	95	3	30	84	2	27
Refer students for extra help outside the classroom	70	2	17	64	4	23	66	2	18
Plan different assignments or lessons based on performance	68	3	17	81	5	29	69	0	18
Reteach topics because performance on assignments or assessments did not meet expectations	95	4	24	93	4	30	87	0	16
Review assessment results to identify individual students who need supplemental instruction	84	3	17	89	2	26	75	1	15
Review assessment results to identify topics requiring more or less emphasis in instruction	86	1	19	90	1	28	83	2	19
Conduct a preassessment to find out what students know about a topic	49	5	9	65	4	21	41	4	20

NOTE: Response options for frequency questions included never, rarely (a few times a year), sometimes (once or twice a month), and often (once a week or more). Response options for the questions about change from previous year included less than 2003–2004, about the same as 2003–2004, and more than 2003–2004. Used technique columns show percentages reporting that they engage in each practice sometimes or often. See Table B.59 in Appendix B for standard errors and additional information.

Among all math teachers, 80 percent or more reported reteaching math topics because student performance on assessments or assignments did not meet expectations, reviewing math assessment results to identify topics requiring more or less emphasis in instruction and to identify those students who needed supplemental instruction, and having students help other students learn mathematics content. Lower percentages of elementary and middle school mathematics teachers reported using extended mathematics investigations or projects, conducting a preassessment to find out how much a student knew, and referring students for extra help outside of the classroom.

The introduction of content through direct instruction or formal presentations was commonly used in science (90 percent or more), though the percentages of teachers who reported using the other instructional practices tended to be lower in science than mathematics. For example, 70 percent or more of elementary school mathematics teachers reported providing extra help to students outside of the classroom, whereas about 25 to 41 percent of elementary school science teachers across the three states reported providing such help in science (see Table B.60 in Appendix B).

Although teachers reported using almost all strategies more frequently in 2004–2005 than in the past, the largest reported increases tended to be for practices related to individualization of instruction and use of data. For example, roughly 20 percent or more of mathematics teachers reported increasing their use of the following strategies: providing individual help to students outside of class time, conferring with another teacher about ways to present specific topics or lessons, having students help other students learn the content, planning different assignments or lessons based on student performance, reteaching mathematics topics because student performance on assessments or assignments did not meet expectations, and reviewing assessment results to identify individual students who need supplemental instruction. Although the increased use of many of these activities was also reported in science, the increases were not as great, particularly among elementary school science teachers (see Table B.60 in Appendix B). Unlike the practices discussed in the previous section, the survey questions on general instructional practices did not ask teachers to attribute these changes to NCLB. However, these results do provide some information that can be helpful for understanding changes that have taken place in the wake of NCLB. In particular, there is a clear trend toward greater attention to individual students' needs, and teachers' reports of their practices are consistent with many of the school-improvement initiatives described in Chapter Five.

Summary

State standards and assessments appear to be influencing decisions made at the school and classroom levels in all three states. In particular,

- although instructional time devoted to most subjects remained relatively constant between 2003–2004 and 2004–2005, time devoted to subjects that state NCLB accountability systems tested was more likely to increase than decrease over the past year. There were some reported decreases in time spent on nontested subjects, particularly social studies in California and Pennsylvania.

• most teachers reported aligning their instruction with both standards and state assessments, even though teachers were not always convinced that the standards and assessments were well aligned with one another.

• majorities of teachers, regardless of state, level, or subject, reported that state assessments influenced their practices in a variety of ways. Some teacher responses are consistent with SBA advocates' claims regarding the benefits of accountability, whereas others raise concerns about excessive narrowing of curriculum and instruction.

• teachers use a wide variety of instructional strategies. Between 2003–2004 and 2004–2005, the strategies that were most likely to increase in use were those that emphasized individualization of instruction and use of achievement data, a finding that is consistent with many of the school-improvement initiatives described in Chapter Five.

For the most part, there were not major differences in findings between the states, but those differences that existed were consistent with states' accountability systems. For example, Pennsylvania science teachers were less likely than other teachers to report aligning instruction with state standards, which probably reflects the fact that Pennsylvania had not yet administered a science test. Similarly, Georgia middle school science teachers were more likely than were middle school science teachers in the other two states to report increasing the amount of time spent on science instruction, which is consistent with the fact that Georgia had more extensive science testing requirements in place.

For SBA to have the desired effects on student achievement, teachers and other educators must respond to the standards, assessments, and other components of NCLB in educationally productive ways. The results presented in this chapter suggest that some NCLB goals are being realized—educators are aligning their instruction with state standards, are using achievement data to make decisions about instruction, and are working to improve student achievement on state tests. In the next chapter, we examine educators' perceptions of factors that hinder their efforts to improve student achievement in their schools.

CHAPTER SEVEN

Perceived Barriers to School Improvement

Although teachers and administrators reported extensive efforts to improve their schools' performance, they also identified factors that they believed made it difficult to achieve the desired levels of improvement. Some of these factors relate to resources or other conditions that might be affected by school or district policy, whereas others, such as lack of support from parents, are more difficult for schools to influence.

Funding

Both fiscal and physical capital limitations impeded school improvement, according to administrators, but fiscal constraints were more widespread. Almost all of the superintendents in all three states identified lack of adequate funding as a moderate to great hindrance to their efforts to improve student performance, as shown in Table 7.1.[1] In fact, lack of funding was the most frequently cited hindrance out of the 13 options included on surveys to superintendents. When asked specifically about whether they had adequate funding to implement the NCLB requirements, fewer than one-fourth of superintendents in each state said that they did (3 percent in Pennsylvania, 15 percent in Georgia, and 23 percent in California) (see Table B.62 in Appendix B for standard errors). Many principals also expressed concerns about funding, particularly in California, where 80 percent of principals at both the elementary and middle school levels identified lack of funding as a moderate to great hindrance to school improvement, compared with 68 percent in Pennsylvania and 49 percent in Georgia.

Administrators at both the district and school levels were far less likely to cite physical capital factors as impediments to improvement. Across all three states, fewer than one-third of superintendents and principals reported inadequate school facilities as significant hindrances.

---

[1] We asked principals and superintendents to what extent various factors hindered their efforts to improve the performance of students in their schools or districts; we asked teachers to what extent various factors hindered their students' academic success.

Table 7.1
Administrators Reporting Inadequate Fiscal or Physical Capital as a Moderate or Great Hindrance to Their Improvement Efforts

Hindrance	California (%)			Georgia (%)			Pennsylvania (%)		
	Supt.	Principal Elem.	Principal Middle	Supt.	Principal Elem.	Principal Middle	Supt.	Principal Elem.	Principal Middle
Lack of adequate funding	98	81	80	99	43	67	98	66	72
Inadequate school facilities	10	3	8	19	23	1	26	16	31
Shortage of standards-based curriculum materials	14	NA	NA	46	NA	NA	34	NA	NA

NOTE: See Table B.63 in Appendix B for standard errors and additional information.

Instructional Resources

Superintendents also perceived lack of instructional materials as a barrier to improvement, particularly in Georgia. Approximately half the Georgia superintendents and one-third of Pennsylvania superintendents identified lack of standards-based curriculum material as a hindrance, while fewer than 15 percent of superintendents in California identified this as a problem. Similarly, many teachers viewed lack of materials as a problem: Approximately one-third of teachers surveyed at both levels in all three states identified this as a moderate to great hindrance to their students' academic success (see Table 7.2). Several teachers in the case study schools noted in particular a need for more hands-on materials to ensure improved student learning and performance.

Some teachers also identified other classroom conditions as barriers to student learning. Approximately one-third or more of teachers surveyed identified as a hindrance a lack of school resources to provide extra support for students who need it. Some teachers also cited large class sizes as a barrier to student learning. This was particularly true for teachers in California and middle school teachers, of whom more than half identified this as a moderate to great hindrance in all three states. Given California's state-level investments in reducing class sizes in kindergarten through third grade over the past decade, it may be surprising that more than half the elementary teachers in California identified large class size as an impediment to student success. However, grade-level breakdowns indicate that third-grade teachers—a grade level covered by the state's policy—were much less likely than fourth- and fifth-grade teachers to report this as a hindrance: 39 percent compared to 67 percent and 79 percent, respectively.

Table 7.2
Teachers Reporting Inadequate Physical Classroom Resources as a Moderate or Great Hindrance to Students' Academic Success

Hindrance	California (%)		Georgia (%)		Pennsylvania (%)	
	Elem.	Middle	Elem.	Middle	Elem.	Middle
Large class size	59	69	39	58	48	57
Inadequate instructional resources (e.g., textbooks, equipment)	33	34	28	35	33	33
Lack of school resources to provide the extra help for students who need it	42	37	23	34	32	31

NOTE: See Table B.64 in Appendix B for standard errors and additional information.

Staffing

Nearly 30 percent of superintendents indicated that shortages of qualified principals created barriers to improvement (Table 7.3). One-third or more of the superintendents, however, noted that shortages of particular content area teachers hindered efforts to improve student performance. Almost 70 percent of Georgia superintendents reported that shortages of highly qualified math and science teachers were hindrances, compared with approximately 40 percent in California and 30 percent in Pennsylvania. In response to a slightly different question about all teachers, principals generally did not view teacher shortages as an impediment, particularly at the elementary school level. Fewer than 15 percent of elementary school principals and approximately one-third of middle school principals in each state identified shortages of highly qualified teachers as a moderate to great hindrance to improvement efforts. Most principals did not view teacher turnover as a major impediment to improvement. Fewer than one-fourth of all principals cited teacher turnover as a moderate to great hindrance. This is consistent with teacher reports: Fewer than a third of elementary and middle school teachers in all three states identified teacher turnover as a moderate to great hindrance.

Principals in all three states did, however, indicate concerns over having adequate clerical staff to handle the high volume of administrative tasks. This was especially true in California, where 70 percent of principals identified insufficient staff time to meet administrative responsibilities as a moderate to great hindrance, compared with slightly more than half in Georgia and Pennsylvania. Superintendents echoed this concern over capacity to handle administrative tasks, particularly as it related to implementing NCLB. Majorities of superintendents in all three states reported needing additional staff to comply with the law's program and reporting requirements.[2]

---

[2] Eighty-six percent of superintendents in Georgia, 80 percent in California, and 64 percent in Pennsylvania agreed or strongly agreed with the statement.

Table 7.3
Administrators Reporting Inadequate Human Capital as a Moderate or Great Hindrance to Their Improvement Efforts

Hindrance	California (%)			Georgia (%)			Pennsylvania (%)		
	Supt.	Principal Elem.	Principal Middle	Supt.	Principal Elem.	Principal Middle	Supt.	Principal Elem.	Principal Middle
Shortage of qualified principals	22	—	—	36	—	—	29	—	—
Shortage of highly qualified teachers	—	12	39	—	7	32	—	10	25
Shortage of highly qualified mathematics teachers	40	—	—	69	—	—	33	—	—
Shortage of highly qualified science teachers	43	—	—	69	—	—	28	—	—
Shortage of highly qualified teacher aides and paraprofessionals	—	22	28	—	9	8	—	27	34
Teacher turnover	—	20	12	—	15	25	—	14	21
Shortage or lack of high-quality PD opportunities for teachers	47	32	38	45	16	17	39	22	19
Shortage or lack of high-quality PD opportunities for principals	37	29	40	45	10	10	51	34	22
Insufficient staff time to meet administrative responsibilities	—	71	72	—	56	43	—	55	63

NOTE: See Table B.65 in Appendix B for standard errors and additional information.

Skills and Knowledge

Superintendents' reports about staff skills and knowledge shed some light on their perceptions of factors hindering improvement efforts. As discussed in Chapter Five, use of data for decisionmaking was one of the most widely used school improvement strategies, so teachers' and administrators' ability to use data is likely to be an important determinant of the success of these efforts. Most principals agreed or strongly agreed that teachers had the skills and knowledge to analyze and make use of test results; however, the consensus in Pennsylvania (64 percent for elementary school principals) was considerably lower than that in California and Georgia (each 92 percent) (see Table B.66 in Appendix B for standard errors and additional information). A similar pattern emerged at the district level, where more than half of all superintendents reported that their districts had sufficient staff with the necessary skills to help schools analyze data for school improvement (see Table 7.4). Once again, however, the numbers were slightly lower in Pennsylvania. One possible explanation for these differences is that the state test was not yet administered in all grades and that, until recently, the Pennsylvania state testing and accountability system was more limited than in the other two states and created less pressure and opportunity for educators to examine state test results. Educators in the other states had either a more comprehensive school-level accountability system (California) or a more extensive testing system (Georgia) in place prior to NCLB and therefore more time and incentives to become familiar with their tests and to build the capacity to analyze test results. In addition, Pennsylvania offered less technical assistance in this area (see Chapter Five).

Table 7.4 also illustrates a difference across the states in the district staff's perceived capacity to help with school improvement. Most notably, fewer than a third of Pennsylvania superintendents reported having adequate capacity among their staff to facilitate improvements in low-performing schools, compared with more than 60 percent in the other two states. Again, this difference may be because, unlike the other two states, Pennsylvania has not had a school-level accountability system in place until recently.

Table 7.4
Superintendents Reporting That the District Has Adequate Staff Capacity in Certain Areas

Staffing Need	Calif. (%)	Ga. (%)	Pa. (%)
Facilitate improvements in low-performing schools	62	68	32
Help schools to analyze data for school improvement	68	66	56
Help schools identify research-based strategies for improvement	57	73	58
Conduct PD tailored to teacher needs	35	68	74
Conduct PD tailored to the needs of principals	27	64	48
Align curriculum with state content standards and state assessments	52	70	86

NOTE: The question asked, "Does the district have sufficient staff with the necessary skills to perform the following school improvement functions?" See Table B.67 in Appendix B for standard errors and additional information.

Professional Development

One approach to enhancing human capital and thus the capacity for school improvement is through PD, but superintendents and principals had different views on the availability of needed PD. Superintendents were more likely than principals in their respective states to report problems with availability of PD opportunities. For example, as shown in Table 7.3, approximately 40 percent or more of superintendents in all three states identified shortages of high-quality PD opportunities for teachers and principals as moderate to great hindrances to improvement efforts. In California, a majority of superintendents also reported a lack of adequate capacity within the central office to conduct PD tailored to the needs of teachers and principals, as shown in Table 7.4. Superintendents in the other two states were much more confident in their central office staff's ability to conduct PD. In contrast, approximately one-third or fewer of principals in California, Georgia, and Pennsylvania reported insufficient PD as a moderate to great hindrance to school improvement. Thus, principals in Georgia and Pennsylvania were less likely than superintendents in those states to perceive staff development as a problem.

Instructional and Planning Time

More than half the elementary school teachers in all three states identified insufficient class time to cover the entire curriculum as a moderate to great hindrance to their students' academic success (Figure 7.1). This is consistent with teachers' reports that standards covered more content than they could address in a year (reported in Chapter Four). Administrators and teachers, particularly in California, also expressed concern about a lack of teacher planning time built into the school day. About one-half or more of elementary school teachers in all three states cited lack of planning time as an impediment to their students' academic success. Elementary school principals were more likely than their middle school counterparts to report problems due to a lack of planning time. More than 40 percent of elementary school principals in Georgia and Pennsylvania and 71 percent in California identified this as a moderate to great hindrance to improving student performance in their schools.

Figure 7.1
Teachers Reporting Inadequate Time as a Moderate or Great Hindrance to Students' Academic Success

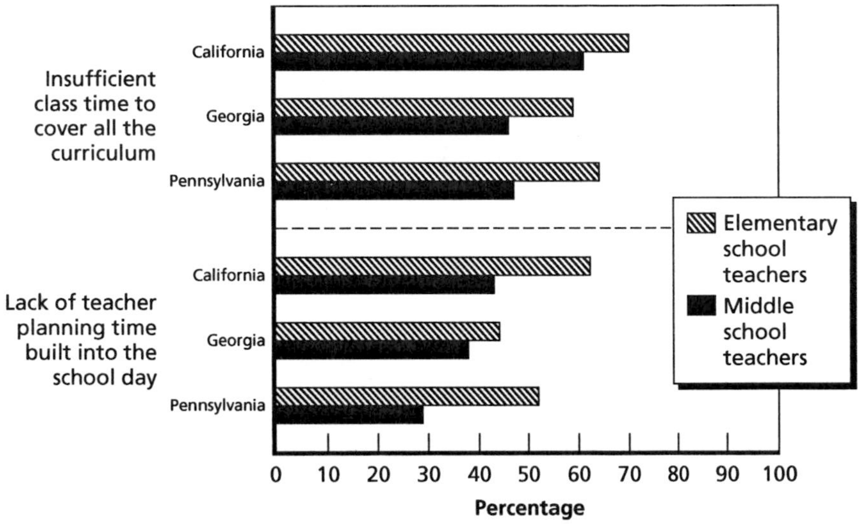

NOTE: See Table B.68 in Appendix B for standard errors and additional information.
RAND MG589-7.1

Finally, more than half of the superintendents and approximately one-third of the principals in all three states identified inadequate lead time to prepare before implementing reforms as a moderate to great hindrance to their reform efforts, as shown in Figure 7.2. These numbers are even greater among some California administrators. Compared to their counterparts in Georgia and Pennsylvania, California superintendents and elementary school principals were more likely to identify inadequate lead time as a hindrance. Compared with last year (2003–2004), however, administrators were slightly less likely to identify this as a hindrance.[3]

Conditions Outside of School

Majorities of teachers at both levels in all three states reported that inadequate basic skills and prior preparation, lack of support from parents, and student absenteeism and tardiness were moderate to great hindrances to students' academic success (Figure 7.3). Middle school teachers were more likely to cite factors such as these as barriers than were their elementary school counterparts in all three states. More teachers saw these

---

[3]   For example, last year, 92 percent of superintendents in California, 86 percent in Georgia, and 64 percent in Pennsylvania cited inadequate time to plan before implementing reforms as a moderate to great hindrance.

Figure 7.2
Administrators Reporting Inadequate Time as a Moderate or Great Hindrance to Improvement Efforts

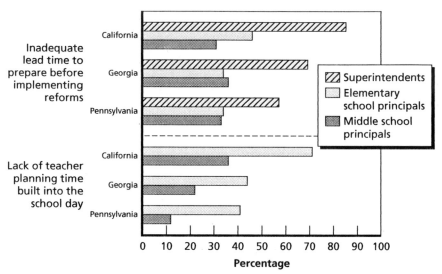

NOTE: See Table B.69 in Appendix B for standard errors and additional information.
RAND *MG589-7.2*

student background factors as barriers than the school and classroom conditions also included in the survey.

During case study visits, teachers reported that factors such as poverty, problems at home (including alcohol and drugs), lack of parental involvement, health issues, and special needs exerted a powerful effect on students' performance. For example, one teacher said that only about 25 percent of parents attended a recent open house, so it was difficult for teachers to establish relationships with parents. Teachers also noted that, when students fell behind in the very early grades, it was almost impossible for teachers to bring them up to the proficient level of performance because of achievement deficits that had been compounding over time. In addition, teachers expressed concerns about students who experienced test anxiety and did not perform well on state tests even though their performance in the classroom was strong. As a result, teachers felt they were often blamed for factors over which they had no control. As one middle school teacher expressed it,

> The problem is I'm not in control of the sociological factors that are out there that is keeping Hector or little Johnny down there [in performance on state tests], or little Samantha from handing in her stuff [homework]. And it's all psychological. It's the very stuff that I can't control. And so what am I supposed to do?

Figure 7.3
Teachers Reporting Student Background Factors and Conditions Outside of School as Moderate or Great Hindrances to Students' Academic Success

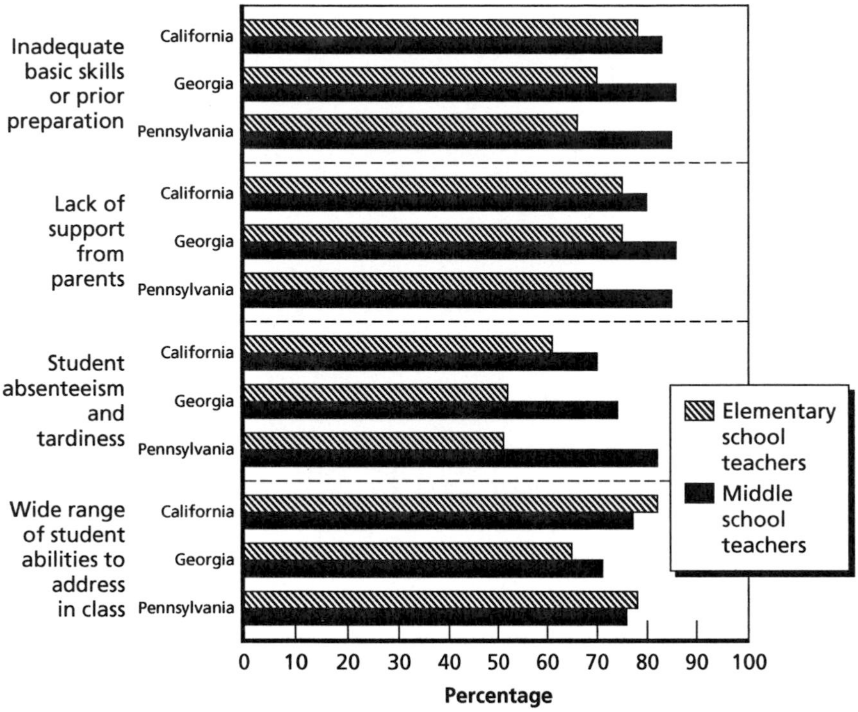

NOTE: See Table B.70 in Appendix B for standard errors and additional information.
RAND MG589-7.3

Similarly, an elementary school teacher in the same district reported,

> These kids are going home and they're putting themselves to bed. They're the baby-sitters. They don't read a story before they go to bed. They're lucky that they're in bed at two in the morning. Then they come here and they don't have breakfast and they probably don't have dinner and they're supposed to worry about tests?

Parents interviewed during case study visits also identified the influence of conditions outside of school on student achievement. A parent in Pennsylvania explained,

> I don't see it as the school. I mean, everybody's blaming it on the schools; it's our society, it's our neighborhood, that's what needs improvement. You really want to do an assessment test? Go door to door. That's where you're going to find these problems. It's not the school, it's not the teaching, it's not the children not wanting to learn: it's what they learn outside the school. That puts us where we're at, as a school.

Similarly, another parent in Pennsylvania stated,

I don't feel like it's the teaching that's keeping them from passing the tests. I think a lot of it starts at home. A lot of parents are lacking in the area of staying on their children, coming here, finding out what they're doing. It starts at home, to me. Because a lot of them come here and disrupt the class so the teachers spend half of the day trying to get them in order instead of this time that she could be teaching the kids.

In some schools, parents placed the responsibility for lack of student progress on parents themselves. As one Georgia parent explained, "I think any school that fails, it's the parents. If you want your school to [succeed], you've got to be involved, period." Others pointed to the potential lack of parent follow-through with obtaining additional support and supplemental services their children need. One California parent explained,

There are kids who have the need for the extra help, but if the parent doesn't authorize it, it's not going to happen. So no matter what you call it, or you make these vast declarations that no child will be left behind, it's just theoretical. Still, so much of it is going to be based on what the parents are doing.

Students with Special Needs or Limited English Proficiency

Another issue that may influence the response of educators to NCLB is the treatment of students with disabilities and students with limited English proficiency. Under the law, these students are included in school and district scores and, when numbers are sufficient, must meet subgroup targets as well. Educators at all levels had doubts about the appropriateness of this policy. More than 80 percent of superintendents in all three states believed that special education students should not be included in AYP calculations (see Table B.71 in Appendix B). Similarly, more than 80 percent of principals agreed that the system of accountability did not allow sufficient flexibility for meeting the needs of students in special education programs and students who were ELLs.

Administrators and teachers in case study schools expressed skepticism that high percentages of students with special needs could meet AYP targets. Teachers reported concerns about the negative effects of SBA on the self-esteem of special education students who they felt were being blamed for the school's failure to meet AYP. An elementary school principal in Pennsylvania attributed some of her school's difficulty in meeting AYP to the fact that they were the district's "Mecca for special education," a reference to the high number of special education students attending the school who did not live within its attendance boundaries. Teachers in case study schools also expressed concerns about the wisdom of testing special education students using grade-level tests. One California elementary school teacher stated,

> [My students] are working on a second grade level, then four times a year I'm giving them district tests on a fifth grade level. They can't read the words. I can't read them to them. They can't understand the vocabulary because learning disabled says that they have a processing disorder in a basic function. And if it's reading, then why am I testing them at their present grade level as opposed to their present level of performance?

Several parents in case study schools also reported skepticism about a school's ability to make future targets when faced with the special education students requirements. A parent in Pennsylvania explained,

> I think that it [NCLB] imposed standards on the school that sometimes are going to be impossible, especially in the coming years. . . . [I]t just seems impossible that any school . . . would be able to push up to the highest level when you have students who don't speak English, when you have students who are Special Ed. It seems like that later . . . the goals are unattainable for some schools.

Other parents questioned the expectation that special education students meet grade-level standards. As one parent stated,

> The state gives the special education kids the same grade [level test] as regular education, which is wrong, because if they're expected to take the same test as the 5th graders and the 3rd graders they should be in regular classrooms. They're in special education for a reason. So, they shouldn't be taking the same test because they're in special education.

In addition, almost one-half of the principals in California (and about one-quarter in the other two states) cited lack of guidance for teaching grade-level standards to English learners as moderate to great hindrances to their school improvement efforts (see Figure 7.4).

Many teachers reported lacking adequate knowledge of how to modify curriculum and instruction for English learners. As one California middle school principal told us,

> I wish somebody could give me the magic wand that I need to get my English Language Learners to the levels that the federal government thinks they should be. . . . Is there a pill? Is there a silver bullet. . . ? . . . I mean I can get these kids in middle school probably to basic or maybe the higher ranges of basic, but to get to proficient is really difficult because they're starting so low. . . . And a lot of principals that are high urban impact schools feel that way, that we're making incredible

Figure 7.4
Principals Reporting Lack of Guidance for Teaching Standards to Students with Disabilities and ELLs as a Moderate or Great Hindrance to Their School Improvement Efforts

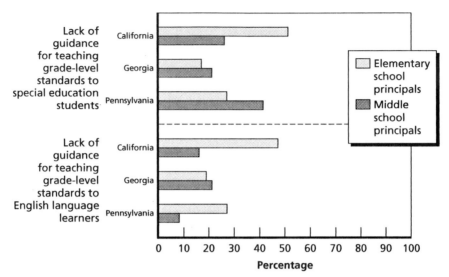

NOTE: See Table B.72 in Appendix B for standard errors and additional information.
RAND *MG589-7.4*

improvement . . . but I want to know, how do I get these kids that just came here a year and a half, two years ago, to be proficient in language arts? . . . And half my kids are English language learners.

Teachers also questioned the appropriateness of NCLB's expectations for these students. As might be expected, concerns about English learners were especially common in case study schools in California. Many teachers reported not being able to use district curriculum guides and tests with their ELL students because they were so far below grade level. Others noted that these students lacked the language skills and vocabulary to perform well on state tests. It was also common to hear that test results did not accurately reflect students' true knowledge and skills. As one California elementary school teacher commented,

> I find that the exams for the lower level kids are a lot more difficult because of the language. So, sometimes I feel that my students really know a lot more than they're showing. But if I could explain it or change the language in it, they could get it. . . . It's not true to what their capabilities are.

A math teacher from a California middle school made a similar observation, questioning the entire accountability system:

I have to teach them really [the] structure of math language, not just the word "ratio," but how then that word fits in a sentence. Because if I teach them ratios and they know how to do ratios, but they see the word in a word problem [on the state test] that's described as opposed to just given a ratio to solve, it creates an entirely different situation for them because they're not able as easily as students with language proficiency to then answer that problem. . . . [T]his speaks to the limitations of No Child Left Behind. . . . [T]he disadvantage that these students face is not relative to whether they know the content. It's whether they know the language and how to decode the language in order to prove they know the content.

Even the case study schools that felt they had done well with their ELL students expressed discontent with the way NCLB deals with ELLs. They felt that their progress with ELL students was not being recognized, since students who can pass the test are no longer designated as language learners.

We met every single area except for one. . . . Our English learner population didn't make it in English language arts. Go figure. . . . What they don't see . . . is we're actually doing extremely well with that population, because if you look at how many kids we're re-designating before middle school, the majority of them are re-designated within the correct time frame. . . . We start with maybe a hundred and fifty at the bottom grades, and they all get filtered through at the appropriate time frame. I keep trying to point that out to people, saying, look, we're being really successful. . . . That part's frustrating, because I think it's very unreasonable the way No Child Left Behind works.

The challenges of addressing the needs of ELL students are also interacting with ethnic tensions, at least in California. At some of our case study schools, ELLs are bussed to the school (due to NCLB choice provisions or local programs) and, when they are a subgroup that is seen to cause the school to fail to meet AYP, parents of local children begin to put pressure on the principal to find a way to exclude the ELLs from the school. One principal at a California school described her experiences with this issue:

Parents the minute they see [our school] as failing, they go, "See!" Then, of course, what eventually they go to—and it gets there pretty quick—is, "Oh, it's because of all those Mexican kids." It will go to a race issue real quickly and that's the sad part, because I've had parents scream at me in this office about how "it's because you let all those Mexicans come to this school that we're a failing school," how bad a principal you are.

Finally, most teachers also found the wide range of student abilities in their classes to be a hindrance to improving student achievement.[4] Some of the challenges associated with variation in ability were described by case study teachers who noted the challenges of keeping the advanced students interested and motivated while maintaining an appropriate pace for students who had not yet mastered the standards.

Changes in Policy and Leadership

Majorities of superintendents in all three states reported that unstable policy environments, i.e., frequent changes in state policy or leadership, impeded their improvement efforts (see Table 7.5). This concern was particularly strong in Pennsylvania, where 98 percent identified this as a moderate to great hindrance.

District leaders in California and Pennsylvania also identified teacher unions as an obstacle. Seventy-one percent of California superintendents and 51 percent in Pennsylvania reported that complying with teacher association policies was a moderate

Table 7.5
Administrators Reporting Frequent Changes in Policy or Leadership as a Moderate or Great Hindrance to Their Improvement Efforts

Hindrance	California (%)			Georgia (%)			Pennsylvania (%)		
	Supt.	Principal Elem.	Principal Middle	Supt.	Principal Elem.	Principal Middle	Supt.	Principal Elem.	Principal Middle
Frequent changes in state policy or leadership	71	—	—	79	—	—	98	—	—
Frequent changes in district policy and priorities	—	46	14	—	11	19	—	19	15
Frequent changes in district leadership	—	30	20	—	14	10	—	14	9
Complying with teacher association rules and policies	71	—	—	7	—	—	51	—	—
Disagreements with district school board over policies	2	—	—	17	—	—	21	—	—

NOTE: See Table B.73 in Appendix B for standard errors and additional information.

---

[4] Although our surveys classified "wide range of student abilities" as a classroom-level factor, an exploratory factor analysis of these items showed that this item clustered with the student-level factors, suggesting that the teachers who perceive student-level factors as barriers also tend to find the range of student abilities difficult to handle.

to great hindrance to their efforts to improve student performance (as a right-to-work state, this was not a factor in Georgia). Very few superintendents in all three states reported disagreements with school board members as hindrances.

Similarly, some principals found changes in district policy to be a problem. California elementary school principals, like California superintendents, were more likely than those in the other two states to report perceived hindrances emanating from the local policy environment. Almost half the elementary school principals reported frequent changes in district policy and priorities and 30 percent cited frequent changes in district leadership as moderate to great hindrances to improvement efforts. One case study principal in California explained how the district's "state of flux" affected his morale:

> I just see so much that could be done that's not getting done. And with the change of leadership in the district, and knowing who the board is and who's selecting, I don't know. Because of the state of flux I'm in, I'm wondering what may happen with the superintendent in the district and I quite honestly wonder whether I want to continue this line of work. Especially if I'm not going to have the support for the kind of work I feel is important to do. . . . I love the school. I love the potential and I [hate] my desire to leave that but I feel so crippled.

Summary

Administrators and teachers across the three states identified five sets of factors as hindrances to student performance and school improvement:

- The number one hindrance that superintendents and principals reported across the states was the lack of adequate funding.
- Many administrators also cited a lack of qualified, trained personnel with the skills and expertise that schools and districts need to bring about improved student achievement.
- Many principals and teachers identified insufficient class time to cover curriculum and a lack of teacher planning time as impediments at the school and classroom levels. More than half the districts across the states cited inadequate lead time to prepare before implementing reforms as an impediment to improvement. Elementary teachers and principals were more likely than their middle school counterparts to perceive these factors as hindrances.
- Most teachers perceived student and family background conditions to be significant barriers to meeting their accountability goals. Middle school teachers were more likely than elementary teachers to mention these conditions as hindrances.

- Local contextual factors further influenced district and school improvement efforts, including frequent changes in state policy or leadership (in all three states) and complying with teacher association rules or policies (in California and Georgia).
- States differed in a number of areas, including administrators' perceptions of staff capacity and other hindrances to school improvement.

These findings suggest that educators believe that factors outside their control play important roles in student success, but they also suggest that improvements in state-level implementation of NCLB might increase educators' acceptance of the law and its goals, which, in turn, might promote more effective responses to the law's SBA provisions. We discuss the implications of these findings in the final chapter of this monograph.

CHAPTER EIGHT

Conclusions and Implications

This study was designed to examine the implementation of NCLB as an example of an SBA system. We hypothesized a multilevel implementation process unfolding incrementally from states to districts to schools to classrooms. We also hypothesized that local contextual factors would influence the manner in which the policies evolved and were translated into practice. The evidence presented in the previous four chapters shows that NCLB has clearly influenced educational practice at all levels; some of the effects appear to be beneficial for student learning, whereas others raise concerns about possible negative consequences. In this final chapter, we reflect back on our initial framework and draw some broader conclusions about the multilevel implementation of NCLB. We also discuss the implications of our findings for policymakers who are responsible for adopting and adapting SBA systems and for educators who must respond to them.

Key Findings

Accountability Systems Enacted in Response to NCLB Differed Across the Three States

Although the states were following the same NCLB guidelines, they created SBA systems that varied on a number of dimensions, leading to somewhat different responses among educators at both the district and school levels. State systems differed with respect to the content of their academic standards, the level of their performance standards, their choice of additional indicators, their methods for calculating AYP and their AYP trajectories, and their school and district support and technical assistance mechanisms, just to name a few. These differences have historical, philosophical, and financial antecedents as well as different consequences. For example, California was building a growth-based accountability system that included norm-referenced tests and used different criteria for success from those that NCLB used. The state had to adopt the NCLB criteria, speed its adoption of standards-based tests, and relegate its own system to the role of additional indicator. Educators in California seemed to prefer the approach embodied in their existing system. In contrast, Georgia did not yet have an accountability system in operation when NCLB was enacted, and the state was testing all students in grades three through eight in reading, mathematics, social studies, and science. The state did not have to make major changes to accommodate NCLB. Similarly, Pennsylvania was testing only in reading and mathematics in a sample of grade levels prior to NCLB, and many educators there responded negatively to the new accountability requirements. They objected, in part, to the additional testing burden and, in part, to the imposition of a top-down system that threatened the state's tradition of local control. These histories might explain why educators in Georgia were more likely than educators in the other two states to report that their state's test results were accurate and useful.

Between-state differences in implementation and impact were greater in science than in mathematics, reflecting greater pre-NCLB differences in this subject (including science standards and assessments). For example, we found more evidence of science curriculum alignment and greater use of progress tests in science in Georgia than in the other two states, which is consistent with the fact that only Georgia had developed science standards and assessments in grades three through eight. As might be expected, we also found differences among the states in administrators' and teachers' opinions about their state's SBA system. Overall, the findings from these three states suggest that differences in the features of state accountability systems should not be ignored when studying the implementation of NCLB or when drawing conclusions about its impact.

Districts and Schools Responded to the New State Accountability Systems

The survey results indicate that districts and schools responded actively to state SBA policies and that majorities of superintendents and principals focused on similar types of activities. For example, most districts reported that they undertook efforts to make sure curriculum aligned with standards, provided a wide range of technical assistance to help schools improve, and offered a variety of PD opportunities for principals and teachers. Districts also instituted policies to increase instructional time for low-performing students.

Principals reported that schools were also active in responding to SBA and that they emphasized similar actions. For example, schools took steps to ensure that instruction aligned with state standards and with state assessments. Some schools focused more instructional time on reading and mathematics, and large numbers reported providing more learning opportunities for low-performing students. Other common improvement strategies included promoting the use of student test results for instructional planning, implementing test preparation activities, and adopting progress tests to provide more frequent assessment information. These findings are consistent with other recent research on district responses to NCLB (e.g., Center on Education Policy, 2006).

Although district and school actions were broadly similar across states, there were a few ways in which district and school efforts differed in the three states. Most notably, Georgia districts and schools were more active than districts or schools in California and Pennsylvania in promoting science instruction and in adopting progress tests. The emphasis on science instruction is consistent with Georgia's extensive science testing program, mentioned above.

It is important to note that many of the changes reported by district and school administrators are likely to have the effect of increasing teachers' attention to tested content. In particular, efforts to align curriculum with state tests, the adoption of interim assessments that mirror the state test, and the distribution of test preparation materials increase the likelihood of some of the narrowing activities discussed in the next section.

Reported Changes at the Classroom Level Included Both Desirable and Undesirable Responses

Teachers reported making a variety of changes in their instructional programs in response to the new accountability systems and in their efforts to improve student achievement. Many of these changes, such as aligning instruction with standards and improving teachers' own practices, indicate that NCLB has led to some beneficial outcomes.

At the same time, teachers described some potentially negative effects, especially on curriculum and instruction. Although we did not see dramatic changes in time spent on various subjects, most teachers reported that their math and science instruction was affected in various ways by state tests and reported changes that are likely to lead to a narrowing of curriculum and instruction toward tested topics and even toward certain problem styles or formats. Teachers also reported focusing more on students near the proficient cut score (i.e., "bubble kids"), and expressed concerns about negative effects of the accountability requirements on the learning opportunities given to high-achieving students—they do not need as much help to reach proficiency and there is no incentive in the system to make extra effort to move them to the advanced level. The focus on students near the proficient cut score also raises concerns about detrimental effects on low-performing students who are not seen as likely to achieve proficiency in one year. In the absence of incentives for raising their scores, there is a risk that resources will be diverted away from them as well.

Educators Expressed Support for NCLB Goals but Had Concerns About Specific Features and Effects

Most superintendents, principals, and teachers supported the idea of SBA. However, responses from these groups suggest that teachers were less supportive of specific features or effects of their state accountability systems than were administrators. For example, most administrators, but fewer teachers, thought that state test scores accurately reflected student achievement. Similarly, administrators were more likely than teachers to report that accountability pressures led to improvement in curriculum and student learning. Teachers were particularly attuned to lack of consistency between state accountability requirements and local resources and programs. For example, many teachers believed that there were substantial mismatches between state standards and tests and their curriculum. How such concerns influence teachers' practices will depend, in part, on administrators' reactions and especially on the support that administrators provide. Despite administrators' generally positive views of NCLB, superintendents reported negative effects on morale among principals and principals reported negative effects on morale among teachers. Apparently, subordinates' concerns are being heard, but we do not know whether they are heard with sympathetic or unsympathetic ears.

Despite these concerns, teachers' reports suggest that the emphasis on state standards and assessments has led to some beneficial outcomes. Teachers reported an increased focus on student achievement in their schools as a result of NCLB, as well as other beneficial changes including increased curriculum coordination and increased rigor of the school's curriculum. These responses suggest that teachers are not necessarily opposed to all aspects of their states' SBA systems but have some specific concerns that stem from perceived pressure to raise test scores.

Several Perceived Hindrances May Stand in the Way of the Effective NCLB Implementation

Respondents identified a variety of factors that were barriers to achieving NCLB goals. Most administrators thought that inadequate funding hampered their school improvement efforts, and many said they did not have adequate numbers of highly qualified teachers in mathematics or science. Administrators and teachers alike saw insufficient instructional time and insufficient planning time as barriers. In addition, teachers reported that students' lack of basic skills, support from parents, and student absenteeism and tardiness hampered their efforts. One of the underlying principles of NCLB is that educators are expected to promote high levels of achievement despite these conditions, but our findings suggest that large numbers of educators have not adopted this view. All these factors will have an impact on school outcomes and the success of NCLB. Some are more easily influenced by educators than others, but all are likely to influence the implementation of the law.

Implications

Alignment Efforts at All Levels Need to Be Improved

Alignment of curriculum and instruction with state standards and tests was a primary strategy adopted by teachers, principals, and superintendents. Whether the benefits of these alignment efforts outweigh any adverse consequences (such as excessive focus on tested content) is likely to depend to some degree on the quality of those standards and assessments. Several organizations have examined features of standards in each state (American Federation of Teachers [AFT], 2006; "Quality Counts at 10," 2006; Finn, Petrilli, and Julian, 2006). Although these studies do not always agree with one another, they illustrate the tremendous variability in the content, format, and quality of state standards, and they indicate areas in which further work may be needed to create standards that promote high-quality instruction.

Teachers in the ISBA study echoed some of the concerns that have been raised in published reviews of state standards. In particular, many teachers claimed that the standards included more content than they could cover. While this perception might stem in part from lack of experience implementing standards, it might also reflect a problem with the standards themselves. Standards that are too broad or numerous to guide decisions about what to teach might lead to negative consequences, such as excessive reliance on the test rather than the standards to decide what to teach. States have begun trying to address these problems; Pennsylvania, with its assessment anchors, exemplifies an approach designed to make it easier for teachers to teach to the standards. The effects of these initiatives should be carefully monitored as they move forward.

The quality of state assessments also varies as a result of decisions about content, item format, methods for setting cut scores, and other factors. In an SBA environment, a critical aspect of assessment quality is the degree to which the assessments align with state standards. A recent review of alignment by the American Federation of Teachers (2006) indicated variability among states in their efforts to conduct and publish alignment studies (though the AFT did not look at the quality or methods used in these alignment studies). The AFT judged 100 percent of California's assessments to be aligned with standards, compared with 60 percent and 53 percent for Georgia and Pennsylvania, respectively.

Educators in the ISBA study expressed some concerns about the validity of state test scores and were especially concerned about the extent to which the tests were good measures of the state standards (Table 4.1). To the extent that standards and tests are misaligned, teachers' use of tests as a means of determining what should be taught raises concerns about the possibility that teachers will adopt practices designed to raise test scores without necessarily promoting the standards. The ISBA data are based on perceptions rather than on actual validity studies, but there are still some potentially important implications. Perceptions of low test validity or lack of alignment might reduce educators' buy-in to the accountability system. They might also lead to inappropriate test preparation if teachers believe that the test does not accurately measure the knowledge and skills that the curriculum promotes. The states in our study have taken steps to evaluate the validity and alignment of their assessments. States need to address any validity problems that these evaluations reveal but also need to communicate to teachers and administrators the work they have done to ensure validity so that educators can be confident that the tests used to evaluate their schools are high-quality measures. State officials and other users of state test results must understand and acknowledge the fact that it is virtually impossible to create a test that adequately assesses all of the content and skills described in the standards and that the higher-level reasoning constructs are most likely to be omitted from the tests (Rothman et al., 2002). Alignment is desirable, but perfect alignment is an unattainable goal, and educators and policymakers using information from tests need to recognize their limitations as measures of students' mastery of standards.

In addition to promoting alignment between state standards and tests, school improvement efforts at all levels of the system need to address alignment between these state initiatives and local curriculum and instruction. Despite the prevalence of reports from ISBA survey respondents that alignment was a focus of school improvement efforts, majorities of teachers reported mismatches between their curriculum and state standards and tests. Educators at the local level often need assistance in making decisions about curriculum and instruction to ensure that they are adequately covering the standards. The perceived lack of alignment may just reflect the long lead time necessary to change curriculum, but it may also reflect shortcomings in the quality of standards or assessments or in the ways that information about them is communicated to local educators. Ensuring appropriate alignment will require efforts at all levels of the system and is necessary to achieve the vision of standards-based reform put forth more than a decade ago, which emphasized the value of coherence across all components of the educational system (Smith and O'Day, 1991).

Teacher and Administrator Capacity for Improvement Needs to Be Developed

Educators identified several areas in which capacity was lacking and in which additional technical assistance might be beneficial. In particular, assistance for helping teachers and other school and district staff use data for decisionmaking, devise strategies for improving the learning of low-performing students, and identify effective instructional practices could increase the likelihood that they will respond effectively to information and incentives provided by state accountability systems. These are areas that received extensive emphasis in school improvement efforts. Educators hope that these strategies will promote improvement, but, at the same time, they acknowledge that they are not fully equipped to implement these strategies effectively. Because school and district staff have expressed support for these strategies, the provision of technical assistance in these areas would probably influence practices and could contribute to more effective school improvement efforts.

The use of data for educational decisionmaking deserves special attention because of policymakers and administrators' widespread efforts to promote it. As noted previously, data-driven decisionmaking is often cited as a key characteristic of successful districts and schools. Educators in all three states described extensive efforts to use data from state tests and other sources, and districts are supporting these efforts by adopting interim assessment systems and providing PD focused on interpretation of test scores. A need remains, however, for guidance to help educators figure out what to do with the large amounts of data they receive. Although our study did not ask participants directly about what kind of assistance they would like with respect to data use, other RAND research as well as work by a number of other researchers suggests that teachers often lack the time and know-how to deal with all of the data they receive (see Marsh, Pane, and Hamilton, 2006, for a review of this work). Guidance is needed to help teachers and administrators address individual student needs while avoiding the temptation to focus excessively on tested content or on specific groups of students.

Educators also need assistance to understand when data quality is sufficient to support decisions and when it is not. For example, teachers tended to rate information on subtopics or skills as being more useful than other types of information, but, if those subscores are based on a small number of items, they might not be sufficiently reliable to warrant strong conclusions about student strengths and weaknesses. Better use of data requires assistance to help educators understand the advantages and limitations of various data sources. More appropriate use of data could also be promoted by improvements in the measures used to evaluate school and district performance, which we discuss in the next section.

Teachers expressed a need for assistance with teaching ELLs and students with special needs. The subgroup reporting requirements of NCLB have drawn educators' attention, as well as the public's, to the performance of these groups of students, but teachers reported a lack of capacity and a lack of PD focusing on these groups. This is clearly an area in which capacity-building efforts are needed.

A primary tension related to capacity building is the fact that insufficient funding was the most frequently mentioned barrier to improvement among school and district leaders. An analysis of NCLB costs is beyond the scope of our study, and the question of whether NCLB is adequately funded is being debated in the policy and research communities. What is clear from this study, however, is that administrators view lack of adequate funding as a hindrance to their improvement efforts. Even if NCLB provided sufficient funding for activities such as standards and assessment development, administrators might perceive a need for additional resources to help low-performing schools and students meet their targets. Whether help comes in the form of more money or guidance to help educators and administrators use existing funds effectively, such assistance seems to be needed based on the responses of administrators in all three states.

Better Methods for Measuring School and Student Performance Should Be Explored

One of the most widespread criticisms of NCLB is its reliance on measures of achievement that represent performance at a single point in time. The U.S. Department of

Education has signaled a willingness to consider alternatives and has recently funded several states to participate in a pilot program to use measures based on growth in individual achievement. The California API system is another approach that is based on growth, in this case cohort-to-cohort change in aggregate school scores. In both cases, the target for performance is defined in terms of improvement rather than a fixed level of attainment. Individual growth models are generally preferred because they follow the same students over time. Although they tend to require sophisticated data systems and advanced analytic tools, they are becoming increasingly feasible with advances in information technology.

Many of the findings described in this monograph provide support for the importance of exploring growth-based measures. Responses to our surveys, as well as interviews with teachers and principals, indicated concerns about the validity of the AYP measure. Teachers were especially concerned that AYP determinations would be influenced by student background characteristics and other outside-of-school factors beyond their control. Adopting performance indicators that mitigate the influence of these factors, such as the growth models or value-added indicators that some states are currently exploring, might increase the likelihood that teachers will view the performance metric as reflecting their own efforts rather than preexisting student characteristics. And, given the widespread skepticism that targets could be reached over the next five years, a growth-based AYP measure might increase the likelihood that educators will view their targets as attainable and therefore could improve their motivation and the quality of their responses to NCLB pressures.

Improved performance indices could also address the problems associated with excessive focus on bubble kids and teachers' concerns about negative effects on high achievers. The current focus on the proficient level of performance creates incentives to move students from below to above proficient but does not reward effective teaching that does not result in students crossing this threshold (whether because their prior performance was far below it or above it). A growth-based measure that provided credit for movement all along the achievement scale could be devised to reflect state or national priorities without ignoring certain types of achievement gains—for example, by incorporating weights that create extra incentives for movement at the lower end of the scale.

Performance measures also need to encourage educators' focus on students who are at high risk of not reaching goals, including ELLs and students with disabilities. Earlier, we noted the importance of increasing teachers' capacity to educate these students, but it is also worth considering the extent to which existing AYP measures create incentives for focusing on these students. On the one hand, the requirement for subgroup reporting has undoubtedly promoted teachers' and administrators' attention to the needs of these and other traditionally low-performing groups of students. At the same time, the use of the percent-proficient metric might decrease the likelihood that teachers will devote extra attention in the first few years of NCLB to students scoring far below the threshold. A measure that incorporates a subgroup component but that includes information about gains throughout the test-score distribution could send a powerful message about expectations for all students, while also providing useful information to policymakers and the public.

Even if all of these improvements are made, a measure that relies primarily or exclusively on test scores is likely to lead to some undesirable consequences. This does not mean that test-based measures should be abandoned altogether, but it does suggest the need for vigilance and for continued exploration of additional measures to supplement the test-based metrics that currently dominate accountability systems.

Teachers' Concerns Should Be Examined and Addressed

Administrators are generally more positive toward NCLB than are teachers. There are a number of reasons for the difference in attitudes between these groups, but, because any effects of NCLB are ultimately going to occur as a result of what teachers do in the classroom, it is critical to ensure that teachers are responding to state accountability requirements in educationally productive ways. As noted in Chapter One, teachers' support for policy goals is an important facilitator of high-quality implementation (McLaughlin, 1987; Odden, 1991). Some of the steps suggested earlier—particularly the adoption of growth models and the provision of appropriate assistance—are likely to help improve teachers' support for the law. At the same time, it is important to recognize that teachers are in a unique position to see the effects of accountability policies on teaching and learning and to take their concerns seriously when considering revisions to those policies.

Conclusions

One of the key challenges facing those who are responsible for designing, implementing, or responding to SBA systems is to identify ways to increase the prevalence of the desirable responses and minimize the undesirable ones. Some of the suggestions we provided in this chapter are intended to do that, but continued monitoring of responses at all levels of the system will be needed to evaluate the effects of NCLB on both actions and outcomes. This study, along with several others that are currently being conducted, should help provide the information needed by policymakers and others to inform future changes and adjustments to the law and its implementation.

As noted earlier, this monograph provides interim findings from the ISBA study. Future reports will provide information about implementation in the 2005–2006 school year and will examine three-year trends for teachers, principals, and superintendents. We will also explore relationships among responses to NCLB at each level of the education system and will examine how these responses are related to student achievement gains.

Sampling and Survey Responses

Sampling

This section describes the procedures that were used to select districts and schools in California, Georgia, and Pennsylvania to participate in the ISBA study. (These three states were selected to represent a range of approaches to implementing NCLB and to provide both geographic and demographic diversity.)

District Sample

To sample districts and schools, we obtained from the National Center for Education Statistics (NCES) Common Core of Data for 2001–2002 a comprehensive list of schools and districts for each of the three states. To obtain our sampling frames, we restricted our attention to the populations of "regular" schools by eliminating vocational, charter, alternative, and special education schools. As noted in Chapter Two, these exclusions reduced the numbers of eligible schools by 4 percent in Georgia, 3 percent in Pennsylvania, and 22 percent in California (though the total count of students in eligible schools in California dropped by only 6 percent).

We included in the district sampling frames all districts that contained regular schools. Power calculations assuming various configurations of between and within district variances indicated that taking fewer than 25 districts per state would not provide sufficient power to detect significance of district-level relationships. We classified our districts based on the number of elementary schools and middle schools (roughly proportional to the size of the district) and, for each state, divided the districts into five strata based on this cross-classification. Stratification was necessary to obtain sufficient representation of the many small districts, while at the same time ensuring a sufficient number of total schools in our sample. The Los Angeles Unified district in California was sampled with probability 1.

We sampled 27 districts per state, anticipating that we would gain cooperation from almost all of them. However, we could not enroll as many of these districts as we hoped. Refusals were particularly high in California. Districts' reasons for not participating included additional pressures related to NCLB. As a result, we drew a supplemental sample of 23 districts to replace those that refused, and we extended recruitment efforts. Eventually, we recruited 68 districts to participate in the 2003–2004 school year, representing an overall cooperation rate of 65 percent (see Table A.1).

For the 2004–2005 school year, we added to the sample of districts drawn for the 2003–2004 school year both to increase the overall number of districts and to increase the number of districts in which high percentages of schools were not meeting NCLB achievement goals. For this refresher sample, we used the same stratified sampling techniques as in the first year but restricted the sample to districts with lower-achieving schools. The refresher sample contained 28 districts, increasing the total sample for 2004–2005 to 132 districts. Ninety-two districts agreed to cooperate, yielding a cooperation rate of about 70 percent (see Table A.2.)

School Sample

The study design called for 100 cooperating schools per state. Anticipating a school cooperation rate of about 80 percent, we initially sampled 125 schools per state. To select schools, we first designated each school in a sampled district as an elementary school, a middle school, or a combined school. Elementary schools contained grades three and four, middle schools contained grades seven and eight, and combined schools contained grades three, four, seven, and eight. We excluded very small schools by requiring that schools have on average 10 or more students in each of these grades.[1]

Table A.1
District Sample and Cooperation, 2003–2004

Sampling	California	Georgia	Pennsylvania	Total
Initial sample	27	27	27	81
Replacement sample	13	5	5	23
Total sample	40	32	32	104
Cooperation	19	25	24	68
Cooperation rate (%)	47.5	78.1	75	65.4

Table A.2
District Sample and Cooperation, 2004–2005

Sampling	California	Georgia	Pennsylvania	Total
Total sample	56	37	39	132
Cooperation	31	30	31	92
Cooperation rate (%)	55	81	80	70

[1]   In California, the criterion was 11 or more students per grade to mirror a limit that California used for reporting purposes.

Then we randomly sampled elementary and middle schools from the sampled districts, selecting between one and five schools of each type from each district according to a prearranged pattern based on district size. We did not contact schools until districts agreed to participate. In California, a larger percentage of districts declined to participate than in Georgia or Pennsylvania. As a result, the California sample was smaller than the sample in the other two states. Districts usually assume responsibility for approving research requests, and, once district cooperation is obtained, school cooperation is easier to obtain. Overall, we recruited 267 schools to participate in the study in 2003–2004, representing a school cooperation rate of 90 percent (see Table A.3).

We followed the same strategy in 2004–2005 for new districts. For continuing districts, we recontacted the same schools. In the second year, we recruited 301 schools to participate in the study, representing a school cooperation rate of 85 percent (see Table A.4).

Survey Response Rates

Superintendent Survey

Table A.5 shows the response rates for superintendents in participating districts by state for 2003–2004, and Table A.6 shows the comparable data for 2004–2005.

Table A.3
School Sample and Cooperation, 2003–2004

Sampling	California	Georgia	Pennsylvania	Total
Sample	78	116	103	297
Cooperation	63	108	96	267
Cooperation rate (%)	80.7	93.1	93.2	89.9

Table A.4
School Sample and Cooperation, 2004–2005

Sampling	California	Georgia	Pennsylvania	Total
Sample	122	124	107	353
Cooperation	91	111	99	301
Cooperation rate (%)	75	90	93	85

Table A.5
Superintendent Survey Responses, 2003–2004

Respondent	California	Georgia	Pennsylvania	Total
Cooperating districts	19	25	24	68
Completed superintendent survey	18	20	22	60
Survey response rate (%)	94.7	80	91.6	88.2

Table A.6
Superintendent Survey Responses, 2004–2005

Respondent	California	Georgia	Pennsylvania	Total
Cooperating districts	31	30	31	92
Completed superintendent survey	24	24	19	67
Survey response rate (%)	77.4	80.0	61.3	72.8

Principal and Teacher Surveys

Table A.7 shows the survey response rates for principals and teachers in cooperating schools for 2003–2004.

Table A.8 shows the response rates for principals and teachers in cooperating schools during the second year of the study, 2004–2005.

Table A.7
Principal and Teacher Survey Responses, 2003–2004

Sampling	California	Georgia	Pennsylvania	Total
Cooperating schools	63	108	96	267
Principal survey responses	51	88	88	227
Principal response rate (%)	80.9	81.5	91.7	85.3
Teacher sample	692	1,522	1,073	3,287
Teacher survey responses	487	1,318	926	2,731
Teacher response rate (%)	70.4	86.6	86.3	83.1

Table A.8
Principal and Teacher Survey Responses, 2004–2005

Sampling	California	Georgia	Pennsylvania	Total
Cooperating schools	91	111	99	301
Principal survey responses	78	95	87	260
Principal response rate (%)	86	86	88	86
Teacher sample	1,013	1,605	1,050	3,668
Teacher survey responses	826	1,409	938	3,173
Teacher response rate (%)	81.5	87.8	89.3	86.5

Supplementary Tables

In all tables in this appendix, *SE* indicates standard error.

Table B.1
Schools Failing to Meet Specific Targets, as a Percentage of All Schools Not Meeting AYP

	California				Georgia				Pennsylvania			
	2003		2004		2003		2004		2003		2004	
Target	%	SE	%	SE	%	SE	%	SE	%	SE	%	SE
Participation rates	15	7	2	2	45	11	6	4	39	9	4	4
Additional indicator	0		0		35	9	36	10	46	11	15	11
Schoolwide AMOs	60	17	30	9	11	8	7	5	26	11	55	15
Subgroup AMOs	95	4	100		77	8	81	9	83	9	100	

Table B.2
Superintendents Reporting Difficulty Hiring and Retaining Teachers Due to NCLB Requirements

	California				Georgia				Pennsylvania			
	2004		2005		2004		2005		2004		2005	
Decision	%	SE	%	SE	%	SE	%	SE	%	SE	%	SE
Retain existing teachers	34	14	16	8	17	9	18	11	11	7	9	5
Hire new teachers	38	14	18	8	26	11	44	14	13	7	19	10

NOTE: Response options included not a hindrance, a minor hindrance, a moderate hindrance, and a major hindrance. Percentages represent the sum of responses that NCLB requirements were a moderate or major hindrance.

Table B.3
Superintendents Reporting More Difficulty Hiring or Retaining Teachers Due to NCLB Requirements, by Teacher Type, 2003–2004

Teacher Type	California		Georgia		Pennsylvania	
	%	SE	%	SE	%	SE
Elementary school	15	8	41	14	0	
Middle school	73	11	51	14	52	13
High school	47	26	61	14	15	7
ELA	46	15	39	14	6	4
Mathematics	66	12	66	13	17	9
Science	66	12	68	13	26	11

NOTE: Response options included easier, no change, slightly more difficulty, and considerably more difficulty. Percentages represent the sum of responses that NCLB requirements generated slightly or considerably more difficulty.

Table B.4
Principals Taking Specific Actions to Meet Requirements for Highly Qualified Teachers, Among Principals Who Took Any Action, 2004

Action	California				Georgia				Pennsylvania			
	Elem.		Middle		Elem.		Middle		Elem.		Middle	
	%	SE	%	SE	%	SE	%	SE	%	SE	%	SE
Change classroom assignments	7	7	47	15	38	11	61	8	16	11	25	11
Increase class size	2	2	0		13	7	7	5	5	3	8	6
Impose stricter hiring rules	83	10	83	7	62	8	74	7	26	10	78	9
Increase use of substitute teachers	0		6	4	5	5	0		12	9	10	5
Require current teachers to obtain certification	80	9	79	6	67	10	81	7	72	12	81	8
Fire or transfer teachers who are not highly qualified	17	9	15	6	18	8	27	8	5	5	17	9
Require current teachers to pass subject-matter tests	35	11	56	8	53	10	68	8	52	16	60	16

NOTE: Response options included yes and no.

Table B.5
Teachers Agreeing with Statements Regarding the Features of Content Standards in Math and Science

| | California | | | | Georgia | | | | Pennsylvania[a] | | | |
| | Elem. | | Middle | | Elem. | | Middle | | Elem. | | Middle | |
Statement	%	SE	%	SE	%	SE	%	SE	%	SE	%	SE
Math standards include more content than can be covered adequately in the school year	81	3	85	3	68	3	72	3	64	4	74	6
Math standards do not cover some important content areas	20	3	21	4	21	2	24	2	22	2	35	5
Math standards are useful for planning my lessons	90	2	83	4	88	1	87	2	75	3	51	6
Science standards include more content than can be covered adequately in the school year	65	4	79	3	54	3	78	3	55	4	62	6
Science standards do not cover some important content areas	19	3	37	4	36	2	34	4	22	4	37	9
Science standards are useful for planning my lessons	83	3	91	1	84	3	88	2	39	3	55	6

NOTE: Response options included strongly disagree, disagree, agree, strongly agree, and don't know. Percentages reflect only those teachers who teach the subject in question. Percentages represent the sum of agree and strongly agree responses.
[a] In Pennsylvania, we asked about the assessment anchors rather than the standards.

Table B.6
Superintendents and Principals Agreeing That State Assessment Scores Accurately Reflect Student Achievement

| | California | | Georgia | | Pennsylvania | |
Respondent	%	SE	%	SE	%	SE
District superintendents	65	12	68	13	49	15
Elementary school principals	34	10	75	6	56	10
Middle school principals	64	11	64	8	40	13

NOTE: Response options included strongly disagree, disagree, agree, and strongly agree. Percentages represent the sum of agree and strongly agree responses.

Table B.7
Superintendents and Principals Agreeing That State Assessment Scores Accurately Reflect Student Achievement, by District AYP Status

| | California | | | | Georgia | | | | Pennsylvania | | | |
| | Met AYP | | Did Not Meet AYP | | Met AYP | | Did Not Meet AYP | | Met AYP | | Did Not Meet AYP | |
Respondent	%	SE	%	SE	%	SE	%	SE	%	SE	%	SE
Superintendents	71	13	18	17	93	6	51	16	70	15	6	7
Principals	47	11	29	10	73	6	61	10	56	8	16	12

NOTE: Response options included strongly agree, agree, disagree, and strongly disagree. Percentages represent the sum of agree and strongly agree responses.

Table B.8
Teachers Agreeing with Statements About State Assessments

| | California | | | | Georgia | | | | Pennsylvania | | | |
| | Elem. | | Middle | | Elem. | | Middle | | Elem. | | Middle | |
Statement	%	SE	%	SE	%	SE	%	SE	%	SE	%	SE
The mathematics assessment												
is a good measure of students' mastery of content standards	42	4	38	4	60	3	57	3	45	4	50	5
is too difficult for the majority of my students	47	5	65	4	31	3	46	3	47	4	64	4
includes considerable content that is not in our curriculum	33	3	32	4	24	2	27	3	25	3	43	6
omits considerable content that is in our curriculum	35	3	30	3	26	2	37	3	27	3	49	5
The science assessment												
is a good measure of students' mastery of content standards	21	8	30	10	46	3	47	4	NA		NA	
is too difficult for the majority of my students	64	7	73	18	43	3	45	3	NA		NA	
includes considerable content that is not in our curriculum	44	7	54	11	34	3	39	3	NA		NA	
omits considerable content that is in our curriculum	36	7	28	10	28	2	45	3	NA		NA	

NOTE: Response options included strongly disagree, disagree, agree, strongly agree, and don't know. Percentages include only teachers in tested grades and represent the sum of agree and strongly agree responses.

Table B.9

Math Teachers Reporting That State Assessment Omits Considerable Content in the Local Curriculum or Includes Considerable Content Not in the Local Curriculum

Statement	California				Georgia				Pennsylvania			
	Elem.		Middle		Elem.		Middle		Elem.		Middle	
	%	SE	%	SE	%	SE	%	SE	%	SE	%	SE
The math assessment includes considerable content not in our curriculum and/or omits considerable content in our curriculum	59	4	53	4	42	3	54	3	42	3	61	4

NOTE: Response options included strongly disagree, disagree, agree, strongly agree, and don't know. Percentages include only teachers in tested grades and represent the sum of agree and strongly agree responses.

Table B.10

Superintendents, Principals, and Teachers Agreeing with Statements About Understanding AYP and the State's Accountability System

Statement	California		Georgia		Pennsylvania	
	%	SE	%	SE	%	SE
I have a clear understanding of AYP criteria.						
Superintendents[a]	80	14	77	13	100	
Elementary school principals	92	4	100		96	4
Middle school principals	95	4	88	6	94	6
The district and/or state helps me to understand the state accountability system requirements.						
Elementary school principals	81	9	86	4	84	9
Middle school principals	82	8	81	6	99	1
The state's accountability system is so complicated it is hard for me to understand.						
Elementary school teachers	52	4	39	2	45	3
Middle school teachers	55	4	44	2	48	3

NOTE: Response options included strongly agree, agree, disagree, and strongly agree. Percentages represent the sum of agree and strongly agree responses.

[a] Superintendent results come from 2003–2004; all other results come from 2004–2005.

Table B.11
Superintendents and Principals Agreeing That Their Districts or Schools Would Meet AYP Targets

Respondent	California		Georgia		Pennsylvania	
	%	SE	%	SE	%	SE
My district/school can attain the AYP targets in the 2004–2005 school year						
Superintendents	88	6	69	11	58	15
Elementary school principals	72	9	100		93	4
Middle school principals	66	10	93	4	74	17
My district/school can attain the AYP targets for the next five years						
Superintendents	29	12	35	13	39	15
Elementary school principals	44	11	87	6	51	10
Middle school principals	44	10	71	8	49	15

NOTE: Response options included strongly agree, agree, disagree, and strongly disagree. Percentages represent the sum of agree and strongly agree responses.

Table B.12
Superintendents and Principals Agreeing That District or School AYP Status Accurately Reflects Overall Student Performance

Respondent	California		Georgia		Pennsylvania	
	%	SE	%	SE	%	SE
Superintendents	60	12	44	14	30	14
Elementary school principals	63	10	77	6	62	10
Middle school principals	55	12	46	8	43	13

NOTE: Response options included strongly disagree, disagree, agree, and strongly agree. Percentages represent the sum of agree and strongly agree responses.

Table B.13
Superintendents and Principals Agreeing That District or School AYP Status Accurately Reflects Overall Student Performance, by AYP Status

	California				Georgia				Pennsylvania		
	Met AYP		Did Not Meet AYP		Met AYP		Did Not Meet AYP		Met AYP		Did Not Meet AYP
Respondent	%	SE	%	SE	%	SE	%	SE	%	SE	%
Superintendents	68	12	0		93	6	12	7	45	18	0
Principals	64	11	53	14	80	5	2	2	61	8	0

NOTE: Response options included strongly agree, agree, disagree, and strongly disagree. Percentages represent the sum of agree and strongly agree options.

Table B.14
Administrators and Teachers Agreeing That, Because of Pressure to Meet AYP, They or Their Staff Are Focusing More on Improving Student Achievement

	California		Georgia		Pennsylvania	
Respondent	%	SE	%	SE	%	SE
Superintendents	43	12	67	13	84	9
Elementary school principals	58	11	58	9	68	10
Middle school principals	44	10	73	8	53	14
Elementary school teachers	79	3	85	2	81	3
Middle school teachers	70	4	84	2	76	3

NOTE: Response options included strongly disagree, disagree, agree, and strongly agree. Percentages represent the sum of agree and strongly agree responses.

Table B.15
Administrators Reporting Changes in Their Schools or Districts as a Result of the State's Accountability System

Respondent	California				Georgia				Pennsylvania			
	For Better		For Worse		For Better		For Worse		For Better		For Worse	
	%	SE	%	SE	%	SE	%	SE	%	SE	%	SE
Academic rigor of the curriculum												
Supts.	61	12	2	2	76	10	0		61	15	9	8
Elem. school principals	61	10	10	6	62	11	0		68	8	3	2
Middle school principals	79	8	2	2	40	11	4	4	38	12	2	2
Elem. school teachers	42	4	16	3	48	3	12	1	32	3	26	3
Middle school teachers	39	4	10	2	42	3	11	1	25	3	15	2
Principal/teacher focus on student learning[a]												
Supts.	68	12	0		84	8	0		87	8	12	8
Elem. school principals	81	9	0		77	6	2	2	74	8	4	3
Middle school principals	79	10	5	4	80	8	0		46	13	7	4
Elem. school teachers	44	5	12	3	59	3	3	1	46	3	8	2
Middle school teachers	49	5	6	2	63	3	8	2	36	7	12	2
Students' focus on school work[b]												
Elem. school principals	30	11	0		51	8	0		21	6	7	4
Middle school principals	51	11	2	2	42	10	0		27	11	3	2
Elem. school teachers	23	4	9	2	36	3	5	1	15	2	10	2
Middle school teachers	20	2	10	2	21	2	16	2	10	3	10	2
Students learning of important skills and knowledge[b]												
Elem. school principals	60	9	1	1	72	7	0		57	8	7	5
Middle school principals	66	11	2	3	56	10	0		33	12	23	17
Elem. school teachers	36	4	8	2	49	3	4	1	31	3	8	2
Middle school teachers	37	3	10	2	37	2	9	2	25	7	12	5

NOTE: Response options included changed for the worse, did not change due to accountability system, and changed for the better.

[a] We asked superintendents about principals' focus on student learning. We asked principals about teachers' focus.

[b] We did not ask superintendents this question.

Table B.16
Teachers Indicating Various Changes in Their Schools as a Result of the State's Accountability System

Respondent	California				Georgia				Pennsylvania			
	For Better		For Worse		For Better		For Worse		For Better		For Worse	
	%	SE	%	SE	%	SE	%	SE	%	SE	%	SE
Elementary school teachers												
The principal's effectiveness as an instructional leader	31	5	11	3	46	3	8	2	27	2	9	2
Teachers' relationships with their students	22	4	14	3	34	3	5	1	16	2	11	2
My own teaching practice	43	5	10	2	59	4	5	1	40	3	11	2
Middle school teachers												
The principal's effectiveness as an instructional leader	30	3	8	2	44	3	13	2	21	3	19	7
Teachers' relationships with their students	18	3	11	2	33	3	10	2	14	2	6	2
My own teaching practice	45	4	6	2	56	3	4	1	32	5	4	1

NOTE: Response options included changed for the worse, did not change due to accountability system, and changed for the better.

Table B.17
Administrators Reporting Changes as a Result of the State's Accountability System

	California				Georgia				Pennsylvania			
	For Better		For Worse		For Better		For Worse		For Better		For Worse	
Respondent	%	SE	%	SE	%	SE	%	SE	%	SE	%	SE
Coordination of mathematics curriculum across grade levels												
Superintendents	74	10	0		50	14	2	2	76	14	2	2
Elementary school principals	50	12	0		51	8	0		76	8	1	1
Middle school principals	67	10	0		46	9	0		82	8	0	
Coordination of science curriculum across grade levels												
Superintendents	54	12	1	1	43	14	4	3	42	15	2	2
Elementary school principals	27	10	0		33	9	0		30	10	9	7
Middle school principals	45	10	0		20	5	0		45	14	0	
Extent to which innovative curricular programs or instructional approaches are used												
Elementary school principals	32	10	19	9	64	6	0		42	9	9	5
Middle school principals	26	7	20	10	38	9	2	2	38	13	4	3

NOTE: Response options included changed for the worse, did not change due to accountability system, and changed for the better.

Table B.18
Administrators and Teachers Reporting Changes in Staff Morale as a Result of the State's Accountability System

	California				Georgia				Pennsylvania			
	For Better		For Worse		For Better		For Worse		For Better		For Worse	
Respondent	%	SE	%	SE	%	SE	%	SE	%	SE	%	SE
Superintendents	0		77	11	12	11	76	13	10	9	77	12
Elementary school principals	5	4	65	11	20	5	27	5	8	5	53	10
Middle school principals	22	8	34	10	19	7	41	8	13	8	53	13
Elementary school teachers	10	3	48	4	20	2	39	4	6	1	63	4
Middle school teachers	11	2	49	4	15	2	50	3	4	1	67	3

NOTE: Response options included changed for the worse, did not change due to accountability system, and changed for the better. We asked superintendents about principal morale; we asked principals and teachers about morale of school staff.

Table B.19
Teachers and Principals Agreeing That the State's Accountability System Has Benefited Students

	California		Georgia		Pennsylvania	
Respondent	%	SE	%	SE	%	SE
Elementary school principals	51	13	77	6	67	9
Middle school principals	77	7	60	9	56	15
Elementary school teachers	28	3	54	2	30	3
Middle school teachers	34	3	50	2	29	3

NOTE: Response options included strongly disagree, disagree, agree, and strongly agree. Percentages represent the sum of agree and strongly agree responses.

Table B.20
Principals Employing School Improvement Strategies

	California				Georgia				Pennsylvania			
	Elem.		Middle		Elem.		Middle		Elem.		Middle	
Strategy	%	SE	%	SE	%	SE	%	SE	%	SE	%	SE
Matching curriculum and instruction with standards and/or assessments	100		100		97	3	100		100		99	1
Using existing research to inform decisions about improvement strategies	100		94	5	100		99	1	94	4	94	5
Providing additional instruction to low-performing students	96	4	95	3	98	2	100		97	2	98	3
Increasing the use of student achievement data to inform instruction	93	7	100		100		94	5	92	7	100	
Increasing the quantity of teacher PD	89	5	90	6	95	3	96	3	64	9	94	4
Improving the school planning process	74	10	85	8	100		84	7	81	6	99	1
Providing before- or after-school, weekend, or summer programs	84	8	92	6	87	5	86	5	77	7	59	15
Promoting programs to make the school a more attractive choice for parents	60	9	70	10	74	6	62	9	43	8	71	11
Restructuring the day to teach content in greater depth (e.g., a literacy block)	63	9	36	10	79	7	53	9	61	9	43	13
Increasing instructional time (lengthening school day or year or shortening recess)	8	5	23	8	58	7	35	8	26	9	20	8

NOTE: Response options included not employed, employed and not useful, employed and minimally useful, employed and moderately useful, and employed and very useful. Percentages represent not employed responses.

Table B.21
Principals Identifying School Improvement Strategies as Most Important

	Elementary						Middle					
	Calif.		Ga.		Pa.		Calif.		Ga.		Pa.	
Strategy	%	SE	%	SE	%	SE	%	SE	%	SE	%	SE
Matching curriculum and instruction with standards and/or assessments	58	11	62	6	63	9	57	10	46	8	59	13
Using existing research to inform decisions about improvement strategies	40	11	23	5	22	6	37	11	25	8	18	8
Providing additional instruction to low-performing students	40	11	38	6	50	9	55	11	46	10	71	10
Increasing the use of student achievement data to inform instruction	71	8	68	7	52	11	44	11	66	9	34	11
Increasing the quantity of teacher professional development	36	11	23	5	25	9	25	9	21	7	19	9
Improving the school planning process	2	1	22	8	17	8	16	7	32	8	22	10
Providing before- or after-school, weekend, or summer programs	18	6	19	6	19	5	27	10	13	6	26	10
Promoting programs to make the school a more attractive choice for parents	0		3	3	2	1	21	8	14	8	19	16
Restructuring the day to teach content in greater depth (e.g., a literacy block)	13	8	24	7	26	6	8	5	20	8	18	9
Increase instructional time (lengthening school day or year or shortening recess)	2	2	17	5	3	3	2	2	5	3	1	1

NOTE: We asked principals to identify the three most important strategies.

Table B.22
Elementary School Principals Reporting That State Test Results Are Useful
(2003–2004 state test results)

| | California | | | | Georgia | | | | Pennsylvania | | | |
| | Available | | Useful | | Available | | Useful | | Available | | Useful | |
Results	%	SE	%	SE	%	SE	%	SE	%	SE	%	SE
Reports of last year's test results for the students at your school last year	98	1	81	8	98	2	92	4	97	3	84	8
Reports of last year's test results for the students at your school this year	100		86	8	98	2	98	2	99	1	93	4
Test results summarized for each student subgroup	100		72	9	92	4	91	4	100		59	8
Test results summarized by subtopic or skill	89	8	71	10	96	3	94	3	100		85	8

NOTE: Response options included not available, available and not useful, available and minimally useful, available and moderately useful, and available and very useful. Percentages in the useful columns represent the sums of the moderately useful and very useful responses from principals who reported that the resource was available.

Table B.23
Middle School Principals Reporting That State Test Results Are Useful
(2003–2004 state test results)

| | California | | | | Georgia | | | | Pennsylvania | | | |
| | Available | | Useful | | Available | | Useful | | Available | | Useful | |
Results	%	SE	%	SE	%	SE	%	SE	%	SE	%	SE
Reports of last year's test results for the students at your school last year	93	7	74	11	98	2	89	6	81	16	77	16
Reports of last year's test results for the students at your school this year	100		92	4	100		92	5	100		72	16
Test results summarized for each student subgroup	100		89	7	96	3	89	6	100		59	14
Test results summarized by subtopic or skill	96	3	82	8	94	4	87	6	100		84	9

NOTE: Response options included not available, available and not useful, available and minimally useful, available and moderately useful, and available and very useful. Percentages in the useful columns represent the sums of the moderately useful and very useful responses from principals who reported that the resource was available.

Table B.24
Elementary School Teachers Reporting Availability and Usefulness of Math and Science State Test Results

Results	California				Georgia				Pennsylvania			
	Available		Useful		Available		Useful		Available		Useful	
	%	SE	%	SE	%	SE	%	SE	%	SE	%	SE
Math teachers												
Math test results summarized by student subgroup	86	2	36	4	88	2	51	3	81	3	27	2
Math test results disaggregated by subtopic/skill	88	2	68	3	94	1	80	2	82	3	66	3
Science teachers												
Science test results summarized by student subgroup	27	4	17	5	73	3	35	3	NA	NA	NA	NA
Science test results disaggregated by subtopic/skill	28	5	25	8	78	3	55	3	NA	NA	NA	NA

NOTE: Response options included not available, available and not useful, available and minimally useful, available and moderately useful, and available and very useful. Percentages in the useful columns represent the sums of the moderately useful and very useful responses from teachers who reported that the resource was available. Georgia tested students in all grades in math and science. California and Pennsylvania did not test students in some grades, but percentages include all teachers who reported that the resource was available, regardless of grade level.

Table B.25
Middle School Teachers Reporting Availability and Usefulness of Math and Science State Test Results

| | California | | | | Georgia | | | | Pennsylvania | | | |
| | Available | | Useful | | Available | | Useful | | Available | | Useful | |
Results	%	SE	%	SE	%	SE	%	SE	%	SE	%	SE
Math teachers												
Math test results summarized by student subgroup	89	3	30	5	82	3	57	4	79	5	27	4
Math test results disaggregated by subtopic/skill	82	2	59	4	90	3	83	2	75	6	65	7
Science teachers												
Science test results summarized by student subgroup	38	4	21	5	77	4	50	4	NA	NA	NA	NA
Science test results disaggregated by subtopic/skill	36	5	43	8	82	4	70	3	NA	NA	NA	NA

NOTE: Response options included not available, available and not useful, available and minimally useful, available and moderately useful, and available and very useful. Percentages were restricted to teachers who reported that the resource was available and represent moderately and very useful responses. Georgia tested students in all grades in math and science. California and Pennsylvania did not test students in some grades, but percentages include all teachers who reported that the resource was available, regardless of grade level.

Table B.26
Principals and Teachers Agreeing with Statements About Timeliness of State Test Results, 2004–2005

| | California | | | | Georgia | | | | Pennsylvania | | | |
| | Elem. | | Middle | | Elem. | | Middle | | Elem. | | Middle | |
Statement	%	SE	%	SE	%	SE	%	SE	%	SE	%	SE
Principals: The information we receive about our school's performance is timely	44	10	23	7	51	8	39	9	13	5	64	5
Teachers: I received the test results in a timely manner	58	4	70	2	71	3	69	4	36	3	64	5

NOTE: Response options included strongly agree, disagree, agree, and strongly agree. Percentages represent the sum of the agree and strongly agree responses.

Table B.27
Superintendents Reporting That State Assessment Data Are Useful for Making Certain Decisions

Decision	Calif.		Ga.		Pa.	
	%	SE	%	SE	%	SE
Developing a district improvement plan	92	4	100		97	2
Focusing principal and/or teacher PD	96	3	100		91	5
Helping individual schools develop school improvement plans	88	7	100		86	9
Making changes to the district's curriculum and instruction materials	89	6	90	6	92	4
Recommending specific instructional strategies	68	11	69	13	80	10
Making policy about how much time is spent on each academic subject	64	11	76	10	72	12
Allocating resources among schools	59	11	52	14	53	15

NOTE: Response options included not useful, minimally useful, moderately useful, and very useful. Percentages represent the sum of the moderately useful and very useful responses.

Table B.28
Principals Reporting That State Assessment Data Are Useful for Making Certain Decisions

Decision	California				Georgia				Pennsylvania			
	Elem.		Middle		Elem.		Middle		Elem.		Middle	
	%	SE	%	SE	%	SE	%	SE	%	SE	%	SE
Developing a school improvement plan	79	8	77	8	100		94	5	70	9	88	7
Focusing teacher PD	73	9	72	9	86	5	83	7	78	8	71	16
Making change to curriculum and instructional materials	69	10	90	5	78	5	83	7	82	6	89	7
Identifying students who need additional instructional support	73	10	85	8	96	3	94	5	63	9	65	15
Making decisions on how much time is spent on each subject	53	12	70	11	71	8	66	11	47	9	49	14
Identifying teacher strengths and weaknesses	47	11	63	9	78	6	60	10	39	9	36	11
Making decisions regarding student promotion or retention	45	12	57	12	79	7	77	8	22	8	36	12
Assigning students to teachers	7	3	47	11	57	7	62	10	10	5	26	10

NOTE: Response options included not useful, minimally useful, moderately useful, and very useful. Percentages represent the sum of the moderately useful and very useful responses.

Table B.29
Math and Science Teachers Agreeing with Statements About the State Tests

| | | California | | | | Georgia | | | | Pennsylvania | | | |
| | | Elem. | | Middle | | Elem. | | Middle | | Elem. | | Middle | |
Statement	Respondent	%	SE	%	SE	%	SE	%	SE	%	SE	%	SE
State test results allowed me to identify areas in which I need to strengthen my content knowledge or teaching skills	Math teachers	70	4	55	4	89	2	79	2	69	4	60	5
	Science teachers	46	8	48	11	83	2	80	2	NA	NA	NA	NA
State test results helped me identify and correct gaps in curriculum and instruction	Math teachers	63	4	53	4	86	2	84	2	63	4	58	4
	Science teachers	38	7	54	12	79	2	74	3	NA	NA	NA	NA
State test results helped me tailor instruction to individual student needs	Math teachers	54	4	35	4	84	2	78	3	40	4	50	5
	Science teachers	30	6	41	11	72	3	58	4	NA	NA	NA	NA

NOTE: Response options included strongly disagree, disagree, agree, and strongly agree. Percentages represent the sum of the agree and strongly agree responses. Results exclude teachers who said that they did not receive test results. Pennsylvania results for 2004–2005 include only math teachers in tested grades (three, five, and eight); Pennsylvania administered no state science tests that year. California administered science tests only in grade five and in high school.

Table B.30
Districts Requiring Some or All Elementary and Middle Schools to Administer Progress Tests in Math and Science, 2004–2005

Test Requirement	California		Georgia		Pennsylvania	
	%	SE	%	SE	%	SE
Math progress tests required at some or all elementary schools	44	13	89	6	38	14
Math progress tests required at some or all middle schools	56	14	89	7	32	13
Science progress tests required at some or all elementary schools	9	5	55	14	NA	NA
Science progress tests required at some or all middle schools	17	8	43	14	NA	NA

NOTE: Response options included none, some, and all. Percentages represent the sum of the some and all responses.

Table B.31
Teachers Required to Administer Math and Science Progress Tests

Progress Test	California				Georgia				Pennsylvania			
	Elementary		Middle		Elementary		Middle		Elementary		Middle	
	%	SE	%	SE	%	SE	%	SE	%	SE	%	SE
Math	62	6	42	8	77	5	62	6	47	6	50	14
Science	9	3	11	4	30	6	44	6	3	1	10	4

NOTE: Response options included yes and no.

Table B.32
Teachers Agreeing with Statements About Math State and Progress Tests

Statement	California				Georgia				Pennsylvania			
	Elem.		Middle		Elem.		Middle		Elem.		Middle	
	%	SE	%	SE	%	SE	%	SE	%	SE	%	SE
State tests are a good measure of students' mastery of state content standards	42	4	38	4	60	3	57	3	45	4	50	5
Progress tests are a good measure of students' mastery of state content standards	57	5	59	5	62	4	68	4	70	3	70	5
State test results help me identify and correct gaps in curriculum and instruction	63	4	53	4	86	2	84	2	63	4	58	4
Progress test results help me identify and correct gaps in curriculum and instruction	76	5	76	5	82	3	82	3	84	3	86	4

NOTE: Response options included strongly agree, agree, disagree, and strongly disagree. Percentages represent the sum of the agree and strongly agree responses.

Table B.33
Math Teachers Reporting Progress Tests with Certain Features

Feature	California Elem. (n = 450)		California Middle (n = 113)		Georgia Elem. (n = 626)		Georgia Middle (n = 277)		Pennsylvania Elem. (n = 569)		Pennsylvania Middle (n = 152)	
	%	SE	%	SE	%	SE	%	SE	%	SE	%	SE
District or school requires you to administer a progress test[a]	62	6	42	8	77	5	62	6	47	6	50	14
Progress tests administered two to three times per year[b]	57	8	60	9	36	6	28	5	51	6	36	4
Progress tests administered approximately every six to eight weeks[b]	30	7	21	7	54	6	65	5	32	4	38	4
Progress tests administered approximately every two to four weeks[b]	13	5	20	6	10	2	7	2	17	4	28	6
Results are available the same or next day[c,d]	36	5	53	8	57	6	56	6	56	6	50	11
Results are available within one week[c,e]	30	5	24	8	25	5	24	3	25	4	28	6
There are consequences for teachers associated with performance on the tests[f]	3	1	6	2	9	3	8	3	4	2	7	3

[a] Response options included yes and no.

[b] Response options included two to three times per year, approximately every six to eight weeks, and approximately every two to four weeks.

[c] Response options included the same day administered, the next day, within one week, two to four weeks later, more than four weeks later, and the scores are not available to me.

[d] Percentages represent the sum of the same day and next day responses.

[e] Percentages represent within one week responses.

[f] Response options included yes, no, and don't know. Percentages represent yes responses.

Table B.34
Principals and Superintendents Reporting New Curricula

Response	California				Georgia				Pennsylvania			
	Elementary		Middle		Elementary		Middle		Elementary		Middle	
	%	SE	%	SE	%	SE	%	SE	%	SE	%	SE
Principal reports implementing (2003–2004 or 2004–2005)[a]												
New math curriculum	10	5	30	9	20	5	22	7	30	10	38	15
New science curriculum	14	7	24	12	9	4	8	6	16	8	17	8
Superintendent reports requiring some or all schools to adopt (2004–2005)[b]												
New math curriculum	27	12	35	13	30	11	36	13	24	12	27	12
New science curriculum	13	9	26	13	18	8	20	8	23	13	23	14

[a] Response options included yes and no.

[b] Response options included none, some, and all schools. Percentages represent the sum of the some and all responses.

Table B.35
Districts Taking Certain Steps to Assist Schools with Aligning Math Curriculum and Instruction with Standards in the Past Three Years

Step	California		Georgia		Pennsylvania	
	%	SE	%	SE	%	SE
Monitored or provided feedback on the implementation of state standards in classrooms	98	3	93	4	82	10
Mapped out the alignment of required textbooks and instructional programs to state *standards*	82	11	86	6	54	15
Mapped out the alignment of required textbooks and instructional programs to state *assessments*	68	12	88	6	49	15
Developed pacing plan or instructional calendar aligned with state standards	60	12	83	8	64	15
Established detailed curriculum guidelines aligned with state content standards	48	11	75	13	66	15
Provided sample lessons linked to state standards	65	13	70	13	76	12
Developed local content standards that augment state content standards	62	12	51	14	72	15

NOTE: Response options included mathematics; science; reading, language arts, and English; and none of these subjects. We asked respondents to select at least one option. Percentages represent mathematics responses.

Table B.36
Districts Taking Certain Steps to Assist Schools with Aligning Science Curriculum and Instruction with Standards in the Past Three Years

Step	California %	California SE	Georgia %	Georgia SE	Pennsylvania %	Pennsylvania SE
Monitored or provided feedback on the implementation of state standards in classrooms	43	12	92	4	40	14
Mapped out the alignment of required textbooks and instructional programs to state *standards*	54	13	76	9	34	14
Mapped out the alignment of required textbooks and instructional programs to state *assessments*	48	12	72	11	30	13
Developed pacing plan or instructional calendar aligned with state standards	24	11	72	11	32	12
Established detailed curriculum guidelines aligned with state content standards	27	10	70	11	48	14
Provided sample lessons linked to state standards	38	12	67	13	32	12
Developed local content standards that augment state content standards	35	11	47	14	49	15

NOTE: Response options included mathematics; science; reading, language arts, and English; and none of these subjects. We asked respondents to select at least one option. Percentages represent science responses.

Table B.37
Teachers Reporting That District or State Actions to Align Math Curriculum and Instruction with Standards Were Useful

Action	California Elem. %	California Elem. SE	California Middle %	California Middle SE	Georgia Elem. %	Georgia Elem. SE	Georgia Middle %	Georgia Middle SE	Pennsylvania Elem. %	Pennsylvania Elem. SE	Pennsylvania Middle %	Pennsylvania Middle SE
Detailed curriculum guidelines aligned with state standards	83	2	80	4	90	2	87	2	87	2	84	4
A pacing plan or instructional calendar	70	4	67	7	83	2	81	3	84	2	73	8
Monitoring and feedback on implementation of the state standards	56	5	52	6	63	3	61	4	58	4	51	5
Mapping out alignment of textbooks and instructional programs to state standards	74	2	76	5	77	2	70	3	83	3	61	8

NOTE: Response options included did not occur, occurred and not useful, occurred and minimally useful, occurred and moderately useful, and occurred and very useful. Percentages represent the sum of moderately useful and very useful responses from teachers who said that the action occurred.

Table B.38
Districts Requiring Some or All Elementary and Middle Schools to Offer Remedial Assistance to Students Outside the School Day

School	California		Georgia		Pennsylvania	
	%	SE	%	SE	%	SE
Elementary	61	13	84	12	95	4
Middle	44	12	86	12	82	11

NOTE: Response options included none, some, and all schools. Percentages represent the sum of the some and all responses.

Table B.39
Districts Requiring Some or All Elementary and Middle Schools to Make Changes Targeting Low-Achieving Students, 2004–2005

Change	School	Calif.		Ga.		Pa.	
		%	SE	%	SE	%	SE
Creating separate math classes for low-achieving students required at some or all . . .	Middle	56	14	56	14	51	15
	Elem.	39	13	57	14	54	15
Increasing the amount of time spent on math instruction specifically for low-achieving students required at some or all . . .	Middle	35	13	92	4	49	15
	Elem.	44	13	94	4	63	15
Eliminating some remedial math courses or instruction and requiring all students to take more challenging math courses or instruction required at some or all . . .	Middle	76	10	22	9	32	12
	Elem.	53	14	19	9	11	5
Increasing the amount of time spent on science instruction specifically for low-achieving students required at some or all . . .	Middle	12	7	33	14	0	
	Elem.	6	3	30	14	0	
Requiring all students to take more challenging science courses or instruction required at some or all . . .	Middle	9	5	43	14	28	15
	Elem.	6	4	33	14	17	14
Creating separate science classes for low-achieving students required at some or all . . .	Middle	4	3	16	11	8	8
	Elem.	2	2	3	3	8	8

NOTE: Response options included none, some, and all schools. Percentages represent the sum of the some and all responses.

Table B.40
Teachers Agreeing with Statements About the Impact of the State's Accountability System

| | California | | | | Georgia | | | | Pennsylvania | | | |
| | Elem. | | Middle | | Elem. | | Middle | | Elem. | | Middle | |
Statement	%	SE	%	SE	%	SE	%	SE	%	SE	%	SE
As a result of the state's accountability system, high-achieving students are not receiving appropriately challenging curriculum or instruction	52	3	47	3	49	2	55	2	39	2	52	6
The state's accountability system leaves little time to teach content not on state tests	89	2	90	2	87	1	85	2	88	2	87	2

NOTE: Response options included strongly agree, agree, disagree, and strongly disagree. Percentages represent the sum of the agree and strongly agree responses.

Table B.41
Teachers Reporting Emphasis on PD Activities, 2004–2005

| | California | | | | Georgia | | | | Pennsylvania | | | |
| | Elem. | | Middle | | Elem. | | Middle | | Elem. | | Middle | |
Activity	%	SE	%	SE	%	SE	%	SE	%	SE	%	SE
Aligning curriculum and instruction with state and/or district content standards	68	5	52	5	79	2	68	3	70	3	65	4
Instructional strategies for low-achieving students	57	5	45	5	68	3	57	3	47	3	39	5
Preparing students to take the state assessments	47	6	28	4	74	3	56	3	67	3	58	4
Instructional strategies for ELLs	57	5	40	5	27	2	17	2	14	2	10	3
Mathematics and mathematics teaching	53	4	42	5	57	4	52	3	64	4	44	3
Interpreting and using reports of student test results	44	6	24	3	65	3	45	4	36	4	33	7
Instructional strategies for special education students	25	4	25	4	39	2	42	3	33	3	33	4
Science and science teaching	28	4	26	4	20	2	32	2	23	3	30	5

NOTE: Response options included no emphasis, minor emphasis, moderate emphasis, and major emphasis. Percentages represent the sum of the moderate and major emphasis responses.

Table B.42
Districts Providing Technical Assistance to Principals or Teachers in Some or All Elementary and Middle Schools

Assistance	California %	California SE	Georgia %	Georgia SE	Pennsylvania %	Pennsylvania SE
Helping the school obtain additional PD based on scientifically based research	74	12	100		99	1
Assigning additional full-time school-level staff to support teacher development	22	8	71	13	30	12
Providing a coach or mentor to assist the principal	41	12	82	8	20	11

NOTE: Response options included no schools, low-performing schools, high-performing schools, and all schools. Percentages represent the sum of all responses except no schools.

Table B.43
Principals Reporting Test Preparation Activities

Activity	California Elem. %	California Elem. SE	California Middle %	California Middle SE	Georgia Elem. %	Georgia Elem. SE	Georgia Middle %	Georgia Middle SE	Pennsylvania Elem. %	Pennsylvania Elem. SE	Pennsylvania Middle %	Pennsylvania Middle SE
Helped teachers identify content that is likely to appear on the state test so they can cover it adequately in their instruction	94	3	99	1	100		100		100		99	1
Discussed methods for preparing students for the state test at staff meetings	94	4	95	4	100		100		99	1	100	
Distributed released copies of the state test or test items	61	10	61	11	88	4	98	2	96	3	96	2
Encouraged teachers to focus their efforts on students close to meeting the standards	85	6	94	3	90	4	93	4	77	7	57	15
Distributed commercial test preparation materials (e.g., practice tests)	59	10	61	11	90	5	88	5	93	4	88	8
Encouraged or required teachers to spend more time on tested subjects and less on other subjects	53	11	63	9	47	7	66	8	61	11	45	13
Discussed assessment anchors with teachers (Pa. only)									100		100	

NOTE: Response options included yes and no.

Table B.44
Superintendents Reporting on Various Aspects of the State's Accountability System

Aspect	California		Georgia		Pennsylvania	
	%	SE	%	SE	%	SE
Percentage agreeing or strongly agreeing with the following statements:						
Information from assessments we administer regularly during the year is more useful than state test results[a]	81	11	84	8	100	
We are eliminating programs (e.g., art, music) to provide more instruction in core subjects[b]	42	13	42	14	39	16
Percentage reporting district required some or all elementary schools to make the following changes:[c]						
Increasing instructional time for all students (e.g., by lengthening the school day)	7	4	71	13	15	11
Increasing the amount of time spent on mathematics instruction for all students	10	5	73	13	42	14
Instituting full-day kindergarten	31	12	59	15	63	14
Percentage reporting district required some or all middle schools to make the following changes:[c]						
Increasing instructional time for all students (e.g., by lengthening the school day)	12	7	61	14	16	11
Increasing the amount of time spent on mathematics instruction for all students	18	8	52	15	29	13

[a] Response options included strongly agree, agree, disagree, strongly disagree, and I did not receive this information. Percentages represent the sum of the agree and strongly agree responses.

[b] Response options included strongly agree, agree, disagree, and strongly disagree. Percentages represent the sum of the agree and strongly agree responses.

[c] Response options included none, some, and all schools. Percentages represent the sum of the some and all responses.

Table B.45
Districts Providing Technical Assistance to Low-Performing or All Schools

Assistance	California All %	SE	California Low-Performing %	SE	Georgia All %	SE	Georgia Low-Performing %	SE	Pennsylvania All %	SE	Pennsylvania Low-Performing %	SE
Assisting the school in analyzing assessment data to identify and address problems in instruction	89	8	3	3	100		0		97	3	3	3
Assisting the school in implementing instructional strategies that have been proven effective	89	9	11	9	98	2	0		93	3	0	
Assisting the school in analyzing and revising its budget to use resources more effectively	65	12	16	10	74	10	4	3	54	15	0	
Helping the school with school improvement planning	87	8	2	2	95	4	5	4	64	15	19	12
Helping schools prepare complete and accurate data to comply with NCLB reporting requirements	74	12	3	3	100		0		71	14	15	14
Helping the school obtain additional professional development based on scientifically based research	72	12	2	2	98	2	2	2	98	2	1	1
Providing guidance for teaching grade-level standards to ELLs and/ or special education students	79	8	8	5	90	7	8	7	78	11	0	
Providing before- or after-school, weekend, or summer programs	57	13	18	10	86	11	2	2	39	14	24	13
Providing additional instructional materials and books	57	12	17	9	80	9	18	9	61	15	7	4
Assisting the school in implementing parental involvement strategies	57	13	10	6	94	4	4	4	41	14	33	15

Table B.45—Continued

| Assistance | California | | | | Georgia | | | | Pennsylvania | | | |
| | All | | Low-Performing | | All | | Low-Performing | | All | | Low-Performing | |
	%	SE	%	SE	%	SE	%	SE	%	SE	%	SE
Helping the school obtain more experienced teachers	35	13	3	2	81	12	0		23	14	1	1
Assigning additional full-time school-level staff to support teacher development	12	7	11	5	55	14	15	7	27	12	3	2
Providing a coach or mentor to assist the principal	19	8	22	10	41	14	41	14	11	9	9	8

NOTE: Response options included no schools, low-performing schools, high-performing schools, and all schools.

Table B.46
Principals Agreeing with Statements About District Support

| Statement | California | | | | Georgia | | | | Pennsylvania | | | |
| | Elem. | | Middle | | Elem. | | Middle | | Elem. | | Middle | |
	%	SE	%	SE	%	SE	%	SE	%	SE	%	SE
When schools are having difficulty, the district provides assistance needed to help them improve	66	11	91	6	83	6	82	5	86	8	69	16
District staff provide appropriate support to enable principals to act as instructional leaders	61	13	82	8	80	5	77	5	66	9	58	15
District staff provide appropriate instructional support for teachers	68	12	74	9	84	5	75	7	74	8	90	6
District staff provide support for teaching grade-level standards to special education students (i.e., students with IEPs)	45	11	64	10	77	7	77	8	80	5	80	9
District staff provide support for teaching grade-level standards to ELLs (i.e., limited English proficient students	62	11	74	10	74	7	76	8	84	7	91	4

NOTE: Response options included strongly disagree, disagree, agree, and strongly agree. Percentages represent the sum of the agree and strongly agree responses.

Table B.47
Principals of Schools Identified as Needing Improvement Reporting District or State Assistance

Improvement	Calif. (n = 17)	Ga. (n = 21)	Pa. (n = 8)
Additional PD or special access to PD resources	9	9	7
Special grants to support school improvement	7	10	7
A mentor or coach for you (e.g., a distinguished educator)	6	6	2
School support teams	3	8	4
Additional full-time school-level staff to support teacher development	2	4	3
Distinguished teachers	3	1	1

NOTE: Response options included yes and no.

Table B.48
Principals of Schools in Corrective Action or Restructuring Reporting District Interventions

Intervention	Calif. (n = 9)	Ga. (n = 4)
Extending the school day or school year	2	3
Appointing an outside expert to advise the school	0	2
Reassigning or demoting the principal	0	2
Significantly decreasing management authority at the school level	1	0
Restructuring the internal organization of the school	1	0
Replacing school staff who are relevant to the failure to make AYP	0	1
Replacing all or most of the school staff	0	0
Reopening the school as a public charter school	0	0
Entering into a contract with a private management company to operate the school	0	0

NOTE: Response options included yes and no. No Pennsylvania schools failed to meet AYP for three or more consecutive years (i.e., were in corrective action or restructuring).

Table B.49
Superintendents Reporting Need for and Receipt of Technical Assistance If Needed

Assistance	California				Georgia				Pennsylvania			
	Needed		Received, If Needed		Needed		Received, If Needed		Needed		Received, If Needed	
	%	SE	%	SE	%	SE	%	SE	%	SE	%	SE
Identify effective methods and instructional strategies in scientifically based research	79	9	53	16	70	14	74	13	88	9	38	14
Provide effective PD	74	10	69	16	72	14	92	5	77	12	58	16
Use data more effectively	48	14	57	18	74	13	90	7	87	9	55	16
Clarify accountability system rules and requirements	84	5	96	4	55	15	86	13	57	15	100	
Develop and implement a district improvement plan	43	13	93	6	45	15	6 of 8[a]		50	15	7 of 8[a]	
Develop curriculum guides or model lessons based on state content standards	34	13	31	19	50	15	90	7	86	6	62	13
Promote parent involvement	37	12	42	20	52	14	60	18	70	13	18	14
Help the district work with schools in need of improvement	37	12	78	16	62	14	100		39	15	3 of 7[a]	

NOTE: Response options included yes and no to whether needed, received, and sufficient.

[a] In cases in which fewer than 10 principals reported having needed or received support, we report raw numbers for the state sample rather than estimates for the whole state.

Table B.50
Superintendents Reporting State Assistance for Schools in Need of Improvement

Assistance	Calif. (n = 7)	Ga. (n = 17)	Pa. (n = 5)
Providing special grants for school improvement	4	16	4
Assigning a state-approved support team to review school operations, evaluate school plans, and make recommendations for improvement	2	10	2
Providing assistance to schools through institutions of higher education, educational service agencies, or private providers of scientifically based research	3	9	0
Designating and assigning a distinguished principal and/or teacher to work with school	0	10	0

NOTE: Response options included yes and no.

Table B.51
Superintendents of Districts Identified as in Need of Improvement Reporting NCLB-Defined State Interventions with Their Districts

Intervention	Calif. (n = 4)	Ga. (n = 13)	Pa. (n = 4)
Helping you notify parents that your district needs improvement	2	6	1
Authorizing students to transfer from district schools to schools in a higher-performing district	0	1	2
Instituting and fully implementing a new curriculum based on state and local content standards	0	5	0
Deferring programmatic funds or reducing administrative funds	0	3	0
Replacing district personnel who are relevant to the failure to make AYP	0	0	0
Removing schools from the jurisdiction of the district	0	0	0
Appointing a receiver or trustee to administer district affairs	0	0	0
Restructuring the district	0	0	0

NOTE: Response options included yes and no.

Table B.52
Elementary School Teachers Reporting Changes in Instruction Time from 2003–2004 to 2004–2005

Subject Changed	California						Georgia						Pennsylvania					
	−		=		+		−		=		+		−		=		+	
	%	SE	%	SE	%	SE	%	SE	%	SE	%	SE	%	SE	%	SE	%	SE
Math	5	2	62	3	28	3	6	1	60	3	22	2	3	1	55	5	38	5
Science	19	3	54	4	21	3	10	1	63	3	11	2	22	4	62	4	8	2
Reading or ELA	3	1	59	4	32	4	4	1	62	3	21	2	7	3	63	4	24	3
Social studies	28	5	55	4	10	2	11	1	65	3	9	2	25	4	60	4	6	1
Arts or music	23	4	60	4	9	2	9	2	69	3	4	1	2	1	88	2	3	1
Physical education	23	4	58	5	11	3	5	1	74	3	5	1	3	1	88	2	3	1

NOTE: Response options included decreased by >45 minutes per week, decreased by 1–45 minutes per week, stayed the same, increased by >45 minutes per week, increased by 1–45 minutes per week, and don't know. Percentages for − columns represent the sums of decreased by >45 minutes per week and decreased by 1–45 minutes per week responses. Percentages for + columns represent the sums of increased by >45 minutes per week and increased by 1–45 minutes per week responses. Percentages for = columns represent stayed the same responses.

Table B.53
Middle School Teachers Reporting Changes in Instruction Time from 2003–2004 to 2004–2005

| | California | | | | | | Georgia | | | | | | Pennsylvania | | | | | |
| | − | | = | | + | | − | | = | | + | | − | | = | | + | |
Subject Changed	%	SE	%	SE	%	SE	%	SE	%	SE	%	SE	%	SE	%	SE	%	SE
Math	1	0	67	3	20	3	5	2	53	5	29	6	2	1	78	5	14	4
Science	9	3	63	4	10	3	5	2	52	4	23	5	7	2	77	6	6	3
Reading or ELA	3	1	60	4	14	3	8	2	48	4	23	5	3	1	74	6	9	3
Social studies	13	5	59	4	5	1	5	1	51	4	20	5	9	4	75	6	3	1
Arts or music	14	3	48	4	8	4	9	2	52	3	5	2	5	2	74	4	6	2
Physical education	5	2	68	4	3	1	8	3	55	4	5	2	3	1	75	4	5	2

NOTE: Response options included decreased by >45 minutes per week, decreased by 1–45 minutes per week, stayed the same, increased by >45 minutes per week, increased by 1–45 minutes per week, and don't know. Percentages in − columns represent the sums of the decreased by >45 minutes per week and decreased by 1–45 minutes per week responses. Percentages in + columns represent the sums of the increased by >45 minutes per week and increased by 1–45 minutes per week responses. Percentages for = columns represent the stayed the same responses.

Table B.54
Teachers Reporting Aligning Their Instruction with State Content Standards

| | California | | | | Georgia | | | | Pennsylvania[a] | | | |
| | Elem. | | Middle | | Elem. | | Middle | | Elem. | | Middle | |
Content Standard	%	SE	%	SE	%	SE	%	SE	%	SE	%	SE
Math	95	1	93	2	90	1	90	2	82	2	70	3
Science	82	3	96	2	87	2	90	3	45	4	57	9

NOTE: Response options included strongly disagree, disagree, agree, strongly agree, and don't know. Percentages represent the sum of the agree and strongly agree responses.

[a] In Pennsylvania, this question focused on assessment anchors rather than on Pennsylvania academic standards.

Table B.55
Teachers in Tested Grades Reporting Aligning Their Instruction with State Assessments and State Content Standards

Measure	California				Georgia				Pennsylvania			
	Elem.		Middle		Elem.		Middle		Elem.		Middle	
	%	SE	%	SE	%	SE	%	SE	%	SE	%	SE
Math standards	95	1	93	1	90	1	90	2	82	3	71	4
Math assessments	52	4	51	4	82	3	77	2	87	3	86	3
Science standards	87	4	95	4	87	2	90	3	NA[a]	NA	NA	NA
Science assessments	60	7	65	9	80	3	81	3	NA	NA	NA	NA

NOTE: Response options included strongly disagree, disagree, agree, strongly agree, and don't know. Percentages represent the sum of the agree and strongly agree responses.

[a] Excludes Pennsylvania science teachers because Pennsylvania did not administer a science test.

Table B.56
Elementary School Teachers Reporting That Their Instruction Differs as a Result of Math and Science Assessments

| Difference | California | | | | Georgia | | | | Pennsylvania[a] | |
| | Math | | Science | | Math | | Science | | Math | |
	%	SE	%	SE	%	SE	%	SE	%	SE
Assign more homework	43	4	8	2	29	4	21	3	30	4
Spend more time teaching content	52	4	29	4	58	4	43	4	53	4
Offer more assistance outside of school for students who are not proficient	29	3	8	2	34	4	16	3	21	3
Search for more effective teaching methods	67	3	33	4	74	4	64	6	62	4
Focus more on standards	73	4	45	4	77	3	68	4	76	3
Focus more on topics emphasized in assessment	63	5	35	4	72	3	57	4	73	4
Emphasize assessment styles and formats of problems	55	4	20	4	78	4	60	4	74	3
Spend more time teaching test-taking strategies	53	4	25	4	56	4	42	4	51	3
Focus more on students who are close to proficient	37	5	9	2	36	2	23	3	29	3
Rely more heavily on multiple-choice tests	24	5	19	4	37	4	42	4	18	3
Rely more heavily on open-ended tests	21	4	18	3	23	4	28	3	50	2

NOTE: Response options included not at all, a small amount, a moderate amount, and a great deal. Percentages represent the sum of a moderate amount and a great deal responses.

[a] We did not present these questions to Pennsylvania science teachers because there was no state science test.

Table B.57
Middle School Math and Science Teachers Reporting That Their Instruction Differs as a Result of Math and Science Assessments

Difference	California Math		California Science		Georgia Math		Georgia Science		Pennsylvania[a] Math	
	%	SE	%	SE	%	SE	%	SE	%	SE
Assign more homework	29	4	8	3	29	3	26	3	13	4
Search for more effective teaching methods	58	3	35	6	69	3	67	3	59	7
Focus more on standards	66	4	47	6	72	3	77	3	69	3
Focus more on topics emphasized in assessment	57	5	27	7	73	3	64	4	71	7
Emphasize assessment styles and formats of problems	49	5	23	4	71	3	65	3	62	4
Spend more time teaching test-taking strategies	45	7	26	6	44	3	48	3	39	4
Spend more time teaching content	45	6	24	4	53	3	59	4	46	3
Focus more on students who are close to proficient	19	3	8	2	38	4	30	3	22	5
Offer more assistance outside of school for students who are not proficient	26	3	9	2	41	3	33	3	19	5
Rely more heavily on multiple-choice tests	23	3	20	3	38	4	54	3	9	2
Rely more heavily on open-ended tests	13	2	11	2	23	2	26	3	33	5

NOTE: Response options included not at all, a small amount, a moderate amount, and a great deal. Percentages represent the sum of the a moderate amount and a great deal responses.

[a] We did not present these questions to Pennsylvania science teachers because there was no state science test.

Table B.58
Elementary School Math Teachers Reporting Their Instructional Techniques and How They Have Changed in the Past Year

Technique	California						Georgia						Pennsylvania					
	Use		−		+		Use		−		+		Use		−		+	
	%	SE	%	SE	%	SE	%	SE	%	SE	%	SE	%	SE	%	SE	%	SE
Assign mathematics homework	97	1	1	1	19	2	96	1	3	1	16	2	98	1	1	0	11	2
Have students work on extended mathematics investigations or projects	45	4	8	2	13	3	46	3	9	1	16	2	43	3	5	1	12	2
Introduce content through formal presentations or direct instruction	98	1	2	1	13	3	98	1	3	1	14	2	98	1	1	1	8	2
Provide help to individual students outside of class time	68	4	5	1	19	2	70	3	5	1	25	2	72	4	5	1	17	3
Confer with another teacher about alternative ways to present specific topics or lessons	81	3	4	1	20	3	90	1	2	1	23	3	89	2	2	1	19	3
Have students help other students learn mathematics content	91	2	2	1	18	3	93	1	2	1	27	3	92	2	2	1	23	3
Refer students for extra help outside the classroom	57	4	4	1	14	3	65	4	3	1	21	3	54	4	2	1	16	3
Plan different assignments based on performance	82	2	4	1	27	3	90	2	4	1	29	2	81	2	5	2	18	2
Reteach topics because performance on assignments or assessments did not meet expectations	93	2	3	2	24	3	96	1	2	1	29	2	89	3	7	3	18	3

Table B.58—Continued

Technique	California Use %	SE	− %	SE	+ %	SE	Georgia Use %	SE	− %	SE	+ %	SE	Pennsylvania Use %	SE	− %	SE	+ %	SE
Review assessment results to identify individual students who need supplemental instruction	91	2	2	1	21	3	95	1	1	1	27	3	89	2	2	1	21	3
Review assessment results to identify topics requiring more or less emphasis in instruction	90	2	1	1	20	2	94	1	0	0	26	3	87	1	2	1	20	2
Conduct a preassessment to find out what students know about a topic	65	4	3	1	13	2	67	3	4	1	17	2	60	5	49		11	2

NOTE: Response options for use included never, rarely (a few times a year), sometimes (once or twice a month), and often (once a week or more). Percentages represent the sum of the sometimes and often responses. Response options for − and + included less than 2003–2004, about the same as 2003–2004, and more than 2003–2004.

Table B.59
Middle School Math Teachers Reporting Their Instructional Techniques and How They Have Changed in the Past Year

Technique	California						Georgia						Pennsylvania					
	Use		−		+		Use		−		+		Use		−		+	
	%	SE	%	SE	%	SE	%	SE	%	SE	%	SE	%	SE	%	SE	%	SE
Assign mathematics homework	94	2	2	1	12	2	92	2	4	1	19	3	95	2	1	0	13	4
Have students work on extended mathematics investigations or projects	28	4	9	2	7	2	39	3	12	2	13	2	26	3	11	3	10	3
Introduce content through formal presentations or direct instruction	95	2	4	2	10	2	97	1	1	1	14	2	99	1	2	1	5	2
Provide help to individual students outside of class time	85	4	2	1	20	4	85	2	4	1	32	3	80	11	3	1	24	8
Confer with another teacher about alternative ways to present specific topics or lessons	81	3	7	2	20	5	84	2	4	1	33	3	72	11	1	1	17	4
Have students help other students learn mathematics content	86	2	3	2	17	3	95	1	3	1	30	2	84	4	2	1	27	5
Refer students for extra help outside the classroom	70	3	2	1	17	4	64	4	4	1	23	4	66	4	2	1	18	3
Plan different assignments or lessons based on performance	68	2	3	2	17	3	81	2	5	1	29	3	69	5	0		18	4

Table B.59—Continued

Technique	California Use %	SE	– %	SE	+ %	SE	Georgia Use %	SE	– %	SE	+ %	SE	Pennsylvania Use %	SE	– %	SE	+ %	SE
Reteach topics because performance on assignments or assessments did not meet expectations	95	2	4	1	24	3	93	1	4	1	30	4	87	3	0	0	16	4
Review assessment results to identify individual students who need supplemental instruction	84	3	3	1	17	4	89	2	2	1	26	4	75	6	1	0	15	5
Review assessment results to identify topics requiring more or less emphasis in instruction	86	2	1	1	19	3	90	2	1	1	28	3	83	4	2	1	19	3
Conduct a preassessment to find out what students know about a topic	49	4	5	2	9	2	65	3	4	1	21	3	41	9	4	2	20	6

NOTE: Response options for use included never, rarely (a few times a year), sometimes (once or twice a month), and often (once a week or more). Percentages represent the sum of the sometimes and often responses. Response options for – and + included less than 2003–2004, about the same as 2003–2004, and more than 2003–2004.

Table B.60
Elementary School Science Teachers Reporting Their Instructional Techniques and How They Have Changed in the Past Year

Technique	California						Georgia						Pennsylvania					
	Use		–		+		Use		–		+		Use		–		+	
	%	SE	%	SE	%	SE	%	SE	%	SE	%	SE	%	SE	%	SE	%	SE
Assign science homework	51	4	8	2	11	2	75	3	4	1	17	2	57	4	5	1	6	2
Have students do hands-on laboratory science activities or investigations	72	3	12	3	15	4	82	2	10	2	21	3	84	3	8	2	12	3
Introduce content through formal presentations or direct instruction	93	2	5	2	15	3	99	1	2	1	12	2	97	1	2	1	4	1
Provide help to individual students outside of class time	25	3	7	2	5	1	41	3	6	1	10	2	30	3	2	1	4	1
Confer with another teacher about alternative ways to present specific topics or lessons	62	5	7	2	17	4	83	2	6	1	19	2	68	4	2	1	11	2
Have students help other students learn science content	67	3	4	2	10	2	87	2	2	1	23	3	75	3	1	1	8	2
Refer students for extra help outside the classroom	20	3	8	2	6	4	35	3	3	1	10	2	16	3	3	1	4	1
Plan different assignments or lessons based on performance	38	4	5	2	8	2	64	4	5	1	18	3	37	3	3	1	7	2
Reteach topics because performance on assignments or assessments did not meet expectations	57	4	7	2	12	3	81	3	3	1	15	2	54	4	2	1	8	2

Table B.60—Continued

Technique	California						Georgia						Pennsylvania					
	Use		–		+		Use		–		+		Use		–		+	
	%	SE	%	SE	%	SE	%	SE	%	SE	%	SE	%	SE	%	SE	%	SE
Review assessment results to identify individual students who need supplemental instruction	61	4	7	2	8	2	81	2	2	1	13	2	62	3	2	1	4	1
Review assessment results to identify topics requiring more or less emphasis in instruction	61	4	6	2	10	3	82	2	3	1	15	2	60	3	2	1	4	1
Conduct a preassessment to find out what students know about a topic	42	4	5	2	7	2	53	3	3	1	12	2	43	4	2	1	5	1

NOTE: Response options for use included never, rarely (a few times a year), sometimes (once or twice a month), and often (once a week or more). Percentages represent the sum of the sometimes and often responses. Response options for – and + included less than 2003–2004, about the same as 2003–2004, and more than 2003–2004.

Table B.61
Middle School Science Teachers Reporting Their Instructional Techniques and How They Have Changed in the Past Year

Technique	California Use		California −		California +		Georgia Use		Georgia −		Georgia +		Pennsylvania Use		Pennsylvania −		Pennsylvania +	
	%	SE	%	SE	%	SE	%	SE	%	SE	%	SE	%	SE	%	SE	%	SE
Assign science homework	75	7	3	1	16	4	87	3	4	1	13	3	79	6	3	2	5	3
Have students do hands-on laboratory science activities or investigations	82	5	8	2	16	4	85	2	12	2	19	2	76	6	11	4	20	8
Introduce content through formal presentations or direct instruction	98	1	3	1	7	2	98	1	2	1	11	2	94	4	2	1	5	2
Provide help to individual students outside of class time	65	7	2	1	14	4	76	3	6	1	19	3	56	10	6	5	15	4
Confer with another teacher about alternative ways to present specific topics or lessons	69	5	5	2	16	4	84	2	4	2	27	3	69	6	7	5	9	3
Have students help other students learn science content	80	4	1	1	14	3	90	2	3	1	27	4	74	6	2	1	12	4
Refer students for extra help outside the classroom	43	6	2	1	12	4	57	3	5	1	17	3	39	7	2	1	9	4
Plan different assignments or lessons based on performance	46	7	3	1	12	3	74	3	3	1	27	3	65	6	7	5	20	2
Reteach topics because performance on assignments or assessments did not meet expectations	59	5	3	1	11	3	80	2	5	2	24	3	62	4	3	2	16	5

Table B.61—Continued

Technique	California						Georgia						Pennsylvania					
	Use		–		+		Use		–		+		Use		–		+	
	%	SE	%	SE	%	SE	%	SE	%	SE	%	SE	%	SE	%	SE	%	SE
Review assessment results to identify individual students who need supplemental instruction	66	7	3	1	13	3	80	3	6	2	21	4	79	6	1	0	11	5
Review assessment results to identify topics requiring more or less emphasis in instruction	70	6	3	1	13	3	85	2	2	1	20	4	76	3	1	1	10	3
Conduct a preassessment to find out what students know about a topic	53	5	4	1	13	3	63	3	8	2	24	4	65	3	1	1	9	4

NOTE: Response options for use included never, rarely (a few times a year), sometimes (once or twice a month), and often (once a week or more). Percentages represent the sum of the sometimes and often responses. Response options for – and + included less than 2003–2004, about the same as 2003–2004, and more than 2003–2004.

Table B.62
Superintendents Agreeing That Their Districts Have Adequate Funding to Implement NCLB Requirements

State	California		Georgia		Pennsylvania	
	%	SE	%	SE	%	SE
Response	23	12	15	9	3	3

NOTE: Response options included strongly disagree, disagree, agree, and strongly agree. Percentages represent the sum of the agree and strongly agree responses.

Table B.63
Administrators Reporting Inadequate Fiscal or Physical Capital as a Hindrance to Their Improvement Efforts

Hindrance	California						Georgia						Pennsylvania					
	Supt.		Principal Elem.		Principal Middle		Supt.		Principal Elem.		Principal Middle		Supt.		Principal Elem.		Principal Middle	
	%	SE	%	SE	%	SE	%	SE	%	SE	%	SE	%	SE	%	SE	%	SE
Lack of adequate funding	98	2	81	8	80	8	99	1	43	7	67	8	98	1	66	9	72	10
Inadequate school facilities	10	6	3	2	8	5	19	12	23	7	18	7	26	12	16	6	31	11
Shortage of standards-based curriculum materials	14	9	—	—	—	—	46	14	—	—	—	—	34	13	—	—	—	—
Unanticipated problems with space, facilities, transportation	—	—	28	9	21	7	—	—	18	5	15	5	—	—	23	7	20	9

NOTE: Response options included not a hindrance, a minor hindrance, a moderate hindrance, and a great hindrance. Percentages represent the sum of the moderate and great hindrance responses.

Table B.64
Teachers Reporting Inadequate Physical Classroom Resources as a Hindrance to Students' Academic Success

Hindrance	California				Georgia				Pennsylvania			
	Elem.		Middle		Elem.		Middle		Elem.		Middle	
	%	SE	%	SE	%	SE	%	SE	%	SE	%	SE
Large class size	59	4	69	4	39	3	58	3	48	4	57	4
Inadequate instructional resources (e.g., textbooks, equipment)	33	3	34	3	28	3	35	4	33	4	33	6
Lack of school resources to provide the extra help for students who need it	42	5	37	4	23	3	34	3	32	4	31	6

NOTE: Response options included strongly disagree, disagree, agree, and strongly agree. Percentages represent the sum of the agree and strongly agree responses.

Table B.65
Administrators Reporting Inadequate Human Capital as a Hindrance to Their Improvement Efforts

Hindrance	California						Georgia						Pennsylvania					
	Supt.		Principal Elem.		Principal Middle		Supt.		Principal Elem.		Principal Middle		Supt.		Principal Elem.		Principal Middle	
	%	SE	%	SE	%	SE	%	SE	%	SE	%	SE	%	SE	%	SE	%	SE
Shortage of qualified principals	22	11	—	—	—	—	36	13	—	—	—	—	29	13	—	—	—	—
Shortage of highly qualified teachers	—	—	12	5	39	10	—	—	7	4	32	8	—	—	10	5	25	11
Shortage of highly qualified *math* teachers	40	12	—	—	—	—	69	13	—	—	—	—	33	14	—	—	—	—
Shortage of highly qualified *science* teachers	43	13	—	—	—	—	69	13	—	—	—	—	28	12	—	—	—	—
Shortage of highly qualified teacher aides and paraprofessionals	—	—	22	8	28	9	—	—	9	5	8	5	—	—	27	8	34	11
Teacher turnover	—	—	20	9	12	6	—	—	15	6	25	9	—	—	14	5	21	10
Shortage/lack of high-quality PD opportunities for *teachers*	47	13	32	10	38	10	45	13	16	5	17	6	39	14	22	9	19	9
Shortage/lack of high-quality PD opportunities for *principals*	37	12	29	8	40	10	45	14	10	5	10	4	51	15	34	10	22	9
Insufficient staff time to meet administrative responsibilities	—	—	71	7	72	12	—	—	56	6	43	8	—	—	55	10	63	12

NOTE: Response options included strongly disagree, disagree, agree, and strongly agree. Percentages represent the sum of the agree and strongly agree responses.

Table B.66
Principals Agreeing That Teachers in Their Schools Have the Skills and Knowledge Needed
to Analyze and Make Use of the Test Results They Receive

California				Georgia				Pennsylvania			
Elementary		Middle		Elementary		Middle		Elementary		Middle	
%	SE	%	SE	%	SE	%	SE	%	SE	%	SE
92	4	84	6	92	4	75	7	64	10	76	10

NOTE: Response options included strongly disagree, disagree, agree, and strongly agree. Percentages
represent the sum of the agree and strongly agree responses.

Table B.67
Superintendents Reporting That Their Districts Have Sufficient Staff with Necessary Skills in
Certain Areas

Skill	Calif.		Ga.		Pa.	
	%	SE	%	SE	%	SE
Facilitate improvements in low-performing schools	62	14	68	13	32	15
Help schools to analyze data for school improvement	68	12	66	14	56	16
Help schools identify research-based strategies for improvement	57	12	73	13	58	16
Conduct PD tailored to the needs of teachers	35	11	68	14	74	13
Conduct PD tailored to the needs of principals	27	10	64	14	48	16
Align curriculum with state content standards and state assessments	52	11	70	13	86	10

NOTE: Response options included yes and no.

Table B.68
Teachers Reporting Inadequate Time as a Hindrance to Students' Academic Success

Hindrance	California				Georgia				Pennsylvania			
	Elem.		Middle		Elem.		Middle		Elem.		Middle	
	%	SE	%	SE	%	SE	%	SE	%	SE	%	SE
Insufficient class time to cover all the curriculum	70	3	61	5	59	3	46	2	64	3	47	6
Lack of teacher planning time built into the school day	62	3	43	4	44	3	38	3	52	3	29	6

NOTE: Response options included not a hindrance, a minor hindrance, a moderate hindrance, and a
great hindrance. Percentages represent the sum of the moderate and great hindrance responses.

Table B.69
Administrators Reporting Inadequate Time as a Hindrance to Their Improvement Efforts

	California						Georgia						Pennsylvania					
	Supt.		Principal Elem.		Principal Middle		Supt.		Principal Elem.		Principal Middle		Supt.		Principal Elem.		Principal Middle	
Hindrance	%	SE	%	SE	%	SE	%	SE	%	SE	%	SE	%	SE	%	SE	%	SE
Inadequate lead time to prepare before implementing reforms	85	7	46	10	31	10	69	13	34	7	36	10	57	15	34	7	33	12
Lack of teacher planning time built into the school day	—	—	71	9	36	10	—	—	44	6	22	7	—	—	41	8	12	6

NOTE: Response options included not a hindrance, a minor hindrance, a moderate hindrance, and a great hindrance. Percentages represent the sum of the moderate and great hindrance responses.

Table B.70
Teachers Reporting Student Background Conditions as a Hindrance to Students' Academic Success

	California				Georgia				Pennsylvania			
	Elem.		Middle		Elem.		Middle		Elem.		Middle	
Hindrance	%	SE	%	SE	%	SE	%	SE	%	SE	%	SE
Inadequate basic skills or prior preparation	78	5	83	3	70	4	86	2	66	5	85	2
Lack of support from parents	75	5	80	4	75	5	86	2	69	5	85	2
Student absenteeism and tardiness	61	5	70	4	52	4	74	2	51	6	82	5
Wide range of student abilities to address in class	82	3	77	3	65	3	71	2	78	3	76	4

NOTE: Response options include not a hindrance, a minor hindrance, a moderate hindrance, and a great hindrance. Percentages represent the sum of the moderate and great hindrance responses.

Table B.71

Superintendents and Principals Agreeing with Statements About the Inclusion of Students with Special Needs in AYP Calculations

Statement	California		Georgia		Pennsylvania	
	%	SE	%	SE	%	SE
Special education students should not be included in AYP calculations: superintendents	83	10	92	4	99	2
The system of accountability does not allow sufficient flexibility for meeting the needs of special education students: elementary school principals	76	11	87	5	94	4
The system of accountability does not allow sufficient flexibility for meeting the needs of special education students: middle school principals	82	7	77	9	87	7
The system of accountability does not allow sufficient flexibility for meeting the needs of English learners: elementary school principals	95	20	86	5	87	6
The system of accountability does not allow sufficient flexibility for meeting the needs of English learners: middle school principals	92	5	89	5	83	9

NOTE: Response options included strongly agree, agree, disagree, and strongly disagree. Percentages represent the sum of the agree and strongly agree responses.

Table B.72

Principals Reporting Lack of Guidance for Teaching Standards to Student Subgroups as a Hindrance to Their Improvement Efforts

Hindrance	California				Georgia				Pennsylvania			
	Elementary Principals		Middle Principals		Elementary Principals		Middle Principals		Elementary Principals		Middle Principals	
	%	SE	%	SE	%	SE	%	SE	%	SE	%	SE
Lack of guidance for teaching grade-level standards to special education students	51	10	26	9	17	6	21	8	27	8	41	14
Lack of guidance for teaching grade-level standards to ELLs	47	10	15	7	19	7	21	6	27	8	8	3

NOTE: Response options included not a hindrance, a minor hindrance, a moderate hindrance, and a great hindrance. Percentages represent the sum of the moderate and great hindrance responses.

Table B.73
Administrators Reporting Frequent Changes in Policy or Leadership as a Hindrance to Their Improvement Efforts

Hindrance	California						Georgia						Pennsylvania					
	Supt.		Principal Elem.		Principal Middle		Supt.		Principal Elem.		Principal Middle		Supt.		Principal Elem.		Principal Middle	
	%	SE	%	SE	%	SE	%	SE	%	SE	%	SE	%	SE	%	SE	%	SE
Frequent changes in state policy or leadership	71	12	—	—	—	—	79	12	—	—	—	—	98	1	—	—	—	—
Frequent changes in district policy and priorities	—	—	46	10	14	5	—	—	11	4	19	6	—	—	19	7	15	7
Frequent changes in district leadership	—	—	30	10	20	8	—	—	14	4	10	4	—	—	14	6	9	7
Complying with teacher association rules/policies	71	12	—	—	—	—	7	6	—	—	—	—	51	15	—	—	—	—
Disagreements with district school board over policies	2	2	—	—	—	—	17	9	—	—	—	—	21	11	—	—	—	—

NOTE: Response options included not a hindrance, a minor hindrance, a moderate hindrance, and a great hindrance. Percentages represent the sum of the moderate and great hindrance responses.

Superintendent, Principal, and Teacher Surveys

2/5/05

Implementing
Standards-Based
Accountability

2005 District Superintendent Survey

This is a voluntary survey of Superintendents in a random sample of school districts in California, Georgia and Pennsylvania.

Please answer the survey questions by circling the number that corresponds to your response.

When finished, place the completed survey in the postage paid return envelope and mail it back to RAND.

The time needed to complete this survey is 20 - 30 minutes.

If you have any questions about this survey or about the study, you may contact Mark Hanson at The RAND Corporation, 310-393-0411 ext. 6169, or by email at mhanson@rand.org.

Section I. No Child Left Behind Components

A. Assessments

DEFINITION: "State tests" refer to the set of assessments used in your state for computing adequate yearly progress (AYP). For California, this means the California Standards Tests (CST). For Georgia, this means the Georgia Criterion-Referenced Competency Tests (CRCT). For Pennsylvania, this means the Pennsylvania System of School Assessment (PSSA).

---

1. How useful are the 2003-04 state test results in helping you make the following decisions? (Circle one number in each row.)

		Not useful	Minimally useful	Moderately useful	Very useful	Not applicable
a.	Making changes to the district's curriculum and instructional materials	1	2	3	4	9
b.	Developing a district improvement plan..	1	2	3	4	9
c.	Helping individual schools to develop school improvement plans...	1	2	3	4	9
d.	Making policy about how much time is spent on each academic subject..	1	2	3	4	9
e.	Focusing principal and/or teacher professional development...............	1	2	3	4	9
f.	Recommending specific instructional strategies	1	2	3	4	9
g.	Allocating resources among schools...	1	2	3	4	9

2. To what extent do you agree or disagree with each of the following statements about your district's results from the 2003-04 state tests? (Circle one number in each row.)

	Strongly disagree	Disagree	Agree	Strongly agree	I did not receive this information
a. The information we receive from the state about our district's performance is clear and easy to understand	1	2	3	4	9
b. State test scores accurately reflect the achievement of students in my district	1	2	3	4	9
c. State tests are a good measure of students' progress towards mastering standards	1	2	3	4	9
d. Information from assessments we administer regularly during the year is more useful than state test results	1	2	3	4	9

B. District Adequate Yearly Progress (AYP)

3. Did your district as a whole meet the AYP target for the 2003-04 school year? (Circle one number.)

Yes 1

No 2

We have not been informed yet 3

I don't know 4

3

4. To what extent do you agree or disagree with the following statements about the AYP target for your district as a whole? (Circle one number in each row.)

	Strongly disagree	Disagree	Agree	Strongly agree
a. My district can attain the AYP target for the 2004-05 school year	1	2	3	4
b. My district can attain the AYP targets for the next five years	1	2	3	4
c. It is difficult for my district to meet the 95% participation rate on the state tests	1	2	3	4
d. It is difficult for my district to meet the additional indicator used to calculate AYP in my state (e.g., attendance rate, graduation rate, or API growth)	1	2	3	4
e. My district's AYP status accurately reflects the overall performance of our students	1	2	3	4
f. Because of the pressure to make AYP, my staff and I are focusing more on improving student achievement than we would without the AYP target	1	2	3	4
g. Special education students should not be included in AYP calculations	1	2	3	4

C. Transfers

5. If a Title I school does not meet its AYP target for two years in a row (i.e., is identified as in need of improvement), the district is required to permit students to transfer to another school and to provide transportation. During the current school year (2004-05), were any Title I schools in your district identified as in need of improvement under NCLB, making students eligible to transfer to another school? (Circle one number.)

☐ If there are no Title I students in this district, check this box and skip to Question 16, page 7

Yes .... 1 ➔ Continue with Question 6

No .... 2 ➔ Skip to Question 9, page 5

6. For the 2004-05 school year, approximately how many students in your district were eligible to transfer to another school because their school was identified as in need of improvement under NCLB? (Write your best estimate on the line below, or write "DK" if you don't know.)

_____students

4

7. For the 2004-05 school year, approximately how many <u>students</u> in your district actually <u>transferred</u> to another school because their school was identified as in need of improvement under Title I? (Write your best estimate on the line below. If no students elected to transfer, write "0." Write "DK" if you don't know.)

    _____students

8. To what extent do you agree or disagree with the following statements about the impact of student transfers under NCLB in your district? (Circle one number in each row.)

	Strongly disagree	Disagree	Agree	Strongly agree
a. Transfers make it more difficult to plan for the next school year because we do not know how many students will be attending each school	1	2	3	4
b. The possibility of transfers has increased pressure on district staff to help schools improve	1	2	3	4
c. Students who are eligible to transfer have convenient, high-quality schools available to them	1	2	3	4
d. It is difficult to inform parents of their transfer choices because we do not receive necessary information from the state in a timely manner.............................	1	2	3	4
e. The transfer option creates a large administrative burden for the district..........	1	2	3	4
f. Higher achieving students are more likely to transfer than lower achieving students...	1	2	3	4
g. The transfer policy has not had a noticeable effect on my district...................	1	2	3	4

D. Supplemental Educational Services Outside the School Day

9. If a Title I school does not meet its AYP target for three years in a row (i.e., is identified as in need of improvement for two consecutive years), NCLB requires the district to permit parents of low-income students to request supplemental educational services (e.g., tutoring) from state-approved, third-party providers. Are there any students in Title I schools in your district eligible under NCLB for supplemental educational services in the current school year (2004-05)? (Circle one number.)

    Yes.................................... 1   → Continue with Question 10

    No...................................... 2   → Skip to Question 16, page 7

10. Approximately how many <u>students</u> in your district are <u>eligible</u> for supplemental educational services under NCLB in the 2004-05 school year? (Write your best estimate on the line below or write "DK" if you don't know.)

_____ students

11. Approximately how many students in your district <u>received</u> supplemental educational services under NCLB in the 2004-05 school year? (Write your best estimate on the line below. If no students received supplemental educational services, write "0". Write "DK" if you don't know.)

_____ students

12. Is the district itself an approved provider of supplemental educational services for its own students? (Circle one number.)

Yes, the district is the sole provider 1   ➜   Skip to Question 16, page 7

Yes, the district is one of several providers...........................2   ➜   Continue with Question 13

No...3   ➜   Continue with Question 13

13. How many supplemental educational service providers (excluding the district) are available to students in this district? (Write your best estimate on the line below, or write "DK" if you don't know.)

_____ supplemental educational service providers

14. Approximately what percentage of the students receiving supplemental educational services in the district are served by each type of provider? (Write your best estimates of the percentages on each line below. The percentages should sum to 100%. Write "DK" if you don't know.)

	Percentage
a. The district as supplemental educational service provider..........	_____
b. All other supplemental educational service providers	_____
Total	100%

6

15. To what extent do you agree or disagree with the following statements about the supplemental educational services offered by <u>outside providers</u> (not the district as provider) to students in your district as a result of NCLB? (Circle one number in each row.)

	Strongly disagree	Disagree	Agree	Strongly agree	I don't know or Not applicable
a. I am generally satisfied with the quality of the supplemental educational services that are available to students in my district	1	2	3	4	9
b. Students who are eligible for supplemental services have convenient service providers available to them	1	2	3	4	9
c. Supplemental educational services are effective in meeting the specific needs of English Language Learners (i.e., Limited English Proficient students) in my district	1	2	3	4	9
d. Supplemental educational services are effective in meeting the specific needs of special education students (i.e., students with IEPs) in my district.......................................	1	2	3	4	9
e. We formally review the effectiveness of supplemental service providers operating in our district	1	2	3	4	9
f. The instruction offered by supplemental service providers is well-aligned with state content standards	1	2	3	4	9

E. Highly Qualified Teachers

16. To what extent have the NCLB requirements for highly qualified teachers hindered the district's ability to retain existing teachers and to hire new teachers during the current school year (2004-05)? (Circle one number in each row.)

Effect on the district's ability to:	Not a hindrance	A minor hindrance	A moderate hindrance	A major hindrance
a. Retain existing teachers	1	2	3	4
b. Hire new teachers	1	2	3	4

7

Section II. District Assistance and Interventions

17. During the 2004-05 school year (including the summer of 2004), how many hours are provided by your district for principal and teacher professional development during regular contract hours? (Write your best estimates on the lines below or write "DK" if you don't know.)

_____ hours of professional development for each principal (on average)

_____ hours of professional development for each teacher (on average)

18. In the past three school years, has the district taken any of the following steps to assist schools in aligning curriculum and instruction with state or district content standards in each of the following subjects? (Circle at least one number in each row.)

		Mathematics	Science	Reading/ Language Arts/English	None of these subjects
a.	Developed local content standards that augment state content standards	1	2	3	9
b.	Established detailed curriculum guidelines aligned with state content standards......................................	1	2	3	9
c.	Developed a specific "pacing plan" or "instructional calendar" aligned with state content standards.........	1	2	3	9
d.	Monitored and provided feedback on the implementation of state content standards in classrooms (e.g., by reviewing lesson plans or students' work or by conducting walk-throughs)	1	2	3	9
e.	Provided sample lessons linked to the state content standards	1	2	3	9
f.	Mapped out the alignment of required textbooks and instructional programs to the state content standards	1	2	3	9
g.	Mapped out the alignment of required textbooks and instructional programs to the state assessments...	1	2	3	9

8

19. During the 2004-05 school year, has the district <u>required</u> any elementary schools or middle schools to make the following changes in their general instructional program? (Circle one number for elementary schools and one for middle schools in each row.)

	Elementary Schools			Middle Schools		
	<u>None</u>	<u>Some</u>	<u>All</u>	<u>None</u>	<u>Some</u>	<u>All</u>
a. Increasing instructional time for all students (e.g., by lengthening the school day or year, shortening recess)...	1	2	3	1	2	3
b. Offering remedial assistance to students outside the school day (other than NCLB-required supplemental educational services)............................	1	2	3	1	2	3
c. Instituting full-day kindergarten....................................	1	2	3	1	2	3
d. Adopting a formal school reform model (e.g., Coalition for Essential Schools, Accelerated Schools)	1	2	3	1	2	3

9

20. During the 2004-05 school year, has the district <u>required</u> any elementary schools or middle schools to make the following changes in their <u>mathematics</u> instructional program? (Circle one number for elementary schools and one for middle schools in each row.)

	Elementary Schools			Middle Schools		
	<u>None</u>	<u>Some</u>	<u>All</u>	<u>None</u>	<u>Some</u>	<u>All</u>
a. Adopting a new mathematics curriculum or instructional program (e.g., Saxon Mathematics, Connected Math)	1	2	3	1	2	3
b. Increasing the amount of time spent on mathematics instruction for <u>all</u> students......................	1	2	3	1	2	3
c. Increasing the amount of time spent on mathematics instruction specifically for <u>low-achieving</u> students...	1	2	3	1	2	3
d. Assigning a school-site instructional specialist or coach to support mathematics instruction	1	2	3	1	2	3
e. Administering common "interim" or "progress" tests every few weeks to monitor student progress in mathematics...	1	2	3	1	2	3
f. Implementing focused test preparation materials or activities in mathematics...	1	2	3	1	2	3
g. Eliminating some remedial mathematics courses or instruction and requiring all students to take more challenging mathematics courses or instruction	1	2	3	1	2	3
h. Creating separate mathematics classes for low-achieving students...	1	2	3	1	2	3

21. During the 2004-05 school year, has the district <u>required</u> any elementary schools or middle schools to make the following changes in their <u>science</u> instructional program? (Circle one number for elementary schools and one for middle schools in each row.)

	Elementary Schools			Middle Schools		
	None	Some	All	None	Some	All
a. Adopting a new science curriculum or instructional program (e.g., Full Option Science System-FOSS) ...	1	2	3	1	2	3
b. Increasing the amount of time spent on science instruction for <u>all</u> students	1	2	3	1	2	3
c. Increasing the amount of time spent on science instruction specifically for <u>low-achieving</u> students......	1	2	3	1	2	3
d. Assigning a school-site instructional specialist or coach to support science instruction...........................	1	2	3	1	2	3
e. Administering common "interim" or "progress" tests every few weeks to monitor student progress in science	1	2	3	1	2	3
f. Implementing focused test preparation materials or activities in science..	1	2	3	1	2	3
g. Requiring all students to take more challenging science courses or instruction	1	2	3	1	2	3
h. Creating separate science classes for low-achieving students..	1	2	3	1	2	3

22. During the 2004-05 school year, has your district provided the following types of <u>technical assistance</u> for low performing schools, for high performing schools, for all schools, or for no schools? (Circle one number in each row.)

	No schools	Low performing schools	High performing schools	All schools
a. Assisting the school in analyzing assessment data to identify and address problems in instruction	1	2	3	4
b. Helping with school improvement planning (e.g., guiding the process, identifying strategies, revising the school plan) ..	1	2	3	4
c. Assisting the school in implementing parental involvement strategies	1	2	3	4
d. Helping the school obtain additional professional development based on scientifically based research..............	1	2	3	4
e. Assisting the school in implementing instructional strategies that have been proven to be effective	1	2	3	4
f. Assisting the school in analyzing and revising its budget to use resources more effectively	1	2	3	4
g. Providing additional instructional materials and books	1	2	3	4
h. Assigning additional full-time school-level staff to support teacher development	1	2	3	4
i. Providing before- or after-school, weekend or summer programs	1	2	3	4
j. Helping the school to obtain more experienced teachers........	1	2	3	4
k. Providing a coach or mentor to assist the principal..................	1	2	3	4
l. Helping schools prepare complete and accurate data to comply with NCLB reporting requirements	1	2	3	4
m. Providing guidance for teaching grade-level standards to English Language Learners and/or special education students	1	2	3	4

12

23. During the 2004-05 school year, did your district perform the following NCLB-defined <u>interventions</u> with schools identified for corrective action (i.e., schools that did not make AYP for <u>four or more years</u>)? (Circle one number in each row.)

☐   If there are no schools identified for corrective action under NCLB in this district, check this box and skip to Question 24, page 14.

	Yes	No
a. Significantly decreasing management authority at the school level..	1	2
b. Appointing an outside expert to advise the school..........	1	2
c. Extending the school day or the school year...................	1	2
d. Restructuring the internal organization of the school......	1	2
e. Reassigning or demoting the principal.............................	1	2
f. Replacing school staff who are relevant to the failure to make AYP...	1	2
g. Replacing all or most of the school staff..........................	1	2
h. Reopening the school as a public charter school............	1	2
i. Entering into a contract with a private management company to operate the school..	1	2
j. Other (specify):_____ .	1	2

13

Section III. State Technical Assistance and Interventions

A. State Interactions with Individual Schools

24. During the 2004-05 school year, did the state Department of Education implement any of the following NCLB-defined interventions with <u>individual schools</u> in your district that were identified for improvement (i.e., schools that did not make AYP for two or more consecutive years)? (Circle one number in each row.)

☐   If there are no schools identified for improvement under NCLB in this district, check this box and skip to Question 25, page15.

		<u>Yes</u>	<u>No</u>
a.	Assigning a state-approved school support team to review school operations, evaluate school plans, and make recommendations for improvement...	1	2
b.	Designating and assigning a distinguished principal and/or teacher to work with the school..	1	2
c.	Providing assistance to schools through institutions of higher education, educational service agencies, or private providers of scientifically based technical assistance..	1	2
d.	Providing special grants to support school improvement.................................	1	2

14

B. State Interactions with the District as a Whole

25. Think about the technical assistance your district received from the state Department of Education or from regional educational offices (e.g., County Office of Education, Regional Educational Service Agencies, Intermediate Units) during the 2003-04 school year. For each technical assistance activity please answer three questions:

    A. Did your district need technical assistance in this area?
    B. Regardless of need, did your district receive technical assistance in this area?
    C. If received, was the technical assistance sufficient to meet your district's needs?

    Include all forms of technical assistance (e.g., visits to the district, workshops, video-conferences, and Web-based technical assistance.)

    (In each row, circle one number to indicate whether the assistance was needed, another to indicate if it was received, and if received, circle a number to indicate if it was sufficient to meet your district's needs.)

	Needed? Yes	Needed? No	Received? Yes	Received? No	Sufficient? Yes	Sufficient? No
a. Clarifying accountability system rules and requirements	1	2	1	2	1	2
b. Developing and implementing a district improvement plan	1	2	1	2	1	2
c. Helping the district work with schools in need of improvement	1	2	1	2	1	2
d. Developing curriculum guides or model lessons based on state content standards	1	2	1	2	1	2
e. Using data more effectively	1	2	1	2	1	2
f. Providing effective professional development	1	2	1	2	1	2
g. Identifying effective methods and instructional strategies grounded in scientifically based research	1	2	1	2	1	2
h. Promoting parent involvement	1	2	1	2	1	2

26. Is your <u>district</u> currently identified as in need of improvement under the NCLB accountability system (i.e., the district did not make AYP for <u>two or more consecutive school years</u>)?

Yes.................................... 1   ➔ Continue with Question 27

No...................................... 2   ➔ Skip to Question 29, page 17

27. For how many years has your <u>district</u> been identified as in need of improvement (count the current school year as one whole year)?

_____ years

28. During the 2004-05 school year, did the state Department of Education implement any of the following NCLB-defined interventions with your <u>district</u>? (Circle one number in each row.)

		Yes	No
a.	Helping you notify parents that your district is in need of improvement...........	1	2
b.	Deferring programmatic funds or reducing administrative funds......................	1	2
c.	Instituting and fully implementing a new curriculum based on state and local content standards..	1	2
d.	Replacing district personnel who are relevant to the failure to make AYP	1	2
e.	Removing schools from the jurisdiction of the district	1	2
f.	Appointing a receiver or trustee to administer the affairs of the district	1	2
g.	Restructuring the district..	1	2
h.	Authorizing students to transfer from district schools to schools in a higher-performing district...	1	2

16

Section IV. District Environment

29. Please indicate how, if at all, the following features of your job and your district have changed <u>as a result of the state's accountability system</u> under NCLB. (Circle one number in each row.)

		Changed for the worse	Did not change due to the accountability system	Changed for the better
a.	My ability to be an instructional leader	1	2	3
b.	My relationship with principals	1	2	3
c.	Principals' focus on student achievement	1	2	3
d.	Principals' relationships with their staff	1	2	3
e.	Principals' morale	1	2	3
f	Academic rigor of the curriculum	1	2	3
g.	Coordination of the mathematics curriculum across schools and grade levels	1	2	3
h.	Coordination of the science curriculum across schools and grade levels	1	2	3
i.	Parents' involvement with their children's education	1	2	3
j.	Use of scientifically based research to guide instructional planning	1	2	3
k.	Use of data for decision making throughout the district	1	2	3
l.	Communication between the district and the schools	1	2	3
m.	Our ability to recruit and/or retain principals and teachers to work in low-performing schools	1	2	3

17

30. To what extent does each of the following conditions <u>hinder</u> your efforts to improve the performance of students in your district? (Circle one number in each row.)

	Not a hindrance	Slight hindrance	Moderate hindrance	Great hindrance
a. Shortage of qualified principals	1	2	3	4
b. Shortage of highly qualified mathematics teachers	1	2	3	4
c. Shortage of highly qualified science teachers	1	2	3	4
d. Shortage of highly qualified teachers in other fields	1	2	3	4
e. Inadequate school facilities	1	2	3	4
f. Inadequate time to plan before implementing reforms	1	2	3	4
g. Shortage of high-quality professional development opportunities for <u>teachers</u>	1	2	3	4
h. Shortage of high-quality professional development opportunities for <u>principals</u>	1	2	3	4
i. Lack of adequate funding	1	2	3	4
j. Frequent changes in state policy or leadership (e.g., state superintendent)	1	2	3	4
k. Complying with rules and policies of teacher associations	1	2	3	4
l. Disagreements with district school board over policies or programs	1	2	3	4
m. Shortage of standards-based curriculum materials	1	2	3	4

31. Does the district have sufficient staff with the necessary skills to perform the following school improvement functions? (Circle one number in each row.)

Adequate capacity to:	Yes	No
a. Facilitate improvement in low-performing schools	1	2
b. Help schools to analyze data for school improvement	1	2
c. Help schools identify research-based strategies for improvement	1	2
d. Conduct professional development tailored to the needs of teachers...	1	2
e. Conduct professional development tailored to the needs of principals	1	2
f. Align curriculum with state content standards and state assessments	1	2

32. How centralized or decentralized is your district with respect to decisions about curriculum and instruction?

"Completely centralized" means that all important decisions about curriculum and instruction are made by district administrators. "Completely decentralized" means that all important decisions about curriculum and instruction are made by principals and teachers. (Circle one number.)

Completely Decentralized				Completely Centralized
1	2	3	4	5

33. During the 2003-04 and 2004-05 school years, how has your district changed in terms of decisions about curriculum and instruction? (Circle one number.)

The district has become much more centralized 1

The district has become somewhat more centralized 2

The district has stayed the same 3

The district has become somewhat more decentralized 4

The district has become much more decentralized 5

19

Section V. Title I Resources

34. What is the district doing in the current school year (2004-05) to comply with the NCLB requirement that districts set aside portions of their Title I funds for specific activities (e.g., choice-related transportation, supplemental educational services, professional development)? (Circle one number in each row.)

		Yes	No
a.	Reducing the Title I allocation to all Title I schools	1	2
b.	Reducing the Title I allocation only to Title I schools identified as in need of improvement	1	2
c.	Reducing the Title I allocation only to Title I schools not identified as in need of improvement	1	2
d.	Reducing Title I positions in the district office	1	2
e.	Scaling back other Title I services and expenditures (specify):	1	2

_____

35. To what extent do you agree or disagree with the following statements about the impact of NCLB in the district for the current school year (2004-05)? (Circle one number in each row.)

	Strongly disagree	Disagree	Agree	Strongly agree
a. The requirement to set aside 20% of Title I funds for transfers and supplemental services makes it difficult for us to plan for the next school year........	1	2	3	4
b. Our inability to include administrative costs in the 20% set-aside of Title I funds forces us to cut back on other services......................................	1	2	3	4
c. We have adequate funding to implement the requirements of NCLB	1	2	3	4
d. We need additional staff to comply with the program and reporting requirements of NCLB.......	1	2	3	4
e. We have new technology to comply with the NCLB reporting requirements.................................	1	2	3	4
f. Teachers receive more staff development to improve student achievement and/or to understand the new state accountability system as a result of NCLB...	1	2	3	4
g. We provide more technical assistance to schools to implement the curriculum, hiring, testing and reporting requirements of NCLB..........	1	2	3	4
h. We are eliminating programs (e.g., art, music) to provide more instruction in core subjects	1	2	3	4
i We are increasing our academic expectations for special education students and/or English Language Learners	1	2	3	4
j. There is a decline in community support for our schools..	1	2	3	4

36. During the 2004-05 school year, did your district remove Title I funds from any schools to avoid the consequences of NLCB (e.g., transfers, supplemental educational services)? (Circle one number.)

Yes..................................... 1

No..................................... 2

37. During the 2004-05 school year, did your district transfer special education students from one school to another to reduce the number of schools that would not meet their NCLB targets? (Circle one number.)

Yes..................................... 1

No..................................... 2

21

Section VI: Background Information

38. Please indicate the number of years you have served as an administrator or a teacher in this district or in other districts. (Fill in each space with zero or another number.)

Position	Number of years in THIS district	Number of years at OTHER districts
a. Superintendent	_____	_____
b. Other District Administrative Position	_____	_____
c. Principal or Assistant Principal	_____	_____
d. Teacher	_____	_____

39. How many people (including yourself) have served as Superintendent in this district in the past five school years? (Write in your best estimate on the line below or "DK" if you don't know.)

_____ people

Thank you very much for completing this survey.

Please place your completed survey in the postage paid envelope, seal it, and mail it to RAND.

2/1/05

Implementing
Standards-Based
Accountability

2005 Principal Survey (Georgia Version)

This is a voluntary survey of principals in a random sample of elementary and middle schools in California, Georgia and Pennsylvania.

You should complete this survey if
you are the principal of a school with students in grades 3, 4, 5, 7 or 8.

You should NOT complete this survey if
you are not the school principal, OR if your school does not have any students in grades 3, 4, 5, 7 and 8.

If you fall into the second category, please check here ☐ and return the uncompleted survey in the enclosed envelope.

The time needed to complete this survey is approximately 45 minutes.
We promise to keep your answers confidential.

When finished, place the completed survey in the business-reply envelope, seal the envelope using the security sticker, and return it to your school coordinator. If you prefer, you may return the survey yourself. In either case, we will send you $25 in recognition of your help on this study.

Your questionnaire should be returned to your school coordinator, or if you prefer to mail it yourself you may send it to:

> *RAND Survey*
> *c/o Debbie Alexander*
> *1650 Research Blvd.*
> *Westat*
> *Rockville, MD 20850*

If you have any questions about this survey or about the study, you may contact Ms. Alexander at 1-800-937-8281, ext. 2088 or by email at DebbieAlexander@Westat.com.

Project 7806.01.30.03

Section I: Curriculum and Instruction

1. Does your school operate either a Title I schoolwide program or a Title I targeted assistance program?
    (Circle one number.)

    We do not receive Title I funds.. 1 → Skip to Question 3

    We operate a Title I schoolwide program.. 2 → Skip to Question 3

    We operate a Title I targeted assistance program.. 3 → Continue with Question 2

    I don't know .... 4 → Skip to Question 3

2. How many students receive Title I targeted assistance services?   _____ students

3. Are educators at your school currently implementing a <u>formal school reform model</u> (e.g., Success for All, Accelerated
    Schools, Coalition of Essential Schools, etc.)? (Circle one number.)

    Yes 1   → Continue with Question 4

    No..................................... 2   → Skip to Question 6

4. In what term and year did your school begin implementing the school reform model (e.g., Spring 2001)?
    (Write in the term and the year.)

    _____ term _____ year

5. Did your district or state <u>require</u> your school to adopt the school reform model? (Circle one number.)

    Yes 1

    No..................................... 2

6. Have educators at your school implemented a new mathematics curriculum or instructional program during the 2003-04 or
    2004-05 school year (e.g., Everyday Math, Saxon Math, etc.)? Include here any mathematics programs that may be part
    of a school reform model. (Circle one number.)

    Yes 1   → Continue with Question 7

    No 2   → Skip to Question 9 on page 3

7. In what term and year did your school begin implementing the new mathematics curriculum or instructional
    program (e.g., Fall 2003)? (Write in the term and the year.)

    _____ term _____ year

8. Did your district or state <u>require</u> your school to adopt the new mathematics curriculum or instructional program?
    (Circle one number.)

    Yes 1

    No 2

9. Have educators at your school implemented a new science curriculum or instructional program during the 2003-04 or 2004-05 school year (e.g., new hands-on kits or a new textbook series)?   Include here any science programs that may be part of a school reform model. (Circle one number.)

    Yes .... 1 → Continue with Question 10

    No .... 2 → Skip to Question 12

10. In what term and year did your school begin implementing the new science curriculum or instructional program (e.g., Fall 2003)? (Write in the term and the year.)

    _____ term _____ year

11. Did your district or state require your school to adopt the new science curriculum or instructional program? (Circle one number.)

    Yes 1

    No 2

Section II. Standards, Assessments and Accountability

A. Standards

12. How familiar are you with the Georgia Quality Core Curriculum (QCC) and the Georgia Performance Standards (GPS) in the following subjects? (Circle one number in each row.)

	Never heard of them	Heard of them, but don't know much about them	Am familiar with the main points, but not the details	Have a thorough understanding of them
a. The Georgia Quality Core Curriculum (QCC) for Mathematics	1	2	3	4
b. The Georgia Performance Standards (GPS) for Mathematics..........................	1	2	3	4
c. The Georgia Quality Core Curriculum (QCC) for Science	1	2	3	4
d. The Georgia Performance Standards (GPS) for Science.................................	1	2	3	4
e. The Georgia Quality Core Curriculum (QCC) for English/Language Arts.........	1	2	3	4
f. The Georgia Performance Standards (GPS) for English/Language Arts	1	2	3	4

3

13. How <u>useful</u> are the Georgia Quality Core Curriculum (QCC) and the Georgia Performance Standards (GPS) in each subject for guiding decisions about the school's curriculum? (Circle one number in each row.)

	Not at all useful	Minimally useful	Moderately useful	Very useful	I don't know
a. The Georgia Quality Core Curriculum (QCC) for Mathematics.....	1	2	3	4	9
b. The Georgia Performance Standards (GPS) for Mathematics	1	2	3	4	9
c. The Georgia Quality Core Curriculum (QCC) for Science............	1	2	3	4	9
d. The Georgia Performance Standards (GPS) for Science	1	2	3	4	9
e. The Georgia Quality Core Curriculum (QCC) for English/Language Arts........................	1	2	3	4	9
f. The Georgia Performance Standards (GPS) for English/Language Arts........................	1	2	3	4	9

B. Assessments

14. Has your school and/or district ever done any of the following activities to help teachers prepare students for Georgia Criterion-Referenced Competency Tests (CRCT)? (Circle one number in each row.)

	Yes	No
a. Distributed commercial test preparation materials (e.g., practice tests)..........	1	2
b. Distributed released copies of the CRCT test or items.....................................	1	2
c. Discussed methods for preparing students for the CRCT at staff meetings ...	1	2
d. Encouraged or required teachers to spend more time on tested subjects and less time on other subjects..	1	2
e. Helped teachers identify content that is likely to appear on the CRCT so they can cover it adequately in their instruction	1	2
f. Encouraged teachers to focus on students <u>close</u> to meeting standards (i.e., close to proficient)	1	2

4

15. During this school year, was the following information or assistance regarding last year's (2003-04) CRCT results available to you? If available, how <u>useful</u> was it for guiding instruction and school improvement? (Circle one number in each row.)

	Not available	Available and:			
		Not useful	Minimally useful	Moderately useful	Very useful
a. Reports of last year's test results for the students at your school <u>last</u> year	1	2	3	4	5
b. Reports of last year's test results for the students at your school <u>this</u> year	1	2	3	4	5
c. Test results summarized for each student subgroup (e.g., special education, race/ethnicity, economically disadvantaged)	1	2	3	4	5
d. Test results disaggregated by subtopic or skill	1	2	3	4	5
e. Computer software or systems for re-analyzing test results	1	2	3	4	5
f. Workshops or meetings where test results are presented and explained	1	2	3	4	5
g. Training on how to use test results for instructional planning or school improvement	1	2	3	4	5

5

16. To what extent do you agree or disagree with each of the following statements about your state's accountability system (including standards, assessments, adequate yearly progress targets, rewards, and sanctions) and the results from the CRCT? (Circle one number in each row.)

	Strongly disagree	Disagree	Agree	Strongly agree
a. The test results we receive have explicit links to content standards and/or lesson plans	1	2	3	4
b. The district and/or state helps me understand the state accountability system requirements	1	2	3	4
c. The district and/or state helps my school staff understand the state accountability system requirements ...	1	2	3	4
d. The information we receive about our school's performance is clear and easy to understand......................	1	2	3	4
e. The information we receive about our school's performance is timely	1	2	3	4
f. Teachers in my school have the skills and knowledge needed to analyze and make use of the test results we receive	1	2	3	4
g. Teachers in my school review test results and use them to tailor instruction	1	2	3	4
h. State test scores accurately reflect the achievement of students in my school	1	2	3	4
i. The system of accountability does not allow sufficient flexibility for meeting the needs of special education students (i.e., students with IEPs)	1	2	3	4
j. The system of accountability does not allow sufficient flexibility for meeting the needs of English Language Learners (i.e., Limited English Proficient students)	1	2	3	4
k. Overall, the state's accountability system has been beneficial for students in my school.........................	1	2	3	4

6

17. How useful are the CRCT results in helping you make the following decisions? (Circle one number in each row.)

		Not useful	Minimally useful	Moderately useful	Very useful
a.	Making changes to the school's curriculum and instructional materials	1	2	3	4
b.	Developing a school improvement plan	1	2	3	4
c.	Making decisions regarding student promotion or retention	1	2	3	4
d.	Identifying students who need additional instructional support	1	2	3	4
e.	Making decisions on how much time is spent on each academic subject	1	2	3	4
f.	Assigning students to teachers	1	2	3	4
g.	Focusing teacher professional development	1	2	3	4
h.	Identifying teacher strengths and weaknesses	1	2	3	4

C. Adequate Yearly Progress (AYP) Targets

18. Did your school make adequate yearly progress (AYP) for 2003-04? (Circle one number.)

Yes 1

No 2

I don't know 3

19. Is your school currently in Needs Improvement status for not making AYP for two consecutive school years? (Circle one number.)

Yes 1   → Continue with Question 20 on page 8

No 2   → Skip to Question 21 on page 8

I don't know... 3   → Skip to Question 21 on page 8

20. What year of Needs Improvement status is your school currently in? (Circle one number.)

Year One... 1

Year Two... 2

Year Three 3

Year Four 4

Year Five... 5

Year Six... 6

Year Seven 7

I don't know... 8

21. To what extent do you agree or disagree with the following statements about adequate yearly progress (AYP) targets?
(Circle one number in each row.)

	Strongly disagree	Disagree	Agree	Strongly agree
a. My school can attain the AYP targets for 2004-05	1	2	3	4
b. My school can attain the AYP targets for the next five years	1	2	3	4
c. It is difficult for us to meet the 95% participation rate on the state assessments	1	2	3	4
d. Differences in student characteristics from year to year make it difficult for my school to make AYP	1	2	3	4
e. I have a clear understanding of the criteria our school needs to meet to make AYP	1	2	3	4
f. My school's AYP status accurately reflects the overall performance of our school	1	2	3	4
g. Because of pressure to meet the AYP target, my staff and I are focusing more on improving student achievement than we would without the AYP target	1	2	3	4

8

D. Transfers

22. NCLB requires that Title I students be given the option of transferring to another school if their school does not meet its AYP target for two years in a row (i.e., in Needs Improvement status). Are Title I students in your school eligible under NCLB to transfer to another school in 2004-05? (Circle one number.)

Yes 1	→	Continue with Question 23
No 2	→	Skip to Question 24
There are no Title I students in the school 3	→	Skip to Question 24
I don't know.. 4	→	Skip to Question 24

23. During the current school year (2004-05), approximately how many Title I students from your school exercised the option to <u>transfer to another school?</u> (Write your best estimate on the line below. If no students elected to transfer to another school, write in "0." Write "DK" if you don't know.)

_____ students

24. During the current school year (2004-05), approximately how many Title I students from other schools that are in Needs Improvement status <u>transferred into</u> your school under NCLB rules? (Write your best estimate on the line below. If no students transferred in to your school, write in "0." Write "DK" if you don't know.)

_____ students

25. If no Title I students transferred into your school <u>and</u> no Title I students transferred out of your school under NCLB rules in 2004-05 (i.e., if the answers to Questions 23 and 24 are both zero), check here ❑ and skip to Question 28 on page 10. Otherwise, continue with Question 26.

26. Have any of the following occurred at your school in the 2004-05 school year as a result of <u>student transfers</u> under NCLB? (Circle one number in each row.)

	<u>Yes</u>	<u>No</u>	I don't <u>know</u>
a. We hired additional staff	1	2	9
b. We decreased the number of staff...............................	1	2	9
c. We converted other facilities (e.g., multi-purpose room) into classrooms..	1	2	9
d. We increased class size	1	2	9
e. We decreased class size	1	2	9
f. More students shared textbooks or other curriculum materials..	1	2	9

9

27. To what extent do you agree or disagree with the following statements about the impact of student transfers under NCLB on your school? (Circle one number in each row.)

	Strongly disagree	Disagree	Agree	Strongly agree
a. It has become difficult to plan for the next year, because I do not know how many students will be attending my school...........	1	2	3	4
b. The possibility of transfers has increased pressure on staff to improve student performance.....................................	1	2	3	4
c. It is more difficult to communicate with parents because more students live far away from school.........................	1	2	3	4
d. The NCLB transfer policy has not had a noticeable effect on my school	1	2	3	4

E. Supplemental Educational Services Outside the School Day

28. NCLB requires that parents of Title I students be allowed to request "supplemental educational services" (e.g., tutoring) from a state-approved, third-party provider if their child's school did not make AYP targets for three consecutive years (e.g., in Year Two of Needs Improvement status). Are Title I students in your school eligible under NCLB to receive supplemental educational services (e.g., tutoring) in 2004-05? (Circle one number.)

Yes 1   → Continue with Question 29

No.. 2   → Skip to Question 33 on page 12

There are no Title I students in the school 3   → Skip to Question 33 on page 12

I don't know 4   → Skip to Question 33 on page 12

29. Approximately how many Title I students at your school are eligible for supplemental educational services in 2004-05? (Write your best estimate on the line below, or write "DK" if you don't know.)

_____ students

30. Approximately how many Title I students at your school receive supplemental educational services in 2004-05? (Write your best estimate on the line below, or write "DK" if you don't know.)

_____ students

10

31. Are supplemental educational services available to Title I students in your school in the following subjects? If available, how well are they aligned with your state's academic content standards in each subject? (Circle one number in each row.)

	Not available in this subject	Available and:			
		Not at all aligned	Partially aligned	Well aligned	Don't know
a. Reading/Language Arts/English	1	2	3	4	9
b. Mathematics	1	2	3	4	9
c. Science	1	2	3	4	9

32. To what extent do you agree or disagree with the following statements about supplemental educational services available to your students as a result of NCLB? (Circle one number in each row.)

	Strongly disagree	Disagree	Agree	Strongly agree	Not applicable
a. I am generally satisfied with the quality of the supplemental educational services that are available to students in my school	1	2	3	4	9
b. Supplemental educational services are conveniently located near students in my school who want them.....................	1	2	3	4	9
c. Many of the students in my school who enroll in supplemental educational services do not attend them regularly ..	1	2	3	4	9
d. Supplemental educational services are effective in meeting the specific needs of English Language Learners (i.e., Limited English Proficient students) in my school	1	2	3	4	9
e. Supplemental educational services are effective in meeting the specific needs of special education students (i.e., students with IEPs) in my school..........	1	2	3	4	9

11

F. Qualified Teachers and Paraprofessionals

33. To comply with the new federal requirements for <u>highly qualified teachers</u>, have you done any of the following at your school in 2004-05? (Circle one number in each row.)

		Yes	No
a.	Change teacher classroom assignments	1	2
b.	Increase class sizes	1	2
c.	Impose stricter hiring rules	1	2
d.	Increase the use of substitute teachers	1	2
e.	Require current teachers to obtain certification	1	2
f.	Fire/transfer teachers who are not highly qualified	1	2
g.	Require current teachers to pass subject matter tests	1	2
h.	Other (Specify) _____ ..	1	2

34. In order to meet the new requirements for qualified Title I instructional <u>paraprofessionals</u>, have you done any of the following at your school in 2004-05? (Circle one number in each row.)

If you do not have any Title I instructional paraprofessionals, check this box ☐ and continue with Question 35 on page 13.

		Yes	No
a.	Fire paraprofessionals who did not meet the requirements	1	2
b.	Require paraprofessionals to take classes	1	2
c.	Reconfigure an instructional program	1	2
d.	Shift some paraprofessionals from instructional roles into non-instructional roles	1	2
e.	Other (Specify) _____ ...	1	2

12

Section III. School Improvement Efforts

35. Have you employed any of the following strategies to make your school better in 2004-05? If you have, how useful were they? (Circle one number in each row.)

		Not employed	Employed and:			
			Not useful	Minimally useful	Moderately useful	Very useful
a.	Improving the school planning process	1	2	3	4	5
b.	Increasing the use of student achievement data to inform instruction...	1	2	3	4	5
c.	Increasing the quantity of teacher professional development...............	1	2	3	4	5
d.	Matching curriculum and instruction with standards and/or assessments.....................................	1	2	3	4	5
e.	Providing before- or after-school, weekend, or summer programs.......	1	2	3	4	5
f.	Creating and/or promoting programs to make the school a more attractive choice for parents and their children	1	2	3	4	5
g.	Using existing research to inform decisions about improvement strategies...	1	2	3	4	5
h.	Restructuring the school day to teach content in greater depth (e.g., establishing a literacy block) ..	1	2	3	4	5
i.	Providing additional instruction to low-achieving students....................	1	2	3	4	5
j.	Increasing instructional time for all students (e.g., by lengthening the school day or year, shortening recess)...	1	2	3	4	5

36. Please indicate up to three of the useful strategies in question 35 that were the most important for making your school better in 2004-05? (Circle no more than three letters.)

a   b   c   d   e   f   g   h   i   j

13

37. During the 2004-05 school year, has your school received any of the following kinds of technical assistance for improvement from your district or state? (Circle one number in each row.)

		Yes	No
a.	School support teams	1	2
b.	Distinguished teachers	1	2
c.	Special grants to support school improvement	1	2
d.	Additional professional development or special access to professional development resources	1	2
e.	A mentor or coach for you (e.g., a distinguished principal, a leadership facilitator, or a school improvement specialist)	1	2
f.	Additional full-time school-level staff to support teacher development	1	2
g.	Other (Specify) _____ ...	1	2

38. During the 2004-05 school year, has your district intervened in your school by taking the following NCLB-defined actions? (Circle one number in each row.)

		Yes	No
a.	Significantly decreasing management authority at the school level	1	2
b.	Appointing an outside expert to advise the school	1	2
c.	Extending the school day or the school year	1	2
d.	Restructuring the internal organization of the school	1	2
e.	Reassigning or demoting the principal	1	2
f.	Replacing school staff who are relevant to the failure to make AYP	1	2
g.	Replacing all or most of the school staff	1	2
h.	Reopening the school as a public charter school	1	2
i.	Entering into a contract with a private management company to operate the school	1	2
j.	Other (Specify) _____ ...	1	2

14

39. Please indicate how, if at all, the following features of your job or your school have changed as a result of your state's accountability system (including standards, assessments, adequate yearly progress targets, rewards, and sanctions). (Circle one number in each row.)

	Changed for the worse	Did not change due to accountability system	Changed for the better
a. My ability to be an instructional leader ...	1	2	3
b. Teachers' focus on student learning	1	2	3
c. Teachers' relationships with their students	1	2	3
d. Morale of school staff..............................	1	2	3
e. Students' learning of important skills and knowledge	1	2	3
f. Students' focus on school work...............	1	2	3
g. Academic rigor of the curriculum............	1	2	3
h. Coordination of the mathematics curriculum across grade levels...............	1	2	3
i. Coordination of the science curriculum across grade levels	1	2	3
j. Parents' involvement with their children's education	1	2	3
k. The extent to which innovative curricular programs or instructional approaches are used	1	2	3
l. Our ability to recruit new teachers/paraprofessionals for our school...	1	2	3

15

40. To what extent do you agree or disagree with the following statements about your district's current role in improving schools? (Circle one number in each row.)

	Strongly disagree	Disagree	Agree	Strongly agree
a. District administrators communicate a clear academic vision for schools in our district	1	2	3	4
b. The superintendent of the district is an effective manager who makes the district run smoothly	1	2	3	4
c. When schools are having difficulty, the district provides assistance needed to help them improve	1	2	3	4
d. District staff provide appropriate support to enable principals to act as instructional leaders..	1	2	3	4
e. District staff provide appropriate instructional support for teachers	1	2	3	4
f. District staff provide support for teaching grade level standards to special education students (i.e., students with IEPs)	1	2	3	4
g. District staff provide support for teaching grade level standards to English Language Learners (i.e., Limited English Proficient students).......................................	1	2	3	4
h. District staff understand the particular needs of our school	1	2	3	4

16

41. To what extent is each of the following a hindrance in your efforts to improve the performance of students in your school? (Circle one number in each row.)

	Not a hindrance	A slight hindrance	A moderate hindrance	A great hindrance
a. Teacher turnover	1	2	3	4
b. Shortage of highly qualified teachers..........	1	2	3	4
c. Shortage of highly qualified teacher aides and paraprofessionals.................................	1	2	3	4
d. Inadequate school facilities.........................	1	2	3	4
e. Inadequate lead time to prepare before implementing reforms.................................	1	2	3	4
f. Lack of teacher planning time built into the school day...	1	2	3	4
g. Lack of high-quality professional development opportunities for teachers......	1	2	3	4
h. Lack of high-quality professional development opportunities for principals	1	2	3	4
i. Lack of adequate funding............................	1	2	3	4
j. Insufficient staff time to meet administrative responsibilities (e.g., filling out paperwork)..	1	2	3	4
k. Frequent changes in district policy and priorities..	1	2	3	4
l. Frequent changes in district leadership (e.g., the superintendent)............................	1	2	3	4
m. Unanticipated problems with space, facilities, transportation, etc.	1	2	3	4
n. Lack of guidance for teaching grade-level standards to special education students (i.e., students with IEPs)	1	2	3	4
o. Lack of guidance for teaching grade-level standards to English Language Learners (i.e., Limited English Proficient students)....	1	2	3	4

17

42. Please estimate how much time you spend on the following activities during <u>a typical week</u>. Also, please indicate whether the amount of time has changed this school year (2004-05) compared to last school year (2003-04). (Circle one number for amount of time and one number for change in each row.)

If you were not a school principal last year, check this box ❑ *and answer only Column 1.*

	COLUMN 1 Amount of time per week				COLUMN 2 Change in 2004-05 compared to 2003-04		
	I do not do this on a weekly basis	A small amount (1-4 hours)	A moderate amount (5-15 hours)	A large amount (more than 15 hours)	Less time than 2003-04	About the same as 2003-04	More time than 2003-04
a. Working on administrative duties, including budgets, personnel management, or paperwork......................	1	2	3	4	1	2	3
b. Observing your teachers' classroom instruction	1	2	3	4	1	2	3
c. Providing feedback to teachers regarding curriculum and instruction..	1	2	3	4	1	2	3
d. Reviewing student assessment results	1	2	3	4	1	2	3
e. Talking with parents and/or community members............................	1	2	3	4	1	2	3
f. Addressing student discipline problems.............	1	2	3	4	1	2	3
g. Planning or conducting teacher professional development workshops....	1	2	3	4	1	2	3
h. Monitoring students in the hallways, playground, lunchroom, etc.	1	2	3	4	1	2	3
i. Collaborating with other principals............................	1	2	3	4	1	2	3
j. Meeting with school leadership teams to plan for school improvement	1	2	3	4	1	2	3

18

43. How centralized or decentralized is your district with respect to decisions about curriculum and instruction?

"Completely centralized" means that all important decisions about curriculum and instruction are made by district administrators. "Completely decentralized" means that all important decisions about curriculum and instruction are made by principals and teachers. (Circle one number.)

Completely Decentralized				Completely Centralized
1	2	3	4	5

44. During the 2003-04 and 2004-05 school years, how has your district changed in terms of decisions about curriculum and instruction? (Circle one number.)

The district has become much more centralized 1

The district has become somewhat more centralized 2

The district has stayed the same 3

The district has become somewhat more decentralized 4

The district has become much more decentralized 5

Section IV: Parent Involvement

45. There are many activities that involve parents in student learning. Which of the following opportunities for parent involvement are available at your school, and if available what percent of your students' parents have participated in each during the 2004-05 school year? (Circle one number in each row.)

			Available; and:			
		Not available	10% or less participate	11–25% participate	26-50% participate	51-75% participate	More than 75% participate
a.	Parent-teacher association/ organization (PTA or PTO)	1	2	3	4	5	6
b.	Open house, back-to-school night or other school-wide events	1	2	3	4	5	6
c.	Science fair, math night or other academically focused events	1	2	3	4	5	6
d.	Parent/teacher conferences........	1	2	3	4	5	6
e.	Education programs for parents (e.g., family literacy, homework support workshops)...	1	2	3	4	5	6
f.	Parent resource center (i.e., a place where parents can get information on school-related issues and gather informally)......	1	2	3	4	5	6
g.	Volunteering in the school...........	1	2	3	4	5	6

19

Section V. Professional Development

46. During the 2004-05 school year (including last summer), how many times did <u>you</u> engage in each of the following <u>professional development activities with other administrators</u>? If you participated, how valuable was each for your own professional development? (Circle one number for frequency and, if you participated, circle one number for value in each row.)

		Frequency of Activity					Value of activity for your professional development		
		Never	A few times	Once or twice a month	Once or twice a week	Almost daily	Not valuable	Moderately valuable	Very valuable
a.	Acting as a coach or mentor to another principal.......	1	2	3	4	5	1	2	3
b.	Receiving coaching or mentoring from another principal.......	1	2	3	4	5	1	2	3
c.	Participating in a formal support network	1	2	3	4	5	1	2	3
d.	Visiting other schools within and/or outside your district........................	1	2	3	4	5	1	2	3
e.	Participating on a district or state committee or taskforce	1	2	3	4	5	1	2	3
f.	Attending college courses for school administrators..........	1	2	3	4	5	1	2	3
g.	Attending conferences, seminars, or workshops for school administrators..........	1	2	3	4	5	1	2	3

20

47. During your participation in professional development activities in the 2004-05 school year (including last summer), how much <u>emphasis</u> was placed on the following areas? (Circle one number in each row.)

If you did not participate in any professional development in 2004-05, check this box ☐ and continue with Question 48.

	No <u>emphasis</u>	Minor <u>emphasis</u>	Moderate <u>emphasis</u>	Major <u>emphasis</u>
a. Managing staff effectively	1	2	3	4
b. Preparing budgets and managing school finances	1	2	3	4
c. Understanding the requirements of the accountability system under NCLB	1	2	3	4
d. Using state assessment results to guide school improvement	1	2	3	4
e. Articulating and implementing a vision for your school	1	2	3	4
f. Working to engage parents in support of your school's efforts...	1	2	3	4
g. Helping teachers understand standards and use curriculum materials	1	2	3	4
h. Meeting the needs of low-achieving students	1	2	3	4

Section VI: Background Information About You and Your School

48. Please indicate the number of years you have served as a teacher and/or an administrator in this school or in other schools. (Fill in all six spaces with zero or a number. Please count this school year as one year.)

Position	Years at THIS school	Years at OTHER schools
a. Principal...	_____	_____
b. Assistant Principal	_____	_____
c. Teacher	_____	_____

21

49. Please answer the following questions about student enrollment and mobility in your school during the 2004-05 school year. (Write your best estimate in each row, or write "DK" if you don't know.)

   a. How many students were enrolled in your school on or around October 1, 2004?.............. _____ students

   b. How many additional students entered your school since the start of the school year? ..... _____ students

   c. How many students left your school since the start of the school year? .... _____ students

50. Please answer the following questions about student subpopulations in your school during the 2004-05 school year. (Write your best estimate in each row, or write "DK" if you don't know.)

   a. How many students are English Language Learners (i.e. Limited English Proficient)? .... _____ students

   b. How many students are special education students (i.e. students with IEPs)? .... _____ students

   c. How many students qualify for free or reduced-price lunch?.. _____ students

   d. How many students are migrant students?.. _____ students

51. Please answer the following questions about the regular <u>teaching staff</u> at your school in 2004-05. (Write your best estimate in each row, or write "DK" if you don't know.)

   a. How many full-time regular classroom teachers are on your staff this school year? .... _____ teachers

   b. How many of these teachers are <u>new</u> to your school this year? .... _____ teachers

   c. How many of your regular classroom teachers hold the certification required for their main teaching assignment?... _____ teachers

   d. How many of your regular classroom teachers have been teaching for less than 3 years?.. _____ teachers

Thank you very much for completing this survey.

Place the completed survey in the business-reply envelope, seal the envelope using the <u>security sticker,</u> and return it to your school coordinator. If you prefer, you may return the survey yourself by mailing it to the address printed below.

Your questionnaire should be returned to your school coordinator, or if you prefer to mail it yourself you may send it to:

RAND Survey
c/o Debbie Alexander
1650 Research Blvd.
Westat
Rockville, MD 20850

If you have any questions about this survey or about the study, you may contact Ms. Alexander at 1-800-937-8281, ext. 2088 or by email at DebbieAlexander@Westat.com.

2/1/05

Implementing Standards-Based Accountability

2005 Teacher Survey   (Georgia Version)

This is a voluntary survey of teachers in a random sample of elementary and middle schools in California, Georgia and Pennsylvania.

You should complete this survey if
you regularly teach mathematics or science to students in grades 3, 4, 5, 7 or 8.

You should NOT complete this survey if
you are a short-term substitute teacher or a teacher's aide, or if you are in a non-teaching position such as a counselor, a librarian, or a psychologist, OR if you do not teach mathematics or science to any students in grades 3, 4, 5, 7 and 8.

If you fall into the second category, please check here ❏ *and return the uncompleted survey in the enclosed envelope.*

The time needed to complete this survey is approximately 45 minutes.
We promise to keep your answers confidential.

When finished, place the completed survey in the business-reply envelope, seal the envelope using the <u>security sticker</u>, and return it to your school coordinator. If you prefer, you may return the survey yourself. In either case, we will send you $25 in recognition of your help on this study.

Your questionnaire should be returned to your school coordinator, or if you prefer to mail it yourself you may send it to:

> *RAND Survey*
> *c/o Debbie Alexander*
> *1650 Research Blvd.*
> *Westat*
> *Rockville, MD 20850*

If you have any questions about this survey or about the study, you may contact Ms. Alexander at 1-800-937-8281, ext. 2088 or by email at DebbieAlexander@Westat.com.

Project 7806.01.30.03

Section I: Your Students and Your Class(es)

1. What grade(s) do you currently teach? (Circle all that apply.)

   K 1 2 3 4 5 6 7 8 9

> *We recognize you may be teaching more than one grade level and your approach may be different for different grade levels. Please answer the survey questions based on what is typical of your teaching overall.*

2. Which statements describe the way the majority of your teaching at your school is organized? (Circle one number in each row.)

	Yes	No
a. I teach multiple subjects to the same class of students (i.e., self-contained classroom)......	1	2
b. I teach courses in a single subject to several different classes of students...........................	1	2
c. I teach multiple subjects to multiple groups of students	1	2
d. I share instructional responsibilities with one or more teachers in teaching multiple subjects to a shared group of students...	1	2
e. I provide instruction (e.g., special education, remedial mathematics) to certain students, who are released from their regular classes	1	2
f. I may teach in more than one of the above arrangements in a single day	1	2
g. Other (Specify:_____) ..	1	2

3. In a typical week, how many students do you teach in total? (Write in a number. Please count each student only once.)

   _____ students in total

4. In a typical week, to how many students do you teach mathematics, science, or reading/language arts/English? (Write a number in each row. Please count each student only once per row.)

   a. Mathematics _____ students

   b. Science _____ students

   c. Reading/Language Arts/English _____ students

5. How many of the students you teach in a typical week have the following characteristics? (Write a number in each row. Please count each student only once per row.)

   a. Classified as English Language Learners
      (Limited English Proficient students) _____ students

   b. Participate in an official Gifted and Talented
      Education (GATE) program _____ students

   c. Classified as Special Education students with
      Individualized Education Plans (IEPs) _____ students

   d. Pulled out of regular class for remedial instruction _____ students

2

6. How has the amount of instruction your students receive in a typical week changed from last school year (2003-04) to this school year (2004-05) in each of the following subjects regardless of who is teaching them? (Circle one number in each row.)

	Decreased by more than 45 minutes per week	Decreased by 1-45 minutes per week	Stayed the same	Increased by 1-45 minutes per week	Increased by more than 45 minutes per week	I don't know
a. Mathematics	1	2	3	4	5	9
b. Science	1	2	3	4	5	9
c. Reading/Language Arts/English	1	2	3	4	5	9
d. Social Studies	1	2	3	4	5	9
e. Art/Music	1	2	3	4	5	9
f. Physical Education/Health	1	2	3	4	5	9

7. How familiar are you with the Georgia Quality Core Curriculum (QCC) and the Georgia Performance Standards (GPS) in the following subjects? (Circle one number in each row.)

	Never heard of them	Heard of them, but don't know much about them	Familiar with the main points, but not the details	Have a thorough understanding of them
a. The Georgia Quality Core Curriculum (QCC) for Mathematics	1	2	3	4
b. The Georgia Performance Standards (GPS) for Mathematics	1	2	3	4
c. The Georgia Quality Core Curriculum (QCC) for Science	1	2	3	4
d. The Georgia Performance Standards (GPS) for Science	1	2	3	4
e. The Georgia Quality Core Curriculum (QCC) for English/Language Arts	1	2	3	4
f. The Georgia Performance Standards (GPS) for English/Language Arts	1	2	3	4

3

Section II: Mathematics Instruction

*Questions 8 to 20 ask about your mathematics instruction. If you do **not** teach mathematics to any students in grades 3, 4, 5, 7, or 8, please check here ☐ and skip to Question 21 on page 11.*

In the following questions, "Georgia standards in mathematics" refers to the Georgia Quality Core Curriculum (QCC) and, to the extent they have been implemented, the Georgia Performance Standards (GPS). When answering questions, please respond in terms of the current Georgia standards in mathematics you are working toward this year.

8. Did your district or state ever take any of the following actions to assist schools and teachers using the Georgia standards in mathematics for improving curriculum and instruction in mathematics? If the action occurred, how useful was it to you as a teacher? (Circle one number in each row.)

	Did not occur	Occurred and it was:			
		Not useful	Minimally useful	Moderately useful	Very useful
a. Established detailed curriculum guidelines aligned with the Georgia standards in mathematics	1	2	3	4	5
b. Established a specific "pacing plan" or "instructional calendar" indicating a schedule of instructional content throughout the year..	1	2	3	4	5
c. Monitored and provided feedback on the implementation of the standards in classrooms (e.g., by reviewing lesson plans or students' work or by conducting walk-throughs)	1	2	3	4	5
d. Mapped out the alignment of textbooks and instructional programs to the Georgia standards in mathematics	1	2	3	4	5
e. Provided sample lessons linked to the Georgia standards in mathematics...	1	2	3	4	5

4

9. To what extent do you agree or disagree with the following statements about the <u>Georgia standards in mathematics</u>? (Circle one number in each row.)

	Strongly disagree	Disagree	Agree	Strongly agree	I don't know
a. The Georgia standards in mathematics include more content than can be covered adequately in the school year...	1	2	3	4	9
b. The Georgia standards in mathematics do not give enough emphasis to mathematical reasoning and problem-solving	1	2	3	4	9
c. The Georgia standards in mathematics do not cover some important content areas.......................	1	2	3	4	9
d. The Georgia standards in mathematics are useful for planning my lessons	1	2	3	4	9
e. I have aligned my teaching with the Georgia standards in mathematics...	1	2	3	4	9

10. To what extent do you agree or disagree with the following statements about the <u>mathematics textbooks and curriculum materials</u> provided by your school? (Circle one number in each row.)

	Strongly disagree	Disagree	Agree	Strongly agree	I don't know
a. I am satisfied with the <u>quality</u> of mathematics textbooks and curriculum materials in my school....	1	2	3	4	9
b. The mathematics textbooks and curriculum materials are well aligned with the Georgia standards in mathematics...	1	2	3	4	9
c. The mathematics textbooks and curriculum materials are too difficult for the majority of my students..	1	2	3	4	9
d. I often need to supplement the mathematics textbooks and curriculum materials with additional material to cover the Georgia standards in mathematics adequately	1	2	3	4	9

5

11. To what extent do you agree or disagree with the following statements about the <u>Criterion-Referenced Competency Test (CRCT) in mathematics</u>? Please answer the questions whether or not your students are tested. (Circle one number in each row.)

	Strongly disagree	Disagree	Agree	Strongly agree	I don't know
a. The mathematics CRCT is a good measure of students' mastery of the Georgia standards in mathematics..	1	2	3	4	9
b. The mathematics CRCT is too difficult for the majority of my students	1	2	3	4	9
c. The mathematics CRCT <u>includes</u> considerable content that is <u>not</u> in our curriculum	1	2	3	4	9
d. The mathematics CRCT <u>omits</u> considerable content that is in our curriculum	1	2	3	4	9
e. I have aligned my teaching with the mathematics CRCT..	1	2	3	4	9
f. The mathematics CRCT adequately measures mathematical reasoning and problem-solving........	1	2	3	4	9
g. I feel a great deal of pressure to improve my students' scores on the mathematics CRCT	1	2	3	4	9

12. During this school year, was the following information or assistance regarding last year's (2003-04) mathematics CRCT results available to you? If available, how useful was it for guiding your instruction? (Circle one number in each row.)

	Not available	Available; and it was				Not applicable
		Not useful	Minimally useful	Moderately useful	Very useful	
a. Reports of last year's mathematics test results for the students you taught <u>last year</u>........	1	2	3	4	5	9
b. Reports of last year's mathematics test results for the students you teach <u>this year</u>	1	2	3	4	5	--
c. Mathematics test results summarized for each student subgroup (e.g., special education, race/ethnicity, economically disadvantaged)	1	2	3	4	5	--
d. Mathematics test results disaggregated by topic or skill	1	2	3	4	5	--
e. Computer software or systems for re-analyzing mathematics test results....................................	1	2	3	4	5	--
f. Workshops or meetings where mathematics test results are presented and explained...............	1	2	3	4	5	--
g. Training on how to use mathematics test results for instructional planning or school improvement	1	2	3	4	5	--

6

13. Think about ways in which your teaching is <u>different</u> because of the mathematics CRCT than it would be without the CRCT. How much do the following statements describe differences in your teaching <u>due to the mathematics CRCT</u>? (Circle one number in each row.)

As a result of the mathematics CRCT:	No difference	Differs by: A small amount	A moderate amount	A great deal
a. I assign more homework or more difficult homework	1	2	3	4
b. I search for more effective teaching methods	1	2	3	4
c. I focus more on the Georgia standards in mathematics............	1	2	3	4
d. I focus more on topics emphasized in the mathematics CRCT (e.g., shifting instructional time from geometry to arithmetic or vice-versa)	1	2	3	4
e. I look for particular styles and formats of problems in the mathematics CRCT and emphasize those in my instruction (e.g., using particular styles of graphs; using specific key phrases)	1	2	3	4
f. I spend more time teaching general test-taking strategies (e.g., time management, eliminating wrong multiple-choice options, filling in answer sheets)	1	2	3	4
g. I spend more time teaching mathematics content (e.g., by replacing non-instructional activities with mathematics instruction)	1	2	3	4
h. I focus more effort on students who are <u>close to proficient</u> (i.e., close to meeting the standard) on the mathematics CRCT than on other students..	1	2	3	4
i. I offer more assistance outside of school to help students who are <u>not proficient</u> (i.e., not meeting the standard) on the mathematics CRCT	1	2	3	4
j. I rely more heavily on multiple-choice tests in my own classroom assessment	1	2	3	4
k. I rely more heavily on open-ended tests (e.g., essays, portfolios) in my own classroom assessment.............................	1	2	3	4

7

14. To what extent do you agree or disagree with each of the following statements about <u>student results</u> from the mathematics CRCT administered last school year (2003-04)? (Circle one number in each row.)

	Strongly Disagree	Disagree	Agree	Strongly agree	I do not have access to the results
a. I received the CRCT results in a timely manner	1	2	3	4	9
b. The CRCT results were clear and easy to understand	1	2	3	4	9
c. The CRCT results helped me identify and correct gaps in curriculum and instruction	1	2	3	4	9
d. The individual student results helped me tailor instruction to students' individual needs	1	2	3	4	9
e. The CRCT results allowed me to identify areas where I need to strengthen my content knowledge or teaching skills	1	2	3	4	9

Questions 15-19 ask about "progress tests." By "progress tests" we mean <u>required</u> tests that are administered periodically (e.g., every six weeks) to monitor your students' progress (also called "interim," "benchmark," or "diagnostic" tests). "Progress tests" do not refer to the annual mathematics CRCT or to the tests that you administer voluntarily on your own in the classroom.

---

15. All teachers monitor their students' progress. Sometimes districts or schools require that additional tests be administered. Are you required by your district or school to administer specific mathematics <u>progress tests</u> (i.e., interim tests, benchmark tests, diagnostic tests) on a periodic basis to monitor your students' progress in mathematics? (Circle one number.)

Yes 1   →   Continue with Question 16

No 2   →   Skip to Question 20 on page 10

16. How often are the required mathematics <u>progress tests</u> administered? (Circle one number.)

Two to three times per year 1

Approximately every six to eight weeks 2

Approximately every two to four weeks 3

17. How soon are the scores from the required mathematics <u>progress tests</u> available to you? (Circle one number.)

The same day I administer them 1

The next day 2

Within one week 3

Two to four weeks later 4

More than four weeks later 5

The scores are not available to me 6

8

18. Please indicate whether the required mathematics <u>progress tests</u> have the following characteristics. (Circle one number in each row.)

		Yes	No	I don't know
a.	The test contains only multiple-choice questions............................	1	2	9
b.	The students take the test on computers...	1	2	9
c.	The results are reported to your principal...	1	2	9
d.	The results are reported to the district..	1	2	9
e.	There are consequences (e.g., rewards or sanctions) for teachers associated with performance on these tests.....................	1	2	9

19. To what extent do you agree or disagree with the following statements about the required mathematics <u>progress tests</u>? (Circle one number in each row.)

		Strongly Disagree	Disagree	Agree	Strongly agree
a.	The mathematics progress tests are a good measure of students' mastery of the Georgia standards in mathematics................................	1	2	3	4
b.	The mathematics progress tests are good preparation for the mathematics CRCT...........	1	2	3	4
c.	The mathematics progress test results help me identify and correct gaps in curriculum and instruction	1	2	3	4

20. How often do you do each of the following activities in your mathematics instruction? How has the frequency changed this school year (2004-05) compared to last school year (2003-04)? (Circle one number for frequency and one number for change in each row. If you teach mathematics to more than one class, answer in terms of your typical practice.)

If you did not teach mathematics last year, please check here❑ and answer only Column 1.

	COLUMN 1 Frequency of Activity				COLUMN 2 Change in 2004-05 compared to 2003-04		
	Never	Rarely (a few times a year)	Sometimes (once or twice a month)	Often (once a week or more)	Less than 2003-04	About the same as 2003-04	More than 2003-04
a. Plan different assignments or lessons for groups of students based on their performance............	1	2	3	4	1	2	3
b. Assign mathematics homework	1	2	3	4	1	2	3
c. Re-teach topics because student performance on assignments or assessments did not meet your expectations.....................................	1	2	3	4	1	2	3
d. Have students work on extended mathematics investigations or projects..	1	2	3	4	1	2	3
e. Introduce content to the whole class through formal presentations or direct instruction ..	1	2	3	4	1	2	3
f. Review assessment results to identify individual students who need supplemental instruction........	1	2	3	4	1	2	3
g. Review assessment results to identify topics requiring more or less emphasis in instruction...........	1	2	3	4	1	2	3
h. Provide help to individual students outside of class time (e.g., during lunch, after school).....	1	2	3	4	1	2	3
i. Confer with another teacher about alternative ways to present specific topics or lessons...............	1	2	3	4	1	2	3
j. Conduct a pre-assessment to find out what students know about a topic	1	2	3	4	1	2	3
k. Have students help other students learn mathematics content (e.g., peer tutoring)	1	2	3	4	1	2	3
l. Refer students for extra help outside of the classroom (e.g., tutoring)	1	2	3	4	1	2	3

10

Section III: Science Instruction

Questions 21 to 30 ask about your science instruction. If you do **not** teach science to any students in grades 3, 4, 5, 7, or 8, please check here ❑ and skip to Question 31 on page 17.

In the following questions, "Georgia standards in science" refers to the Georgia Quality Core Curriculum (QCC) and, to the extent they have been implemented, the Georgia Performance Standards (GPS). When answering questions, please respond in terms of the current Georgia standards in science you are working toward this year.

21. Did your district or state take any of the following actions to assist schools and teachers using the Georgia standards in science for improving curriculum and instruction in science? If the action occurred, how useful was it to you as a teacher? (Circle one number in each row.)

	Did not occur	Occurred and it was:			
		Not useful	Minimally useful	Moderately useful	Very useful
a. Established detailed curriculum guidelines aligned with the Georgia standards in science.........................	1	2	3	4	5
b. Established a specific "pacing plan" or "instructional calendar" indicating a schedule for instructional content throughout the year............................	1	2	3	4	5
c. Monitored and provided feedback on the implementation of the Georgia standards in science in classrooms (e.g., by reviewing lesson plans or students' work or by conducting walk-throughs).........	1	2	3	4	5
d. Mapped out the alignment of textbooks and instructional programs to the Georgia standards in science...	1	2	3	4	5
e. Provided sample lessons linked to the Georgia standards in science	1	2	3	4	5

22. To what extent do you agree or disagree with the following statements about the <u>Georgia standards in science</u>?
(Circle one number in each row.)

		Strongly disagree	Disagree	Agree	Strongly agree	I don't know
a.	The Georgia standards in science include more content than can be covered adequately in the school year..	1	2	3	4	9
b.	The Georgia standards in science do not give enough emphasis to scientific inquiry (including investigation and experimentation)	1	2	3	4	9
c.	The Georgia standards in science do not cover some important content areas	1	2	3	4	9
d.	The Georgia standards in science are useful for planning my lessons...	1	2	3	4	9
e.	I have aligned my teaching with the Georgia standards in science	1	2	3	4	9

23. To what extent do you agree or disagree with the following statements about your <u>science textbooks and curriculum materials</u> provided by your school? (Circle one number in each row.)

		Strongly disagree	Disagree	Agree	Strongly agree	I don't know
a.	I am satisfied with the <u>quality</u> of science textbooks and curriculum materials in my school	1	2	3	4	9
b.	The science textbooks and curriculum materials are well aligned with the Georgia standards in science	1	2	3	4	9
c.	The science textbooks and curriculum materials are too difficult for the majority of my students..............................	1	2	3	4	9
d.	I often need to supplement the science textbooks and curriculum materials with additional material to cover the Georgia standards in science adequately	1	2	3	4	9

24. To what extent do you agree or disagree with the following statements about the <u>Criterion-Referenced Competency Test (CRCT)</u> in science? (Circle one number in each row.)

	Strongly disagree	Disagree	Agree	Strongly agree	I don't know
a. The science CRCT is a good measure of students' mastery of the Georgia standards in science	1	2	3	4	9
b. The science CRCT is too difficult for the majority of my students	1	2	3	4	9
c. The science CRCT <u>includes</u> considerable content that is <u>not</u> in our curriculum	1	2	3	4	9
d. The science CRCT <u>omits</u> considerable content that is in our curriculum	1	2	3	4	9
e. I feel a great deal of pressure to improve my students' scores on the science CRCT	1	2	3	4	9
f. I have aligned my teaching with the science CRCT	1	2	3	4	9
g. The science CRCT adequately measures scientific inquiry (including investigation and experimentation)	1	2	3	4	9

25. During this school year, was the following information or assistance regarding last year's (2003-04) science CRCT results available to you? If available, how useful was it for guiding your instruction? (Circle one number in each row.)

	Not available	Available; and				Not applicable
		Not useful	Minimally useful	Moderately useful	Very useful	
a. Reports of last year's science test results for the students you taught <u>last year</u>	1	2	3	4	5	9
b. Reports of last year's science test results for the students you teach <u>this year</u>	1	2	3	4	5	--
c. Science test results summarized for each student subgroup (e.g., special education, race/ethnicity, economically disadvantaged)	1	2	3	4	5	--
d. Science test results disaggregated by topic or skill	1	2	3	4	5	--
e. Computer software or systems for re-analyzing science test results	1	2	3	4	5	--
f. Workshops or meetings where science test results are presented and explained	1	2	3	4	5	--
g. Training on how to use science test results for instructional planning or school improvement	1	2	3	4	5	--

13

26. Think about ways in which your teaching is <u>different</u> because of the science CRCT than it would be without the CRCT. How much do the following statements describe differences in your teaching <u>due to the science CRCT</u>? (Circle one number in each row.)

As a result of the science CRCT:	No difference	Differs by: A small amount	A moderate amount	A great deal
a. I assign more homework or more difficult homework...............	1	2	3	4
b. I search for more effective teaching methods	1	2	3	4
c. I focus more on the Georgia standards in science...................	1	2	3	4
d. I focus more on material emphasized in the science CRCT (e.g., shifting instructional time from geology to biology or vice-versa)..	1	2	3	4
e. I look for particular styles and formats of problems in the science CRCT and emphasize those in my instruction. (e.g., using particular styles of graphs; using specific key phrases) .	1	2	3	4
f. I spend more time teaching general test-taking strategies (e.g., time management, eliminating wrong multiple-choice options, filling in answer sheets)	1	2	3	4
g. I spend more time teaching science content (e.g., by replacing non-instructional activities with science instruction)	1	2	3	4
h. I focus more effort on students who are <u>close to proficient</u> (i.e., close to meeting the standard) on the science CRCT than on other students..	1	2	3	4
i. I offer more assistance outside of school to help students who are <u>not proficient</u> (i.e., not meeting the standard) on the science CRCT	1	2	3	4
j. I rely more heavily on multiple-choice tests in my own classroom assessment...	1	2	3	4
k. I rely more heavily on open-ended tests (e.g., essays, portfolios) in my own classroom assessment..........................	1	2	3	4

14

27. To what extent do you agree or disagree with each of the following statements about <u>student results</u> from the science CRCT administered last school year (2003-04)? (Circle one number in each row.)

	Strongly Disagree	Disagree	Agree	Strongly agree	I do not have access to the results
a. I received the CRCT results in a timely manner	1	2	3	4	9
b. The CRCT results were clear and easy to understand	1	2	3	4	9
c. The CRCT results helped me identify and correct gaps in curriculum and instruction	1	2	3	4	9
d. The individual student results helped me tailor instruction to students' individual needs...	1	2	3	4	9
e. The CRCT results allowed me to identify areas where I need to strengthen my content knowledge or teaching skills	1	2	3	4	9

Questions 28 and 29 ask about "progress tests". By "progress tests" we mean <u>required</u> tests that are administered periodically (e.g., every six weeks) to monitor your students' progress (also called "interim," "benchmark," or "diagnostic" tests). "Progress tests" do not refer to the annual CRCT assessment or to the tests that you administer voluntarily on your own in the classroom.

28. All teachers monitor their students' progress. Sometimes districts or schools require that additional tests be administered. Are you required by your district or school to administer specific science <u>progress tests</u> (i.e., interim tests, benchmark tests, diagnostic tests) on a periodic basis to monitor your students' progress in science? (Circle one number.)

Yes .... 1 ➜ Continue with Question 29

No .... 2 ➜ Skip to Question 30 on page 16

29. How often are the required science <u>progress tests</u> administered? (Circle one number.)

Two to three times per year 1

Approximately every six to eight weeks 2

Approximately every two to four weeks 3

30. How often do you do each of the following activities in your science instruction? How has the frequency changed this school year (2004-05) compared to last school year (2003-04)? (Circle one number for frequency and one number for change in each row. If you teach science to more than one class, answer in terms of your typical practice.)

If you did not teach science last year, please check here ❑ *and answer only Column 1.*

	COLUMN 1 Frequency of Activity				COLUMN 2 Change in 2004-05 compared to 2003-04		
	Never	Rarely (a few times a year)	Sometimes (once or twice a month)	Often (once a week or more)	Less than 2003-04	About the same as 2003-04	More than 2003-04
a. Plan different assignments or lessons for groups of students based on their performance...........	1	2	3	4	1	2	3
b. Assign science homework	1	2	3	4	1	2	3
c. Re-teach topics because student performance on assignments or assessments did not meet your expectations.....................................	1	2	3	4	1	2	3
d. Have students do hands-on laboratory science activities or investigations	1	2	3	4	1	2	3
e. Introduce content to the whole class through formal presentations or direct instruction ..	1	2	3	4	1	2	3
f. Review assessment results to identify individual students who need additional assistance	1	2	3	4	1	2	3
g. Review assessment results to identify topics requiring more or less emphasis in instruction...........	1	2	3	4	1	2	3
h. Provide help to individual students outside of class time (e.g., during lunch, after school).....	1	2	3	4	1	2	3
i. Confer with another teacher about alternative ways to present specific topics or lessons	1	2	3	4	1	2	3
j. Conduct a pre-assessment to find out what students know about a topic	1	2	3	4	1	2	3
k. Have students help other students learn science content (e.g., peer tutoring).........................	1	2	3	4	1	2	3
l. Refer students for extra help outside of the classroom (e.g., tutoring)	1	2	3	4	1	2	3

16

Section IV: Accountability

31. Please indicate how the following features of your school have changed as a result of the state's accountability system (including standards, assessments, adequate yearly progress (AYP) targets, rewards, and sanctions). (Circle one number in each row.)

    If this is your first year working at this school please check here ❑ *and skip to Question 32.*

As a result of the state's accountability system:	Changed for the worse	Did not change due to accountability system	Changed for the better
a. The principal's effectiveness as an instructional leader ...	1	2	3
b. Teachers' general focus on student learning	1	2	3
c. Teachers' relationships with their students	1	2	3
d. Morale of the school staff	1	2	3
e. Students' learning of important skills and knowledge	1	2	3
f. Students' focus on school work..	1	2	3
g. Academic rigor of the curriculum......................................	1	2	3
h. My own teaching practices	1	2	3

32. To what extent do you agree or disagree with each of the following statements about the state's accountability system under NCLB? (Circle one number in each row.)

	Strongly disagree	Disagree	Agree	Strongly agree
a. The state's accountability system supports my personal approach to teaching and learning	1	2	3	4
b. The state's accountability system leaves little time to teach content not on the state tests	1	2	3	4
c. Because of pressure to meet the AYP target, I am focusing more on improving student achievement at my school	1	2	3	4
d. The possibility of my school receiving rewards or sanctions is a very strong motivator for me	1	2	3	4
e. The state's accountability system is so complicated it is hard for me to understand...	1	2	3	4
f. The accommodation policies regarding testing special education students (students with IEPs) and students who are English Language Learners (Limited English Proficient students) are clear to me	1	2	3	4
g. Overall, the state's accountability system has been beneficial for students at my school.................................	1	2	3	4
h. As a result of the state's accountability system, high-achieving students are not receiving appropriately challenging curriculum or instruction.................................	1	2	3	4

Section V. School Climate

33. To what extent do you agree or disagree with the following statements about the <u>conditions</u> in your school? (Circle one number in each row.)

	Strongly disagree	Disagree	Agree	Strongly agree
a. Most of my colleagues share a focus on student learning ...	1	2	3	4
b. Our school has clear strategies for improving instruction.....	1	2	3	4
c. Teacher morale is high...	1	2	3	4
d. Many new programs come and go in our school	1	2	3	4
e. There is consistency in curriculum, instruction, and learning materials among teachers <u>in the same grade level</u> at our school..	1	2	3	4
f. Curriculum, instruction, and learning materials are well coordinated <u>across different grade levels</u> at our school	1	2	3	4
g. Most of my colleagues share my beliefs and values about what the central mission of the school should be	1	2	3	4
h. I feel accepted and respected as a colleague by most staff members	1	2	3	4
i. There is a great deal of cooperative effort among staff members	1	2	3	4
j. Teachers in our school are continually learning and seeking new ideas..	1	2	3	4

34. There are many conditions that may hinder or prevent students from achieving at high levels in school. To what extent is each of the following factors a <u>hindrance to your students' academic success</u>? (Circle one number in each row.)

	Not a hindrance	Slight hindrance	Moderate hindrance	Great hindrance
Student and Family Conditions				
a. Inadequate basic skills or prior preparation......................	1	2	3	4
b. Lack of support from parents...	1	2	3	4
c. Student absenteeism and tardiness..................................	1	2	3	4
Classroom Conditions				
d. Insufficient class time to cover all the curriculum..............	1	2	3	4
e. Wide range of student abilities to address in class...........	1	2	3	4
f. Large class size..	1	2	3	4
g. Inadequate instructional resources (e.g., textbooks, equipment)	1	2	3	4
School Conditions				
h. Frequent changes in school priorities or leadership	1	2	3	4
i. High rate of teacher turnover...	1	2	3	4
j. Lack of school resources to provide the extra help for students who need it	1	2	3	4
k. Lack of teacher planning time built into the school day	1	2	3	4
l. Other (Specify _____)	1	2	3	4

35. Think about the <u>leadership your principal provides</u> at your school. To what extent do you agree or disagree with each of the following statements about your principal's leadership? (Circle one number in each row.)

The principal at my school...	Strongly disagree	Disagree	Agree	Strongly agree
a. Communicates a clear academic vision for my school.....	1	2	3	4
b. Sets high standards for teaching...	1	2	3	4
c. Encourages teachers to review the Georgia standards and incorporate them into our teaching	1	2	3	4
d. Helps teachers adapt our curriculum based on an analysis of CRCT test results	1	2	3	4
e. Ensures that teachers have sufficient time for professional development..	1	2	3	4
f. Enforces school rules for student conduct and backs me up when needed...	1	2	3	4
g. Makes the school run smoothly..	1	2	3	4

36. Think about the <u>principal's relationship with teachers</u> at your school. To what extent do you agree or disagree with the following statements about this relationship? (Circle one number in each row.)

	Strongly disagree	Disagree	Agree	Strongly agree
a. It's OK in my school to discuss feelings, worries, and frustrations with the principal	1	2	3	4
b. The principal looks out for the personal welfare of the teachers	1	2	3	4
c. I trust the principal at his or her word...............................	1	2	3	4
d. The principal places the needs of children ahead of his or her personal and political interests	1	2	3	4
e. The principal has confidence in the expertise of the teachers	1	2	3	4
f. The principal takes a personal interest in the professional development of teachers	1	2	3	4
g. I really respect my principal as an educator	1	2	3	4

20

Section VI. Parent Engagement and Involvement

37. How often do the following kinds of contact occur between you and the parents of your students? (Circle one number in each row.)

	Never	Rarely	Sometimes	Often
a. I require students to have their parents sign-off on homework..	1	2	3	4
b. I assign homework that requires direct parent involvement or participation	1	2	3	4
c. I send home examples of excellent student work to serve as a model	1	2	3	4
d. For those students who are having academic problems, I provide parents with specific activities they can do to improve their student's performance..................................	1	2	3	4
e. For those students who are having academic problems, I try to make direct contact with their parents...................	1	2	3	4
f. When I contact parents and ask for a face-to-face meeting, they always agree and attend	1	2	3	4
g. For those students whose academic performance improves, I send messages home to parents	1	2	3	4

Section VII. Professional Development

38. During the 2004-05 school year (including last summer), how many times did you engage in each of the following professional development activities with other teachers or administrators? If you participated, how valuable was each for your own professional development? (Circle one number for frequency and, if you participated, circle one number for value in each row.)

	Frequency of activity					Value of activity for your professional development		
	Never	A few times a year	Once or twice a month	Once or twice a week	Daily or almost daily	Not valuable	Moderately valuable	Very valuable
a. Developing lessons or courses with other teachers....	1	2	3	4	5	1	2	3
b. Discussing teaching practices or instructional issues with other teachers	1	2	3	4	5	1	2	3
c. Reviewing state test score results with other teachers......	1	2	3	4	5	1	2	3
d. Observing another teacher for at least 30 minutes at a time.............................	1	2	3	4	5	1	2	3
e. Receiving feedback from another teacher who observed in your class	1	2	3	4	5	1	2	3
f. Acting as a coach or mentor to another teacher	1	2	3	4	5	1	2	3
g. Receiving coaching or mentoring from another teacher	1	2	3	4	5	1	2	3
h. Participating in teacher collaboratives, networks, or study groups	1	2	3	4	5	1	2	3
i. Participating in a school or district committee or task force focused on curriculum and instruction	1	2	3	4	5	1	2	3

39. During the current school year (2004-05) (including last summer), approximately how many hours of formal professional development did you participate in from any source (e.g., district or school workshops, new teacher training, university courses)? (Write a number in each row, as applicable.)

a. Total professional development hours?   _____ hours

   If you wrote zero, → Skip to Question 41 on page 24.

b. How many hours were focused on mathematics or mathematics instruction? _____ hours

c. How many hours were focused on science or science instruction?   _____ hours

22

40. During your participation in professional development activities in the 2004-05 school year (including last summer), how much <u>emphasis</u> was placed on the following areas? If there was emphasis, to what extent did you change your teaching as a result of the professional development? (Circle one number for emphasis and, if there was emphasis, circle one number for instructional change in each row.)

	Amount of emphasis				Change in teaching		
	No emphasis	Minor emphasis	Moderate emphasis	Major emphasis	No change	Moderate change	Major change
a. Mathematics and mathematics teaching..	1	2	3	4	1	2	3
b. Science and science teaching	1	2	3	4	1	2	3
c. Instructional strategies for English Language Learners (i.e., Limited English-Proficient students).............	1	2	3	4	1	2	3
d. Instructional strategies for low-achieving students...........................	1	2	3	4	1	2	3
e. Instructional strategies for special education students (i.e., students with IEPs)..	1	2	3	4	1	2	3
f. Aligning curriculum and instruction with state and/or district content standards	1	2	3	4	1	2	3
g. Preparing students to take the CRCT assessments	1	2	3	4	1	2	3
h. Interpreting and using reports of student test results	1	2	3	4	1	2	3

23

Section VIII: Your Background

41. Including this year, how many years have you taught on a <u>full-time basis</u>? (Write in a number.)

_____ Years

42. What is the <u>highest degree</u> you hold? (Circle one number.)

BA or BS 1

MA or MS 2

PhD or EdD 3

Other (Specify _____) . 4

43. What type of <u>teaching certification</u> do you hold? (Circle one number.)

Not certified 1

Temporary, provisional, or emergency certification 2
  (requiring additional coursework and/or student teaching before regular certification
  can be obtained.)

Regular, standard, or probationary certification in my main teaching assignment 3
  (Probationary certification refers to initial certification issued after satisfying all
  requirements except the completion of a probationary period.)

Regular, standard, or probationary certification <u>not</u> in my main teaching assignment 4
  (Probationary certification refers to initial certification issued after satisfying all
  requirements except the completion of a probationary period.)

Thank you very much for completing this survey.

Place the completed survey in the business-reply envelope, seal the envelope using the <u>security sticker</u>, and return it to your school coordinator. If you prefer, you may return the survey yourself by mailing it to the address printed below.

Your questionnaire should be returned to your school coordinator, or if you prefer to mail it yourself you may send it to:

RAND Survey
c/o Debbie Alexander
1650 Research Blvd.
Westat
Rockville, MD 20850

If you have any questions about this survey or about the study, you may contact Ms. Alexander at 1-800-937-8281, ext. 2088 or by email at DebbieAlexander@Westat.com.

References

AFT—*see* American Federation of Teachers.

American Federation of Teachers, *Smart Testing: Let's Get It Right*, No. 19, July 2006. As of February 26, 2007:
http://www.aft.org/pubs-reports/downloads/teachers/Testingbrief.pdf

Amrein, Audrey L., and David C. Berliner, "High-Stakes Testing, Uncertainty, and Student Learning," *Education Policy Analysis Archives*, Vol. 10, No. 18, March 28, 2002. As of July 20, 2006:
http://epaa.asu.edu/epaa/v10n18

Asimov, Nanette, "'No Child Left Behind' Puts Districts in Bind: Letters Must Offer Transfers from 'Failing' Schools," *San Francisco Chronicle*, September 16, 2003, p. A1.

Bishop, John H., "The Impact of Curriculum-Based External Examinations on School Priorities and Student Learning," *International Journal of Educational Research*, Vol. 23, No. 8, 1995, pp. 653–752.

—————, *The Effect of Curriculum-Based Exit Exam Systems on Student Achievement*, Ithaca, N.Y.: Center for Advanced Human Resource Studies, working paper 97-15, 1998. As of February 20, 2007:
http://www.ilr.cornell.edu/depts/cahrs/downloads/pdfs/workingpapers/WP97-15.pdf

Booher-Jennings, Jennifer, "Below the Bubble: 'Educational Triage' and the Texas Accountability System," *American Educational Research Journal*, Vol. 42, No. 2, Summer 2005, pp. 231–268.

Borko, Hilda, and Rebekah Elliott, "Hands-On Pedagogy Versus Hands-Off Accountability: Tensions Between Competing Commitments for Exemplary Math Teachers in Kentucky," *Phi Delta Kappan*, Vol. 80, No. 5, January 1999, pp. 394–400.

Burch, Tricia, and James Spillane, *Leading from the Middle: Mid-Level District Staff and Instructional Improvement*, Chicago, Ill.: Cross City Campaign for Urban School Reform, 2004. As of March 5, 2007:
http://www.crosscity.org/downloads/Leading%20frm%20the%20Middle.pdf

California Department of Education, "NCLB Teachers and Paraprofessionals Requirements Data," undated Web page. As of February 22, 2007:
http://www.cde.ca.gov/nclb/sr/tq/ap/HQThome.asp

—————, *2003 Adequate Yearly Progress Phase I Report: Information Supplement*, Sacramento, Calif.: California Dept. of Education, August 2003.

—————, *2004 Accountability Progress Report: Information Guide*, Sacramento, Calif.: California Dept. of Education, 2004a.

—————, *California Consolidated State Application Accountability Workbook for State Grants Under Title IX, Part C, Section 9302 of the Elementary and Secondary Education Act (Public Law 107-110)*, Sacramento, Calif.: California Dept. of Education, 2004b.

—————, "O'Connell Releases Data Showing Most California Schools Improve API Scores; Meet Federal AYP Criteria," news release, August 31, 2004c. As of March 6, 2007:
http://www.cde.ca.gov/nr/ne/yr04/yr04rel76.asp

—————, *California Consolidated State Application Accountability Workbook for State Grants Under Title IX, Part C, Section 9302 of the Elementary and Secondary Education Act (Public Law 107-110)*, Sacramento, Calif.: California Dept. of Education, 2005a.

—————, "O'Connell Announces Significant Gains in State API Results, Mixed Progress in Federal AYP Results," news release, August 31, 2005b.

—————, "O'Connell Releases List of 2005–06 PI Schools and Districts; CDE Updates 2005 Accountability Progress Reports," news release, September 20, 2005c. As of March 5, 2007:
http://www.cde.ca.gov/nr/ne/yr05/yr05rel112.asp

—————, *Pocketbook of Special Education Statistics, 2004–05*, Sacramento, Calif.: California Dept. of Education, 2006a. As of March 5, 2007:
http://www.cde.ca.gov/sp/se/ds/documents/pcktbk0405.pdf

—————, "Accountability Progress Reporting (APR)," last modified August 31, 2006b. As of March 5, 2007:
http://www.cde.ca.gov/ta/ac/ar/index.asp

—————, "California Assessment System," last modified December 27, 2006c. As of March 5, 2007:
http://www.cde.ca.gov/ta/tg/sa/caassessment.asp

Carnoy, Martin, and Susanna Loeb, "Does External Accountability Affect Student Outcomes? A Cross-State Analysis," *Educational Evaluation and Policy Analysis*, Vol. 24, No. 4, Winter 2002, pp. 305–331.

Casserly, Michael D., *Beating the Odds: A City-by-City Analysis of Student Performance and Achievement Gaps on State Assessments*, Washington, D.C.: Council of the Great City Schools, 2002. As of February 20, 2007:
http://www.cgcs.org/pdfs/beatodds2.pdf

Center on Education Policy, *From the Capital to the Classroom: Year 2 of the No Child Left Behind Act*, Washington, D.C.: Center for Education Policy, 2004.

—————, *Hope but No Miracle Cure: Michigan's Early Restructuring Lessons*, Washington, D.C.: Center on Education Policy, November 2005.

—————, *From the Capital to the Classroom: Year 4 of the No Child Left Behind Act*, Washington, D.C.: Center on Education Policy, 2006.

Cohen, David K., Milbrey Wallin McLaughlin, and Joan E. Talbert, eds., *Teaching for Understanding: Challenges for Policy and Practice*, San Francisco, Calif.: Jossey-Bass, 1993.

Commonwealth of Pennsylvania, "PA Students Making Progress in Reading and Math: Acting Education Secretary Credits Increased State Investment, Educators, Families and Students," press release, September 2005. As of March 6, 2007:
http://www.state.pa.us/papower/cwp/view.asp?Q=445847&A=11

Corbett, H. D., and B. L. Wilson, "Raising the Stakes in Statewide Mandatory Minimum Competency Testing," in William Lowe Boyd and Charles T. Kerchner, eds., *The Politics of Excellence and Choice in Education: 1987 Yearbook of the Politics of Education Association*, New York: Falmer Press, 1988, pp. 27–39.

Council of Chief State School Officers, and the Charles A. Dana Center, *Expecting Success: A Study of Five High Performing, High Poverty Elementary Schools*, Washington, D.C.: Council of Chief State School Officers, 2002. As of February 20, 2007:
http://www.ccsso.org/publications/details.cfm?PublicationID=39

Darling-Hammond, Linda, and Arthur E. Wise, "Beyond Standardization: State Standards and School Improvement," *Elementary School Journal*, Vol. 85, No. 3, January 1985, pp. 315–336.

Dobbs, Michael, "'No Child' Law Leaves Schools' Old Ways Behind," *The Washington Post*, April 22, 2004, p. A1.

Edmonds, Ronald, "Effective Schools for the Urban Poor," *Educational Leadership*, Vol. 37, No. 1, October 1979, pp. 15–24.

EdSource, *Similar Students, Different Results: Why Do Some Schools Do Better?* Mountain View, Calif.: EdSource, 2005–. As of February 20, 2007:
http://www.edsource.org/pub%5Fabs%5Fsimstu05.cfm

Education Data Partnership, "State of California Education Profile, Fiscal Year 2005–06," revised February 28, 2007. As of March 5, 2007:
http://www.ed-data.k12.ca.us/Navigation/
fsTwoPanel.asp?bottom=%2Fprofile%2Easp%3Flevel%3D04%26reportNumber%3D16

Education Trust, *Telling the Whole Truth (or Not) About Highly Qualified Teachers*, Washington, D.C.: Education Trust, December 2003. As of November 3, 2006:
http://www2.edtrust.org/NR/rdonlyres/C638111D-04E3-4C0D-9F68-20E7009498A6/0/
tellingthetruthteachers.pdf

Education Trust–West, *Achievement in California: How Is Our Progress?* Oakland, Calif.: Education Trust–West, September 1, 2004. As of March 6, 2007:
http://www2.edtrust.org/NR/rdonlyres/34F6021B-51CA-452D-AD29-0F0E374ADC64/0/
Achievement_CA_Progress_.pdf

Educational Resources Information Center, *Results in Education, 1989: The Governors' 1991 Report on Education*, Washington, D.C.: National Governors' Association, U.S. Department of Education, Office of Educational Research and Improvement, Educational Resources Information Center, 1989.

Elmore, Richard F., and Deanna Burney, "Investing in Teacher Learning: Staff Development and Instructional Improvement," in Linda Darling-Hammond and Gary Sykes, eds., *Teaching as the Learning Profession: Handbook of Policy and Practice*, San Francisco, Calif.: Jossey-Bass Publishers, 1999, pp. 263–291.

Finn, Chester E., Jr., Michael J. Petrilli, and Liam Julian, *The State of State Standards 2006*, Washington, D.C.: Thomas B. Fordham Foundation, August 29, 2006. As of September 27, 2006:
http://www.edexcellence.net/foundation/publication/publication.cfm?id=358

Firestone, William A., "Using Reform: Conceptualizing District Initiative," *Educational Evaluation and Policy Analysis*, Vol. 11, No. 2, Summer 1989, pp. 151–164.

Firestone, William A., Lora Monfils, and Gregory Camilli, *Pressure, Support, and Instructional Change in the Context of a State Testing Program*, paper presented at the annual meeting of the American Educational Research Association, Seattle, Wash., April 11, 2001. As of February 20, 2007:
http://www.cepa.gse.rutgers.edu/Pressure.pdf

Fordham Foundation, "Gains on State Reading Tests Evaporate on 2005 NAEP," press release, October 19, 2005. As of November 25, 2005:
http://www.edexcellence.net/foundation/about/press_release.cfm?id=19

Fuhrman, Susan H., *The New Accountability*, Philadelphia, Pa.: Consortium for Policy Research in Education, policy brief RB-27, January 1999. As of February 20, 2007:
http://www.cpre.org/Publications/rb27.pdf

Fuhrman, Susan H., and Richard F. Elmore, "Understanding Local Control in the Wake of State Education Reform," *Educational Evaluation and Policy Analysis*, Vol. 12, No. 1, Spring 1990, pp. 82–96.

Georgia Department of Education, "Adequate Yearly Progress (AYP) 2005," undated(a) Web page. As of March 6, 2007:
http://www.doe.k12.ga.us/aypnclb.aspx

———, "Curriculum Frequently Asked Questions," undated(b) Web page. As of February 22, 2007:
http://www.georgiastandards.org/faqs.aspx

———, "Office of Curriculum and Instruction: Testing," undated(c) homepage. As of March 5, 2007:
http://www.doe.k12.ga.us/ci_testing.aspx

———, *Georgia Consolidated State Application Accountability Workbook for State Grants Under Title IX, Part C, Section 9302 of the Elementary and Secondary Education Act (Public Law 107-110)*, Augusta, Ga.: Georgia Dept. of Education, 2003a.

———, *Adequate Yearly Progress (AYP) FY2003: Calculation Guide for School-Level Data*, version 1.3, Augusta, Ga.: Georgia Dept. of Education, August 14, 2003b. As of February 22, 2007:
http://techservices.doe.k12.ga.us/ayp/aypcalculations.pdf

———, *Georgia Consolidated State Application Accountability Workbook for State Grants Under Title IX, Part C, Section 9302 of the Elementary and Secondary Education Act (Public Law 107-110)*, Augusta, Ga.: Georgia Dept. of Education, 2004.

———, *Georgia Consolidated State Application Accountability Workbook for State Grants Under Title IX, Part C, Section 9302 of the Elementary and Secondary Education Act (Public Law 107-110)*, Augusta, Ga.: Georgia Dept. of Education, 2005.

Goertz, M., D. Massell, and T. Chun, *District Response to State Accountability Systems*, paper presented at the annual meeting of the Association for Public Policy Analysis and Management (APPAM), New York, N.Y., 1998.

Grissmer, David W., and Ann Flanagan, *Exploring Rapid Achievement Gains in North Carolina and Texas: Lessons from the States*, Washington, D.C.: National Education Goals Panel, 1998.

Grissmer, David W., Ann Flanagan, Jennifer H. Kawata, and Stephanie Williamson, *Improving Student Achievement: What State NAEP Test Scores Tell Us*, Santa Monica, Calif.: RAND Corporation, MR-924-EDU, 2000. As of February 20, 2007:
http://www.rand.org/pubs/monograph_reports/MR924/

Hamilton, Laura S., *Assessment as a Policy Tool*, Santa Monica, Calif.: RAND Corporation, RP-1163, 2004. As of March 5, 2007:
http://www.rand.org/pubs/reprints/RP1163/

Hoy, Wayne K., and Anita E. Woolfolk, "Teachers' Sense of Efficacy and the Organizational Health of Schools," *The Elementary School Journal*, Vol. 93, No. 4, March 1993, pp. 355–372.

Huffman, Douglas, Kelli Thomas, and Frances Lawrenz, "Relationship Between Professional Development, Teachers' Instructional Practices, and the Achievement of Students in Science and Mathematics," *School Science and Mathematics*, Vol. 103, No. 8, December 2003, pp. 378–387.

Jennings, Jack, and Diane Stark Rentner, "Ten Big Effects of the No Child Left Behind Act on Public Schools," *Phi Delta Kappan*, Vol. 88, No. 2, October 2006, pp. 110–113.

Jones, M. Gail, Brett D. Jones, Belinda Hardin, Lisa Chapman, Tracie Yarbrough, and Marcia Davis, "The Impact of High-Stakes Testing on Teachers and Students in North Carolina," *Phi Delta Kappan*, Vol. 81, No. 3, November 1999, pp. 199–203.

Kelley, Carolyn, Allan Odden, Anthony Milanowski, and Herbert Heneman III, *The Motivational Effects of School-Based Performance Awards*, Consortium for Policy Research in Education, policy brief RB-29, February 2000. As of February 20, 2007:
http://www.cpre.org/Publications/rb29.pdf

Kim, James S., and Gail L. Sunderman, "Measuring Academic Proficiency Under the No Child Left Behind Act: Implications for Educational Equity," *Educational Researcher*, Vol. 34, No. 8, 2005, pp. 3–13.

Kingsbury, G. Gage, Allan Olson, John Cronin, Carl Hauser, and Ron Houser, *The State of State Standards: Research Investigating Proficiency Levels in Fourteen States*, Lake Oswego, Oreg.: Northwest Evaluation Association, November 21, 2003. As of February 22, 2007:
http://www.nwea.org/research/getreport.asp?ReportID=5

Kirst, Michael W., *Accountability: Implications for State and Local Policymakers*, Washington, D.C.: Information Services, Office of Educational Research and Improvement, U.S. Department of Education, 1990.

Klein, David, *The State of State Math Standards, 2005*, Washington, D.C.: Thomas B. Fordham Foundation, 2005. As of October 2006:
http://www.edexcellence.net/doc/mathstandards05FINAL.pdf

Klein, Stephen P., Laura S. Hamilton, Daniel F. McCaffrey, and Brian M. Stecher, "What Do Test Scores in Texas Tell Us?" *Education Policy Analysis Archives*, Vol. 8, No. 49, October 26, 2000. As of February 20, 2007:
http://epaa.asu.edu/epaa/v8n49/

Koretz, Daniel, and Sheila Barron, *The Validity of Gains in Scores on the Kentucky Instructional Results Information System (KIRIS)*, Santa Monica, Calif.: RAND Corporation, MR-1014-EDU, 1998. As of February 20, 2007:
http://www.rand.org/pubs/monograph_reports/MR1014/

Koretz, Daniel, Sheila Barron, Karen Mitchell, and Brian Stecher, *Perceived Effects of the Kentucky Instructional Results Information System (KIRIS)*, Santa Monica, Calif.: RAND Corporation, MR-792-PCT/FF, 1996. As of February 20, 2007:
http://www.rand.org/pubs/monograph_reports/MR792/

Koretz, Daniel M., and Laura S. Hamilton, *Teachers' Responses to High-Stakes Testing and the Validity of Gains: A Pilot Study,* Los Angeles, Calif.: Center for the Study of Evaluation, National Center for Research on Evaluation, Standards, and Student Testing, Graduation School of Education and Information Studies, University of California, Los Angeles, October 2003. As of April 6, 2007:
http://eric.ed.gov/ERICDocs/data/ericdocs2/content_storage_01/0000000b/80/24/68/92.pdf

———, "Testing for Accountability in K–12," in Robert L. Brennan, ed., *Educational Measurement*, 4th ed., Westport, Conn.: American Council on Education/Praeger, 2006, pp. 531–578.

Koretz, Daniel M., R. L. Linn, S. B. Dunbar, and L. A. Shepard, "The Effects of High-Stakes Testing on Achievement; Preliminary Findings About Generalization Across Tests," paper presented at the annual meeting of the American Educational Research Association, Chicago, Ill., 1991.

Leithwood, Kenneth, *How Leadership Influences Student Learning: Review of Research*, Toronto, Ont.: Ontario Institute for Studies in Education, 2004.

Linn, Robert L., "Assessments and Accountability," *Educational Researcher*, Vol. 29, No. 2, March 2000, pp. 4–16.

——, "Performance Standards: Utility for Different Uses of Assessments," *Education Policy Analysis Archives*, Vol. 11, No. 31, September 1, 2003. As of October 2006:
http://epaa.asu.edu/epaa/v11n31/

——, "Conflicting Demands of No Child Left Behind and State Systems: Mixed Messages About School Performance," *Education Policy Analysis Archives*, Vol. 13, No. 33, June 28, 2005. As of October 2006:
http://epaa.asu.edu/epaa/v13n33/

Loucks-Horsley, Susan, and Carolee Matsumoto, "Research on Professional Development for Teachers of Mathematics and Science: The State of the Scene," *School Science and Mathematics*, Vol. 99, No. 5, May 1999, pp. 258–271.

Marsh, Julie A., John F. Pane, and Laura S. Hamilton, *Making Sense of Data-Driven Decision Making in Education: Evidence from Recent RAND Research*, Santa Monica, Calif.: RAND Corporation, OP-170-EDU, 2006. As of February 26, 2007:
http://www.rand.org/pubs/occasional_papers/OP170/

Marzano, Robert J., *What Works in Schools: Translating Research into Action*, Alexandria, Va.: Association for Supervision and Curriculum Development, 2003.

Massell, Diane, "The Theory and Practice of Using Data to Build Capacity: State and Local Strategies and Their Effects," in Susan Fuhrman, ed., *From the Capitol to the Classroom: Standards-Based Reform in the States*, Chicago, Ill.: National Society for the Study of Education, 2001, pp. 148–169.

Massell, Diane, and Margaret Goertz, "Local Strategies for Building Capacity: The District Role in Supporting Instructional Reform," paper presented at the annual meeting of the American Education Research Association, Montreal, Canada, 1999.

Massell, Diane, Michael W. Kirst, and Margaret Hoppe, *Persistence and Change: Standards-Based Reform in Nine States*, Philadelphia, Pa.: Consortium for Policy Research in Education, University of Pennsylvania, Graduate School of Education, 1997.

McCombs, Jennifer Sloan, Sheila Nataraj Kirby, Heather Barney, Hilary Darilek, and Scarlett J. Magee, *Achieving State and National Literacy Goals, a Long Uphill Road: A Report to Carnegie Corporation of New York*, Santa Monica, Calif.: RAND Corporation, TR-180-1-EDU, 2005. As of February 22, 2007:
http://www.rand.org/pubs/technical_reports/TR180-1/

McKnight, Curtis C., F. Joe Crosswhite, and John A. Dossey, *The Underachieving Curriculum: Assessing U.S. School Mathematics from an International Perspective*, Champaign, Ill.: Stipes Pub. Co., 1987.

McLaughlin, Milbrey Wallin, "Learning from Experience: Lessons from Policy Implementation," *Educational Evaluation and Policy Analysis*, Vol. 9, No. 2, Summer 1987, pp. 171–178.

Mezzacappa, D., "Tutoring Eludes Many of City Poor: Only a Small Number Qualify for Outside Help," *Philadelphia Inquirer*, December 16, 2004, p. A1.

Mirel, J., "High Standards for All: The Struggle for Equality in the American High School Curriculum," *American Educator*, Vol. 18, No. 2, 1994, pp. 40–42.

National Center for Education Statistics, *Common Core of Data (CCD): School Years 2003 Through 2004*, Washington, D.C.: National Center for Education Statistics, Office of Educational Research and Improvement, U.S. Department of Education, 2004.

National Council on Educational Standards and Testing, *Raising Standards for American Education: A Report to Congress, the Secretary of Education, the National Education Goals Panel, and the American People*, Washington, D.C.: U.S. Dept. of Education, 1992.

NCES—*see* National Center for Education Statistics.

No Child Left Behind Act (NCLB) of 2001 (20 U.S.C. § 6311 et seq.).

Novak, John R., and Bruce Fuller, "Penalizing Diverse Schools? Similar Test Scores, but Different Students, Bring Federal Sanctions," *Policy Brief* 03-04, December 2003. As of February 22, 2007:
http://epsl.asu.edu/epru/documents/EPRU-0312-48-RW.pdf

O'Connell, Jack, "A California Perspective on Growth Models and Adequate Yearly Progress (AYP)," written testimony submitted to the Aspen Institute Commission on No Child Left Behind, May 22, 2006. As of February 22, 2007:
http://www.cde.ca.gov/nr/sp/yr06/yr06sp0522.asp

O'Day, Jennifer, Margaret E. Goertz, and Robert E. Floden, *Building Capacity for Education Reform*, Consortium for Policy Research in Education, policy brief RB-18, December 1995. As of February 20, 2007:
http://www.cpre.org/Publications/rb18.pdf

Odden, Allan R., "The Evolution of Education Policy Implementation," in Allan R. Odden, ed., *Education Policy Implementation*, Albany, N.Y.: State University of New York Press, 1991, pp. 1–12.

Olson, L., "Benchmark Assessments Offer Regular Checkups on Student Achievement, Special Report: Testing Takes Off," *Education Week*, November 30, 2005, pp. 13–15.

Pedulla, Joseph J., Lisa M. Abrams, George F. Madaus, Michael K. Russell, Miguel A. Ramos, and Jing Miao, *Perceived Effects of State-Mandated Testing Programs on Teaching and Learning: Findings from a National Survey of Teachers*, Chestnut Hill, Mass.: National Board on Educational Testing and Public Policy, 2003. As of February 26, 2007:
http://www.bc.edu/research/nbetpp/statements/nbr2.pdf

Pennsylvania Department of Education, "Assessment," undated Web page. As of February 22, 2007:
http://www.pde.state.pa.us/a_and_t/site/default.asp

————, *Pennsylvania Consolidated State Application Accountability Workbook for State Grants Under Title IX, Part C, Section 9302 of the Elementary and Secondary Education Act (Public Law 107-110)*, Harrisburg, Pa.: Pennsylvania Dept. of Education, 2003.

————, *Pennsylvania Consolidated State Application Accountability Workbook for State Grants Under Title IX, Part C, Section 9302 of the Elementary and Secondary Education Act (Public Law 107-110)*, Harrisburg, Pa.: Pennsylvania Dept. of Education, 2004a.

————, *Assessment Anchors and Eligible Content*, Harrisburg, Pa.: Pennsylvania Department of Education, November 1, 2004b. As of February 22, 2007:
http://www.pde.state.pa.us/a_and_t/lib/a_and_t/2005AnchorintoFINAL.pdf

————, *Pennsylvania Consolidated State Application Accountability Workbook for State Grants Under Title IX, Part C, Section 9302 of the Elementary and Secondary Education Act (Public Law 107-110)*, Harrisburg, Pa.: Pennsylvania Dept. of Education, 2005a.

————, "Public, Private and Nonpublic Schools Enrollments," last modified February 4, 2005b.

————, *Understanding Adequate Yearly Progress 2005*, Harrisburg, Pa.: Pennsylvania Dept. of Education, May 2005c. As of February 22, 2007:
http://www.pde.state.pa.us/pas/lib/pas/Understanding_AYP_2005_-_May_2005_-_revised_61005.pdf

————, "Academic Achievement Report: AYP Facts," homepage, last updated August 25, 2006a. As of February 22, 2007:
http://www.paayp.com/

————, "Education Empowerment Annual Report 2004–2005," last modified September 13, 2006b. As of March 5, 2007:
http://www.pde.state.pa.us/pas/cwp/view.asp?a=3&Q=116441&pasNav=%7C

————, "English as a Second Language Program Statistics," last modified October 30, 2006c. As of March 5, 2007:
http://www.pde.state.pa.us/esl/cwp/view.asp?a=3&Q=70150&eslNav=|6322|&eslNav=|4974

————, "Assessment Anchors," Web page, January 23, 2007. As of February 22, 2007:
http://www.pde.state.pa.us/a_and_t/cwp/view.asp?a=108&q=103127&a_and_tNav=|6309|&a_and_tNav=|

Peterson, Paul E., and Frederick M. Hess, "Johnny Can Read . . . in Some States," *Education Next*, No. 3, 2005, pp. 52–53. As of February 22, 2007:
http://www.hoover.org/publications/ednext/3219636.html

Popham, W. J., "The Merits of Measurement-Driven Instruction," *Phi Delta Kappan*, Vol. 68, 1987, pp. 679–682.

Porter, Andrew C., Robert L. Linn, and C. Scott Trimble, "The Effects of State Decisions About NCLB Adequate Yearly Progress Targets," *Educational Measurement: Issues and Practice*, Vol. 24, No. 4, 2005, pp. 32–39.

Purves, Alan, and Daniel U. Levine, eds., *Educational Policy and International Assessment: Implications of the IEA Survey of Achievement*, Berkeley, Calif.: McCutchan Pub. Corp., 1975.

"Quality Counts at 10: A Decade of Standards-Based Education," *Education Week*, Vol. 25, No. 17, 2006. As of March 6, 2007:
http://www.edweek.org/ew/toc/2006/01/05/index.html

Resnick, D., "History of Educational Testing," in Alexandra K. Wigdor and Wendell R. Garner, eds., *Ability Testing: Uses, Consequences, and Controversies*, Vol. 2, Washington, D.C.: National Academy Press, 1982, pp. 173–194.

Rothman, Robert, Jean B. Slattery, Jennifer L. Vranek, and Lauren B. Resnick, *Benchmarking and Alignment of Standards and Testing*, Los Angeles, Calif.: Center for the Study of Evaluation, National Center for Research on Evaluation, Standards, and Student Testing, Graduate School of Education and Information Studies, University of California, Los Angeles, 2002.

Schemo, Diana Jean, "States' End Run Dilutes Burden for Special Ed," *The New York Times*, June 7, 2004.

Schmidt, William H., *Facing the Consequences: Using TIMMS for a Closer Look at U.S. Mathematics and Science Education*, Dordrecht and Boston: Kluwer Academic Publishers, 1999.

Shepard, Lorrie A., and Katherine Cutts Dougherty, *Effects of High-Stakes Testing on Instruction*, Chicago, Ill.: Spencer Foundation, 1991.

Simon, Raymond, "Lead and Manage My School: Decision Letter on Request to Amend Pennsylvania Accountability Plan," letter from assistant secretary, office of elementary and secondary education, U.S. Department of Education, to Vicki Phillips, secretary of education, Pennsylvania State Board of Education, June 3, 2004a. As of February 22, 2007:
http://www.ed.gov/admins/lead/account/letters/acpa.html

———, "Lead and Manage My School: Decision Letter on Request to Amend Georgia Accountability Plan," letter from assistant secretary, office of elementary and secondary education, U.S. Department of Education, to Wanda Barrs, chair, Georgia State Board of Education, and Kathy Cox, state superintendent of schools, June 7, 2004b. As of February 22, 2007:
http://www.ed.gov/admins/lead/account/letters/acga.html

———, "Lead and Manage My School: Decision Letter on Request to Amend Georgia Accountability Plan," letter from assistant secretary, office of elementary and secondary education, U.S. Department of Education, to Wanda Barrs, chair, Georgia State Board of Education, and Kathy Cox, state superintendent of schools, August 17, 2004c. As of February 22, 2007:
http://www.ed.gov/admins/lead/account/letters/acca2.html

———, "Lead and Manage My School: Decision Letter on Request to Amend California Accountability Plan," letter from assistant secretary, office of elementary and secondary education, U.S. Department of Education, to Ruth E. Green, president, California State Board of Education, and Jack O'Connell, superintendent of public instruction, October 1, 2004d. As of February 22, 2007:
http://www.ed.gov/admins/lead/account/letters/acga4.html

———, "Lead and Manage My School: Decision Letter on Request to Amend Georgia Accountability Plan," letter from assistant secretary, office of elementary and secondary education, U.S. Department of Education, to Wanda Barrs, chair, Georgia State Board of Education, and Kathy Cox, state superintendent of schools, July 1, 2005. As of February 22, 2007:
http://www.ed.gov/admins/lead/account/letters/acga5.html

Smith, Marshall S., and Jennifer O'Day, *Putting the Pieces Together: Systemic School Reform*, Consortium for Policy Research in Education, policy brief RB-06, April 1991. As of February 20, 2007:
http://www.cpre.org/Publications/rb06.pdf

Smith, Mary Lee, and Claire Rottenberg, "Unintended Consequences of External Testing in Elementary Schools," *Educational Measurement: Issues and Practice*, Vol. 10, No. 4, Winter 1991, pp. 7–11.

Snipes, Jason C., Fred C. Doolittle, and Corinne Herlihy, *Foundations for Success: Case Studies of How Urban School Systems Improve Student Achievement*, Washington, D.C.: Council of the Great City Schools, 2002.

Spillane, James P., "School Districts Matter: Local Educational Authorities and State Instructional Policy," *Educational Policy*, Vol. 10, No. 1, 1996, pp. 63–87.

Spillane, James P., and Charles L. Thompson, "Reconstructing Conceptions of Local Capacity: The Local Education Agency's Capacity for Ambitious Instructional Reform," *Educational Evaluation and Policy Analysis*, Vol. 19, No. 2, Summer 1997, pp. 185–203.

Spillane, James P., and John S. Zeuli, "Reform and Teaching: Exploring Patterns of Practice in the Context of National and State Mathematics Reforms," *Educational Evaluation and Policy Analysis*, Vol. 21, No. 1, Spring 1999, pp. 1–27.

Stecher, Brian M., *The Effects of Standards-Based Assessment on Classroom Practices: Results of the 1996–97 RAND Survey of Kentucky Teachers of Mathematics and Writing*, Los Angeles, Calif.: Center for the Study of Evaluation, National Center for Research on Evaluation, Standards, and Student Testing, Graduate School of Education and Information Studies, University of California, Los Angeles, 1998.

———, "Consequences of Large-Scale, High-Stakes Testing on School and Classroom Practices," in Laura S. Hamilton, Brian M. Stecher, and Stephen P. Klein, eds., *Making Sense of Test-Based Accountability in Education*, Santa Monica, Calif.: RAND Corporation, MR-1554-EDU, 2002, pp. 79–100. As of February 20, 2007:
http://www.rand.org/pubs/monograph_reports/MR1554/

Stecher, Brian M., and Sheila I. Barron, *Quadrennial Milepost Accountability Testing in Kentucky*, Los Angeles, Calif.: National Center for Research on Evaluation, Standards, and Student Testing (CRESST), Center for the Study on Evaluation (CSE), Graduate School of Education and Information Studies, University of California, Los Angeles, 1999.

Stecher, Brian M., Sheila Barron, Tessa Kaganoff, and Joy Goodwin, *The Effects of Standards-Based Assessment on Classroom Practices: Results of the 1996–97 RAND Survey of Kentucky Teachers of Mathematics and Writing*, Los Angeles, Calif.: Center for Research on Evaluation, Standards, and Student Testing, May 1998. As of April 6, 2007:
http://eric.ed.gov/ERICWebPortal/contentdelivery/servlet/ERICServlet?accno=ED426070

Stecher, Brian M., Tammi Chun, Sheila Barron, and Karen E. Ross, *The Effects of the Washington Education Reform on Schools and Classrooms: Initial Findings*, Santa Monica, Calif.: RAND Corporation, DB-309-EDU, 2000. As of February 20, 2007:
http://www.rand.org/pubs/documented_briefings/DB309/

Stecher, Brian M., Laura S. Hamilton, and Gabriella Gonzalez, *Working Smarter to Leave No Child Behind: Practical Insights for School Leaders*, Santa Monica, Calif.: RAND Corporation, WP-138-EDU, 2003. As of March 5, 2007:
http://www.rand.org/pubs/white_papers/WP138/

Stevenson, Harold W., and James W. Stigler, *The Learning Gap: Why Our Schools Are Failing and What We Can Learn from Japanese and Chinese Education*, New York: Summit Books, 1992.

Stodolsky, Susan S., *The Subject Matters: Classroom Activity in Math and Social Studies*, Chicago, Ill.: University of Chicago Press, 1988.

Stullich, Stephanie E., *National Assessment of Title I: Interim Report: A Report Prepared for IES*, Vol. I: *Implementation of Title I*, Washington, D.C.: U.S. Department of Education, Institute of Education Sciences, National Center for Education Evaluation and Regional Assistance, 2006.

Supovitz, Jonathan A., and Valerie Klein, *Mapping a Course for Improved Student Learning: How Innovative Schools Systematically Use Student Performance Data to Guide Improvement*, Philadelphia, Pa.: Consortium for Policy Research in Education, University of Pennsylvania Graduate School of Education, November 2003. As of February 20, 2007:
http://www.cpre.org/Publications/AC-08.pdf

Symonds, Kiley Walsh, *After the Test: How Schools Are Using Data to Close the Achievement Gap*, San Francisco, Calif.: Bay Area School Reform Collaborative, 2003.

Taylor, Grace, Lorrie Shepard, Freya Kinner, and Justin Rosenthal, *A Survey of Teachers' Perspectives on High-Stakes Testing in Colorado: What Gets Taught, What Gets Lost*, Los Angeles, Calif.: Center for Research on Evaluation, Diversity, and Excellence, and Center for the Study of Evaluation, CSE technical report 588, February 2003. As of April 6, 2007:
http://eric.ed.gov/ERICWebPortal/contentdelivery/servlet/ERICServlet?accno=ED475139

Travers, Kenneth J., and Ian Westbury, *The IEA Study of Mathematics I: Analysis of Mathematics Curricula*, Oxford and New York: Pergamon Press, 1989.

U.S. Government Accountability Office, *No Child Left Behind Act: Education Needs to Provide Additional Technical Assistance and Conduct Implementation Studies for School Choice Provision*, Washington, D.C.: U.S. Government Accountability Office, GAO-05-07, 2004. As of February 22, 2007:
http://purl.access.gpo.gov/GPO/LPS56511

Walsh, Kate Burke, and Emma Snyder, *Searching the Attic: How States Are Responding to the Nation's Goal of Placing a Highly Qualified Teacher in Every Classroom*, Washington, D.C.: National Council on Teacher Quality, 2004. As of February 22, 2007:
http://www.nctq.org/nctq/images/housse%5Freport%5F2.pdf

Waters, Tim, Robert J. Marzano, and Brian McNulty, *Balanced Leadership: What 30 Years of Research Tells Us About the Effect of Leadership on Student Achievement*, Aurora, Colo.: Mid-Continent Research for Education and Learning, 2003.

Wolf, Shelby A., and Monette C. McIver, "When Process Becomes Policy: The Paradox of Kentucky State Reform for Exemplary Teachers of Writing," *Phi Delta Kappan*, Vol. 80, No. 5, 1999, pp. 401–406.

Ziebarth, Todd, "State Policies for School Restructuring," *StateNotes*, December 2004. As of February 22, 2007:
http://www.ecs.org/clearinghouse/57/02/5702.pdf